DATE DUE

DEMCO, INC. 38-2931

Forgotten Time

The Yazoo-Mississippi Delta after the Civil War

The American South Series

Edward L. Ayers, Editor

Forgotten Time

The Yazoo-Mississippi Delta after the Civil War

John C. Willis

University Press of Virginia

Charlottesville and London

The University Press of Virginia
Printed in the United States of America

First published in 2000

⊗The paper used in this publication meets the minimum requirements of the
American National Standard for Information Sciences—Permanence of
Paper for Printed Library Materials, ANSI Z39.48-1984.

Library of Congress Cataloging-in-Publication Data
Willis, John C., 1961–
    Forgotten time : the Yazoo-Mississippi Delta after the Civil War / John C. Willis.
     p.   cm.
    Includes bibliographical references (p.   ) and index.
    ISBN 0-8139-1971-1 (alk. paper) — ISBN 0-8139-1982-7 (pbk. : alk. paper)
    1. Delta (Miss. : Region)—History—19th century. 2. Afro-Americans—Mississippi
—Delta (Region)—History—19th century. 3. Reconstruction—Mississippi—Delta
(Region) 4. Delta (Miss. : Region)—Social conditions—19th century. I. Title.

F347.M6 W55 2000
976.2'4—dc21   99-057809

For Laura

Contents

Illustrations

Acknowledgments

Mindful of the many kindnesses I have received during this book's preparation, I would like to acknowledge some of the generous souls who have helped so much.

Ed Ayers has been this study's most constant supporter and most perceptive critic; he has also been a great friend, adviser, and mentor. He helped guide me through graduate school and still provides sage advice with a humorous twist. He has unfailingly seen both the benefits and deficiencies of this subject, and his timely suggestions have helped expand the former at the expense of the latter. I was surprised but gratified when he proposed that *Forgotten Time* might be published as a part of his series at the University Press of Virginia, and I hope the book lives up to his expectations and high standards.

I have also had the good fortune to encounter many helpful and supportive archivists and librarians. I am especially grateful to Hank Holmes and his knowledgeable and friendly colleagues at the Mississippi Department of Archives and History. Their thoughtful assistance opened up many possibilities for my work, and I admire their professionalism as much as I enjoy their company. Research trips to Jackson are always a pleasure, and I look forward to my next chance to be among them and learn with them. Sid Graves and his staff at the Carnegie Library in Clarksdale were kind hosts during my extended stays there; I learned a great deal about my hometown in their collections and at the blues museum. I also spent many long and fruitful days in the Carter Room of Greenville's William Alexander Percy Library and recall the helpful staff with great appreciation. I spent less time at libraries in Cleveland, Indianola, and Greenwood but received great courtesy in each of these repositories. Archivists and librarians at the University of Mississippi, the University of Memphis, and Delta State University also proved extremely accommodating, as did the overburdened staff in the microforms section at the National Archives and Records Administration in Washington, D.C. Michael Plunkett and his colleagues at the University of Virginia Library's Special Collections Department were uniformly supportive, even when my requests were obscure, arcane, or worse; so too was the helpful staff at the Southern Historical Collection at the University of North Carolina in Chapel Hill. Finally, a word of praise for a group of women and men less often exposed to the peculiarities of academic research: the county clerks and courthouse staffs of the Mississippi Delta. In my forays into the records of Washington, Coahoma, and Sunflower Counties, I enjoyed the generous support of knowledgeable, friendly, and patient professionals, many of whom are also active local historians. They saved me countless hours of deed and title research with their suggestions and helped me understand what lay between the lines of decades-old legal instruments.

My thoughts were further refined, and sometimes challenged, by commentators on a series of papers delivered at meetings of the Southern Historical Association, the Organization of American Historians, and in other forums. I greatly appreciate the encouraging perspectives offered by Barbara Fields, Pete Daniel, Steven Miller, Daniel Littlefield, Harold Woodman, Stanley Engerman, and James Oakes. I have also benefited from the suggestions of Paul Gaston, Michael Holt, Nan Woodruff, Jim Cobb, Bertram Wyatt-Brown, Randy Shifflett, Bill Harbaugh, Olivier Zunz, Michael Wayne, John Barry, and Randy Boehm. The insights of the anonymous readers for the University Press of Virginia were particularly appreciated, as were their recommendations that the Press take the book. The "Dixie Diners," a group of rarefied intellects with down-home appetites who met sporadically for lunch and mutual assistance in the late 1980s and early 1990s provided an unfailing source of good cheer and better ideas; the generous critiques and enthusiastic support of Ed Ayers, Janette Greenwood, Larry Hartzell, and Beth Schweiger helped sustain this project in its early stages and remain for me a model of scholarly community. Not that I would have survived graduate school long enough to bask in this congenial inquiry were it not for the support of good friends like Melinda Buza, Elizabeth Van Beek, Wendy and Jack Brown, and Ginny and Doug Lapins. Friends and colleagues at Sewanee—particularly Julie Berebitsky, John Grammer, Woody Register, and Houston Roberson—have also helped me refine my ideas as this work passed from a dissertation toward a monograph and, with my predecessor Joe Cushman and our memories of the late Anita Goodstein, lend this place its touch of arcadia even yet.

I had never expected that working on this project would bring so many new friends in faraway places. Mississippians, I can report from experience, still know the meaning and value of hospitality. Chief among my helpful hosts was Clinton I. Bagley, who provided lodgings (sometimes for weeks on end), the sort of indispensable local historical information that never gets written down, introductions to a host of colorful characters, and his dependable friendship. Through him I came to know and greatly admire the late Baby Jane Burdine, whose many courtesies made my visits so pleasant, and whose absence renders this world a bit less sublime. Clint Bagley also introduced me to the incomparable Betty Werlein Carter, who generously shared her observations of a half century of southern life, her hopes for a better future, and her little-known connection to Isadora Duncan. A series of interviews with two Greenville gentlemen helped me immensely as I came to grips with particular aspects of the Delta's past: the late Wade Wineman patiently explained and even demonstrated the methods of turn-of-the-century lumbermen, while L. B. Stein provided helpful documents and insights into the lives of the Delta Jewry. Local historian Katherine Branton has gathered a great trove of information on the region's families, some of it published with Alice Wade, and I appreciate her willingness to share so generously with me. In Washington, D.C., Linton Weeks provided much-needed encouragement at a critical juncture, while John Colletta's deeply researched manuscript and enthusiastic approach to uncovering the secrets of the past continue to inspire my efforts.

Various cheerful experts came to my aid when it was time to create a book from my welter of notecards, computer printouts, past drafts, and random scribblings. Catherine Clark served admirably in the role of "intelligent reader" once a penultimate draft emerged. Tammy Scissom reformatted the text and notes and helped make my tables and graphs decipherable. Bobby Lawson and Glenn Vanden Bosch of Academic Computing saved me endless time and many embarrassing errors with their prompt attention to the machines that have supported this project. I very much appreciate their aid and hope they are not displeased with my final product.

Little of this would have been possible without the generosity of funders. The University of Virginia supported early investigation of this topic and its presentation in my doctoral dissertation through grants from their Governor's Fellowship, Academic Enhancement Program, and Alumni Association Fellowship. Much of the Delta database was compiled by investigating deeds and other documents in Mississippi county courthouses with the support of the American Historical Association's Littleton-Griswold grant for research in American legal history and the field of law and society. A Summer Stipend from the National Endowment for the Humanities helped me return to the Delta for additional research as I began reshaping the dissertation into a monograph. Dean Robert L. Keele of the College of Arts and Sciences at the University of the South has frequently extended the support of the University's Fund for Faculty Research to help me prepare the manuscript contained herein. None of the individuals and institutions mentioned above should be held accountable for the peculiarities of my interpretations, though all deserve commendation for their professionalism and devotion to scholarship.

Finally, family matters. I owe many debts to my parents and sister; their most direct contributions to my career and this book lay in creating a nurturing home where reading was a prized avocation and gentle disputation was as natural as drawing breath. Although my father's death in 1996 prevented him from joining in the excitement of this work's completion, I remain thankful for the many things we shared, including our curious wonderment of things past but not forgotten. The Delta's history is more closely connected with my mother's forebears, however, for her ancestors lived in the region during the era I have studied. In part, this book became my way of reviving those long-vanished souls and the changeful world they inhabited, to retrieve the joys and sorrows of those farmers, lumbermen, schoolteachers, and storekeepers I am descended from but will never know as men and women.

Now another century dwindles down to close, and I find myself on a mountaintop far from that alluvial plain where the humid air hangs heavy with stories yet untold. I can only wonder if the world I've tried to re-create from the Delta's frontier will make sense to my two sons, boys of the late twentieth century who will become men in a new millennium. For Addison (who wonders why his father's idea of work is strangely confined to reading and talking) and for Aaron (namesake of a great-great-grandfather who lived much of his life in the region's forests), I hope the postbellum Delta might someday seem an approachable, if still foreign, country. At least I trust they will not begrudge me the hours given to re-creating it on these pages. As it is for me, in a small way this is also their story.

But I dedicate this book to Laura, their mother and my truest friend for decades. She understands that the past is only vital when connected to the present; she should know, too, that I would not want to chance the future without her. She sustains and delights me, and I am grateful.

Forgotten Time

The Yazoo-Mississippi Delta after the Civil War

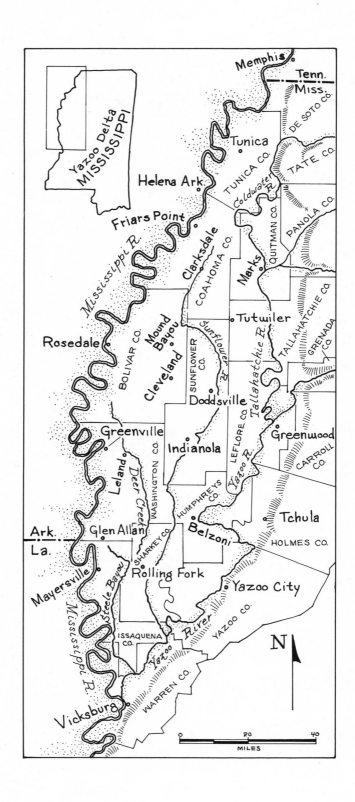

Introduction

With each spring thaw for thousands of years, the Mississippi River carried off the rich topsoil of the Midwest. Then, just south of Memphis, the river predictably bulged out over its banks, hurling water and purloined silt onto a low-lying alluvial basin nearly 200 miles long and up to 70 miles across at its widest point. Later, as the Father of Waters receded early each summer, the river left behind its fertile cargo.[1] Centuries of annual inundation and departure thus deposited a thick, rock-free, and fecund soil upon the Yazoo-Mississippi Delta — conditions fit for a king. King Cotton, that is.

Cotton gave the postbellum Delta its strongest link to the rest of the South, for the region possessed only the slimmest antebellum tradition. Fully 90 percent of its expanse still lay in thick-forested wilderness at the start of the Civil War, and four years of conflict did not spur settlement. By the beginning of the postbellum era, the Delta's plantation districts remained confined to the banks of the Mississippi, Yazoo, and Sunflower Rivers and the ridges along Deer Creek. Beyond this narrow plantation domain stretched miles of inland forest, beckoning or forbidding inhabitants of the settled districts, according to their predilections for rough living and danger. To picture these forests we must banish stereotypical images of southern pines: the trees of the Delta were decidedly deciduous. Myriad varieties of oak, gum, cypress, and cottonwood rose up out of the fertile soil, and thick canebrakes choked the region's "open" places. Anyone arguing that this region typified the South must ignore its land and forests — even the magnolia was an immigrant to the Delta.[2]

But the Delta did not remain a wild corner of the New South. Record numbers of southern farmers planted cotton in the decades following the Civil War, and the Delta, many soon discovered, proved to be the best place in the country for its cultivation. The prospect of riches in this cotton economy drew tens of thousands of immigrants to the area. Former slaves, former masters, foreign-born merchants, and northern men with entrepreneurial schemes all flocked to the region between war's end and the turn of the century. Significantly, most of the newcomers found their main chance in the untamed backcountry. Many realized their dreams of economic independence by growing Delta cotton (or trading with those who did), and thousands more heard of the good fortune and rushed in to try their luck. The Delta's population doubled, and then doubled again.

This fibrous link with the rest of the South initially turned to middling farmers' advantage in the Delta. The labor needs of white planters and the unsettled nature of the country gave tenant farmers unique prospects for success in the last third of the nineteenth century. Former slaves were able to work their way up an "agricultural ladder" toward property ownership in the 1870s and 1880s, and by 1900 two-thirds of the region's farm owners were black, not white. No other part of the South saw comparable black dominance of landowning; nowhere else could ex-slaves reasonably aspire to hold such fertile property.[3]

Yet the people who settled the Delta in this postbellum frontier era are a curiously forgotten generation. No study of the region, the South, or the nation makes more than passing mention of the time when the Delta was the promised land of the New South. Most histories pass quickly over the period. Railroad building and levee construction are recalled from years between the Civil War and the turn of the century, and a few examples of black success are treated as anomalous and isolated occurrences, but little is said of the broad range of opportunity that prevailed in this period. Sharecropping, which did not characterize a majority of Delta farms until 1910, is incorrectly assumed to have been an early and inescapable badge of the Delta's postbellum agriculture. Heavy-handed white planters are presumed to have dominated this alluvial frontier as they did the larger region. And the prospect of reciprocal interests between races, classes, and disparate ethnicities is never considered.[4] Although Delta opposition to desegregation in the mid-twentieth century has become a familiar cautionary tale—the reactionary Citizens' Councils, for example, were spawned in the heart of the Delta—the full story of the frontier generation has been ignored.[5]

The region's labor-poor landowners needed workers after emancipation, and the difficulties of luring laborers to a flood-prone wilderness challenged their traditional notions of plantation management. By the early 1870s planters appreciated the need to encourage black initiative (not repress it as many had while slaveholders) in order to clear, cultivate, and keep their backcountry holdings. Planters realized that they must rent out isolated acreage rather than limit blacks to work as sharecroppers, a tenure distinction that could cost a landlord more than 50 percent of his compensation. Ex-slaves proved willing— even eager—to endure frontier hardships for the chance to rent the rich soil. With its high cotton yield and the money they could earn clearing adjacent tracts, many expected to save a down payment for their own land. The reciprocal interests of black workers and white landowners thus helped to clear and settle a wilderness, and individuals in both groups grew prosperous. African Americans from across the South came to the Delta seeking opportunity, and thousands seized their chance for property ownership. By 1900 blacks dominated the lists of the Delta's landowners.[6]

Just as Delta blacks were more prosperous than one might expect, so too were the origins and occupations of the region's settlers more diverse. Colonies of Austrian barrel-stave makers and Slavonian woodsmen plied their crafts in the backcountry, and even the urban merchants—many of them also European immigrants—defied the New South stereotype. Nor were planters and merchants as restricted to agriculture or commerce as these labels imply. Indeed, it is often difficult to separate the store-tending planters from landholding merchants. The fact that plantation owners were frequently trained in professions complicates matters further, for many practicing lawyers and doctors spent little time on their rural holdings. This broad occupational penumbra was not limited to the wealthier classes. Black and white tenants and small landowners spent months felling timber in the forests, fashioning fences for new fields, and selling garden vegetables in the region's burgeoning towns. The buzzing frontier was too new, its needs and opportunities were too diverse, for any ambitious man to restrict himself to a single endeavor.

The glow of opportunity faded after the turn of the century. Black farmers lost hope of climbing up the agricultural ladder, and whites took political and economic advantage of their greater access to credit. The proportion of black landowners ceased expanding, and many farmers slid swiftly down into tenancy. The region became less a land of hope and more a scene of frustration, and it was here and now that the blues were born. But this unique art expressed more than anger and sadness; it gave vent to powerful disappointment, the sense of a promise betrayed, the knowledge that a unique moment had passed and that the prospects of poor blacks might never soar so high again. When northern factories needed workers during World War I, many left the Delta to follow this siren call. But they did not simply escape the South, they fled shattered dreams and strangled hopes. Their great migration was eager for something better, but it also admitted defeat in the Delta and loss of the best chance.

Introduction

The blues were deepest in the Delta and among its expatriates because they had not simply encountered hardship, they had experienced the sorrow of broken promises. By 1920 nearly three-quarters of Delta farms were operated by sharecroppers.[7]

In both good times and bad, the Delta's history seldom corresponded with the chronologies of the rest of the postbellum South. As the South began to rebuild from the ravages of the Civil War, most of the Delta remained a wilderness. As sharecropping gripped the cotton states, the Delta found it could only develop and prosper with more lenient tenure options. Indeed, the Delta gathered a flood of migrants largely because the pull of its attractions coincided with a push to escape poverty in older sections. Even the Delta's pivot to a thoroughly repressive society after the turn of the century contrasted with the remainder of the old Confederacy, for the shift occurred a decade later and with much greater economic and physical violence in the alluvial basin. Black lynchings became endemic, black farmers found themselves trapped in sharecropping, and business plantations sprouted up where decades of biracial reciprocity had once fostered development.

Although the South's development was not always perfectly mirrored in the Delta, the story of the larger region is incomplete without consideration of "Mississippi's Mississippi." Could we understand the Old Testament without knowing the appeal of the promised land to those who wandered for so long? Closer to home, can we grasp the glories of freedom for America's ex-slaves if we ignore that frontier corner of the South where African Americans gained some fleeting measure of economic independence? We must incorporate the forgotten generation of Delta pioneers into our view of the postbellum South if we are to understand the ambitions, accomplishments, and disappointments of the era.

The Delta's compressed period of development between 1865 and 1920 may best reveal the cotton South through contrast. The headlong scramble to the Delta shows how difficult life in the rest of the South was becoming in the 1870s and 1880s, and the rapid evaporation of prospects after the turn of the century reveals just how fragile were the conditions supporting opportunity in the former Confederacy. The Delta was both in and of the South, but its frequent disjunctures cast the larger region in relief. If we are to tell about the South, we must first understand the Delta. A forgotten time must be recalled.

1

Homecomings

Henry Tillinghast Ireys passed the Civil War avoiding questions about his regional loyalties. He may have felt ties to either the Deep South or the Northeast: his wealthy family lived in Newport, Rhode Island, but owned two large
estates in the Delta's plantation district. When Ireys visited their Mississippi
holdings during a Christmas vacation from school at age fifteen, the trip made
few deep impressions on him. His brief exposure to the Delta and plantation
agriculture failed to engender fealty to slaveholding in young Henry. The Civil
War erupted shortly after his twenty-fourth birthday, and Ireys and his family
repaired to Scotland, where they lived for the duration of hostilities. In the
spring of 1864, after the fall of Vicksburg and the imposition of a patchwork
military occupation of Mississippi, Ireys attempted to return to the Delta for an
inspection of his family's lands. Confederate guerrilla forces prevented the Federal gunboat on which he traveled from landing at Washington County, however, and he returned to Europe without examining the effects of war on the
property.[1]

Despite his neutral status during the conflict, Ireys cast his lot with the South
in 1865. He and his brother John arrived in the Washington County seat,
Greenville, in May 1865, firmly committed to restoring their Mound Place and
Falklands plantations to antebellum prosperity. This resolve was soon tested. "A
desolate scene presented itself," Henry Ireys later recalled; "fields that had been
cultivated . . . were then covered with grass or water; the gin house was out of
repair, fences gone, some of the cabins down, others dilapidated." Although
their manager had remained with the properties throughout the war, both
plantations had fallen into ruin. Regular maintenance work had been abandoned, the incursions of rival armies upset the rhythm of cultivation, and Federal military success encouraged slaves to flee their owners. A private levee, built
by slaves before the war to hold back the Mississippi from the fertile but low-

lying property, had been crevassed by the spring floods. Water poured into the fields. Henry and John realized they would not have the time or laborers to grow a crop after the waters receded, for it was already May, and their plantations were "devoid of labor, [with] only a few of the old hands left." They decided to focus first on repairing their holdings, for with "no labor, no mules, and no forage, nothing could be done on the plantation until Autumn."[2]

Physical damage to their plantation property was the most obvious problem the Ireys brothers faced in 1865, but other implications of slavery's destruction posed difficulties more far-reaching. Many former slave owners recoiled from the prospect that destitute, semiskilled agricultural laborers, individuals who until very recently had been held and treated as human chattel, must be regarded as free people with civil rights. The South's defeated master class was not, however, left to resolve these issues according to its preferences. Unlike other slaveholding societies, "in the United States alone [emancipation] was formulated without the landed elite's direct influence, and, as a consequence, proved the most sweeping and far-reaching." Without precedent in the known world, it was also significant that this "revolution," in the words of historian Harold Woodman, "was imposed from the outside." Many former masters, now reduced to landlords, may be regarded within Woodman's metaphor as counterrevolutionaries, for they did everything in their power to maintain accustomed control over social, political, and economic life in their home territory and as little as possible to comply with the directives of authorities at a distance. If American emancipation was to succeed, it would have to prevail over the wishes of this still potent, if war-diminished, elite; "the building of a free labor economy and society had to be achieved by a population that had not initiated the revolution in the first place—indeed, by a population that included large numbers who actively and violently opposed it."[3] But the fate of this revolution was not simply a struggle between northern enemies of bondage and southern proponents of coercion. A third group, the ex-slaves, was also (indeed, most) concerned with the issue. More than just a prized labor supply to be fought over by white elites, freed people proved eager to determine their own fates and unwilling to accept conditions that smacked of slavery. The Ireys brothers, despite their northern origins, shared this dilemma with other major landholders: they must induce men and women who prized their newfound freedom to rebuild plantations established for slave labor.

Henry Ireys set off for Vicksburg, where many of his former slaves had reportedly established themselves. The young planter hoped to lure the entire workforce back to his plantation but was only partly successful; he "rounded up a few of our old people, but most of them had scattered and were never to be heard from." We do not know what tactics their northern-born former owner used to get these few to return to Washington County. Like ex-masters all over the South, Ireys now had to accommodate labor's wishes as well as his own. He realized that he could not lure them back to the Delta with paternalistic appeals; absentee plantation owners like Ireys had no claim on the loyalty of ex-slaves. Instead, he had to negotiate with the freed men and women. Supervision of the freedmen's labors was one likely point of contention, and the ex-slaves would have argued against the antebellum practice of overseers driving squads of workers at assigned tasks. Compensation was another probable issue. Ireys, like all the South's former labor lords, hoped to limit the workers' recompense to food and lodging, but ex-slaves usually demanded cash for their labors. Freedom—to choose which crops to plant, what tracts to cultivate, and whether wives and children must work in the fields—was another question Ireys and his labor force had to consider. Although Ireys left no account of the negotiation, his concessions were sufficient to convince some of the ex-slaves to return with him to Washington County.[4]

The question of when and how the cotton economy shifted from slave-based cultivation to more or less free labor has generated an academic cottage industry in the last three decades. Although the causes and chronology of gang labor's demise may never be exactly determined, and the strength of planter coercion can never be accurately weighed, we can now discern some important patterns. We know, for example, that ex-slaves actively bargained for a spectrum of rights. Compensation, supervision, and basic freedoms stood at the matrix of any agreement. Some former masters found it difficult to accede to a single demand, construing each appeal for equality as a threat to their own livelihood and a challenge to white supremacy. Others quickly realized that the privileges of antebellum mastery had vanished forever, that they were now bidding for labor in a seller's market, and that refusal to meet the developing price of labor would leave them with crops of worthless Johnson grass, not cotton. African Americans who may have acted submissive in bondage now proved themselves anything but "infantilized." Despite the absence in 1865 of national legislation guaranteeing their economic, legal, and social equality as well as their freedom from slavery, newly emancipated blacks succeeded in wresting some rights from recalcitrant whites.[5]

Ireys's trip to and from Vicksburg revealed to him the "desolate change wrought by war." The young planter discovered that his plantation was not uniquely disadvantaged. The Delta's embryonic levee system was left a shambles in the wake of war, and the few riverside fields that had not been flooded lay untended in the absence of field laborers. Those few mansions that had escaped Federal depredations were frayed by years of neglect. Former masters were desperate for laborers and irate at the sight of ex-slaves freely traversing the countryside. The high price of cotton cried out for large plantings of the staple, but the unpredictable workforce, wartime damages, and shortage of cash and credit prevented many large landowners from pursuing a full crop. War and emancipation changed life for both races, and neither ex-masters nor ex-slaves could confidently predict the road to individual or regional prosperity in 1865. Ireys contrasted the postwar world to the antebellum life he remembered from his 1852 visit to the Delta. "From a scene of plenty and prosperity," he recalled, "there was presented destruction's waste; from a well-stocked plantation, with horses, mules, negroes, and cattle, to a dearth of labor and no stock."[6] Unlike most white Mississippians, Ireys did not feel deep remorse for a war fought and lost, but he did have to contend with the effects of invasion and its disruption of plantation society.

Not that plantations had been well established in the Delta before the war. In fact, the alluvial basin was only thinly inhabited by 1861, despite its fertile soil and the many navigable rivers nearby. At the end of the antebellum era, settlement was confined to a narrow plantation district along the banks of the Mississippi and its tributaries, and few dared travel in the interior, much less attempt to clear and cultivate it. The most prominent settlements were beside the Mississippi River—Greenville and Friars Point—and contained only a few hundred inhabitants each. Although the Delta is just slightly smaller than the state of New Jersey, the region contained fewer than 50,000 settlers in 1860. Of these, 87 percent were enslaved African Americans. Significantly, a mere 10 percent of the Delta's land had been cleared or inhabited before the Civil War. Even those tracts in private hands were largely wooded: barely 28 percent of the 747,995 privately owned acres had been cleared by 1860.[7] A bird's-eye view of the region before the Civil War would have revealed vast stretches of forest broken only at the riverside fringes. This bifurcated development—with heavily capitalized plantations along the major waterways and an untamed wilderness in the backcountry—would play a crucial role in shaping postbellum prospects in the Delta.

The region's few small settlements faced toward rivers—for transportation of goods, persons, and ideas, for mail delivery, and for flood alert—with their backs to the thick forest. In the region's interior one encountered a land little altered from nature's rough plan. Panthers were not uncommon, bears made regular raids on isolated cornfields, and alligators lurked along the slow-moving, tepid streams. Wild cane stood 10 to 20 feet tall, bamboo thickets rose up in the marshy lowlands, and a wide variety of hardwoods grew everywhere else. This persistent flora "necessitated the cutting of trails and roads with cane knives and axes before travel could be carried on," one antebellum settler later recalled. "Great clinging vines of wild grape and muscadine climbing to the tops of tall trees, festooned [the] forests, which, with the giant trees and the undergrowth of cane, created a jungle equal to any of Africa." Several types of oak dominated the drier lands, cypress sprouted among the marshes, and pecan, hickory, gum, elm, hackberry, and cottonwood trees, among others, filled out the forests. In 1883 the wilderness still covered 75 to 80 percent of the Delta, with trees from 2 to 4 feet thick standing 30 to 100 feet tall. [8]

Although prized as verdant arboreal habitats or valuable wetlands today, uncontrolled forests and waterways were the most persistent challenges to nineteenth-century Delta agriculture. Most of that era's farmers began removing trees and canebrakes when they initiated settlement and continued the practice until departing the region, either in death or frustration. As humans will, they looked for means of subduing the forest that did not require too much exertion. Few farmers actually cut down all the trees on their land before planting crops. Instead, they girdled large stands of oaks, hickories, cottonwoods, and other deciduous growth. Trees usually lost most of their leaves within a few weeks of having a ring cut through their bark; branches and trunks fell unpredictably to earth in these "deadenings" over the subsequent months and years. Farmers commenced planting a first crop of cotton and corn among the bare and crumbling reminders of the great forest and removed deadfalls and stumps as they found the time.[9]

Even when trees made way for agriculture, water threatened to claim a farmer's fields. As Ireys learned after the war, spring brings flood danger along the Mississippi River and its tributaries. The burden of protecting farmers against loss of crops, livestock, implements, and other property rested upon a comprehensive network of levees and drainage canals. Antebellum levee efforts were suspended during the war (due to hostilities and the bankruptcy of the regional levee-building authority), and the postbellum inhabitants of the Delta were left to devise their own systems of flood control. Continuous erosion of riverbanks posed another problem for settlers. The Mississippi has always been cavalier in its course, departing accustomed beds with disturbing frequency in its search for more amenable paths. Dry fields one day became riverbed the next; farmers might retire to sleep as Mississippians and awake to find themselves in Arkansas. The river chewed constantly at the shore — acre-sized chunks of land sometimes plunged unexpectedly into the Mississippi. "In every sharp bend the banks caved rapidly into the river, with a sound like artillery where timber stood; but with a dull, muffled sound where the land was cleared." Merchants at steamboat landings and in towns, where riverfront space was at a premium, were even more threatened than most farmers. Stores and houses were frequently removed from their foundations and carried away from the river's uncertain course: it was not uncommon for a merchant to reposition his store three or four times in a decade. When Leopold Alexander built his house in Greenville soon after the Civil War, for example, it stood more than 400 yards from the Mississippi's banks. When he pulled it down in 1877, the river ran within six feet of his front door. Those who had time to move their structures were fortunate; whole villages, like Bolivar County's aptly styled Riverton, were swallowed by the capricious Mississippi. But those perched alongside the river were not the only settlers to dread high water; backcountry pioneers had to deal with overflown streams and semipermanent swamps.[10]

Nor were collapsed banks and flooding the only waterborne menaces of the Delta. Frequent overflows of the region's rivers and streams, the persistence of standing water, and the area's near-tropical climate all combined to breed disease. Visitors often described the Delta as malarial, but yellow fever actually posed the greatest danger. Like malaria, yellow fever is spread by mosquitoes, a salient fact not discovered until after 1900. Thousands died of the disease in the late nineteenth century, and its pernicious effects were felt most strongly in 1878. In that year yellow fever's deadly effects on Grenada, a railroad town on the Delta's eastern edge, made the village internationally infamous. Lesser-known locations were similarly affected. Terrene, a small riverside town in Bolivar County, was ravaged by the disease in 1878, as was Greenville in Washington County. All but one of Greenville's elected officials died of yellow fever in that plague year; the sole survivor was fortunate enough to be away from the city at the time of its infestation. Nearly 300 of the town's citizens, approximately 20 percent of its population, perished in the scourge. When rumors of an outbreak of yellow fever at Memphis reached Greenville the next year, all who could escape the town (nearly half of the town's white citizens) did so. Business was almost entirely suspended until the perceived threat passed, and many stores remained closed for weeks.[11] Although the disease was never again as virulent as in 1878, the danger of yellow fever was not eradicated for decades.

The same waters that exacerbated the ills of the region also should have eased the transportation of goods and persons. In fact, steamboats regularly plied the Mississippi and most of its larger tributaries. But almost all of these rivers and creeks flowed from north to south, and commerce and travel east and west between them were impeded by forests, sloughs, and mud. Even the navigable waterways were sometimes undependable. One of the region's main rivers, the Sunflower, was so heavily dependent on rainfall runoff to augment its flow that shallow-draft steamboats could navigate the river for only six months each year. Some sections of the Sunflower refused to accommodate any but the smallest craft, even when the river was at its height. The Mississippi River was notoriously susceptible to snags. Steamboat travel became hazardous late each summer, when low water exposed sandbars and uprooted trees lodged in the riverbed.[12] Winter could bring even more dangerous developments. The semitropical climate that bred yellow fever in the summer suffered icy waterways from December through February. At times the Mississippi froze solid from bank to bank, and riverside communities were cut off from the water traffic that justified their slender existence. Foot and wheel travel between the rivers was no better. Even publications intended to boost settlement of the region warned travelers of the dangers of inland transportation: "Winters are characterized by dampness overhead and slushiness underfoot," announced one optimistic interpreter. The same admonition applied during spring floods and the heavy rains of summer and fall. Urban roads were not much better than the isolated and seldom-repaired rural paths. One Greenville wag reflected that "no good Methodist can sing 'How Firm a Foundation' in confident tones when traveling through our streets." But muddy (or alternately, dusty) roads characterized the region for decades: the first gravel roads were not constructed until 1915.[13]

Given the danger of flooding, lack of open land, transportation difficulties, and prevalence of disease, it might seem a wonder that the Delta was ever settled. But one factor prevented the region from being overlooked as King Cotton's empire expanded after the Civil War: the Delta's unusually fertile soil. For thousands of years the floods that washed over the basin each April and May carried fine, rich earth to the region. This aggregation of silted nutrients was lauded in the 1880s for supporting the world's highest proportion of plant food in its soil. Yet landowners like Henry Ireys faced the possibility of losing their verdant property from a lack of labor. They might own the richest soil in the world, but what did that profit them if no one worked the land? What good was a fertile plantation sitting idle, what value a rich tract covered with un-cleared hardwoods or threatened by flooding? After the Civil War white Deltans who had always been able to command labor along the riversides real-ized that they had to appeal actively to their former slaves and other potential settlers. Without laborers to grow their crops and purchasers to buy their unim-proved lands, the rich landowners of the Delta might be ruined. This was no idle possibility: cash-strapped former members of the region's planting elite sur-rendered tracts amounting to hundreds of square miles of land after the Civil War. In Washington County alone, 35 percent of the land (over 165,000 acres) was forfeited for back taxes by 1870.[14]

If the former Rhode Islander and his new allies, most of them ex-Confederates, failed to enhance the Delta's allure, they would be among those surrendering homes, land, and status. If they succeeded, the Delta might be newly populated by men and women from across the South and the nation, and immigrants might journey from other continents to share in building a new society. Only by making the region into an agricultural promised land could the Delta's planters save themselves. In their efforts, and in the responses of the thousands of newcomers to the alluvial wilderness, we discover a new tale to tell about the South.

2

Reconstructing the
Plantation District

Edmund Richardson attained levels of wealth, power, and influence beyond most planters' wildest dreams in the decades following the Civil War. Adept at navigating the roiled waters of Mississippi partisanship during the war and in the Federal occupation that followed, Richardson emerged from the late 1860s with a sizable fortune. He invested heavily in choice properties along the Mississippi River, expanding his domain despite the economic morass of his section and the national panic of 1873. By the end of Reconstruction, Richardson owned fertile plantations in four Delta counties and was hailed as "the largest cotton planter in the world—except, perhaps, the Khedive of Egypt." In 1881 total cotton production on Richardson's Delta properties was reported at 11,500 bales.[1]

Richardson harbored few illusions regarding the means to wealth and influence in postbellum Mississippi. He had little desire to preside over peaceful estates tended by grateful servants and no need to prove himself genteel by affecting the manners of the British gentry. A persistent craving for power drove him, not visions of moonlight and magnolias.

His resourcefulness matched his ambitions. Other planters might strive to emulate the antebellum elite's style of life and labor relations, but Richardson broke cleanly with the past. He mocked his neighbors' paternal concern for "their people," scorned Mississippians' traditional separation of agriculture and industry, and ignored cooperative rail and levee improvement projects proposed for the Delta. On his lands Richardson integrated agriculture, industry, and steam-powered transportation, intimidated competitors and business allies, and threatened the survival of nearby towns.[2] He left a clear model of action for the agribusinessmen who emerged to dominate the region after the turn of the century, but his reputation was sullied, despite his Midas touch.

Richardson pursued vertically integrated cotton production at Refuge, his incongruously styled Washington County headquarters plantation. The property was immense, and he aimed to control every aspect of the growth, processing, shipping, and marketing of his cotton. With Refuge and nearby tracts, Richardson owned ten square miles of land "in state of perfect improvement" by 1877, not counting three other plantations a few miles away. Although the size of his holdings was exceptional and their percentage of cleared land unparalleled in the Delta, the industrial plant Richardson installed at Refuge was the plantation's most distinguishing feature. Richardson erected the most capacious and intricate cottonseed oil mill north of New Orleans in order to squeeze every last penny of profit from his cotton; the machinery alone cost $40,000. He then linked oil mill, headquarters, and distant lands with a private railroad line stretching four miles. Refuge was so profitable that when Richardson considered extending his railroad eastward to the Delta's interior plantation corridor, the bustling entrepôt of Greenville justifiably feared its position as the region's trading and transshipping center might be supplanted.[3]

Although no other Delta planter equaled Richardson's array of enterprises or approached his wealth, many exhibited one or more of his characteristics. Coahoma County's James L. Alcorn, for example, rivaled Richardson's diversity of interests. Before the Civil War, Alcorn opened up Delta cotton lands, established a law practice, sought political office, and supervised the state's first regional levee authority. After the conflict Alcorn expanded into transportation as an influential stockholder in two railroad companies, operated a plantation store, and augmented his cotton acreage with a second Coahoma County estate. Although Alcorn was elected governor, served in the United States Senate, and was the wealthiest inhabitant of Coahoma County, his property and influence were eclipsed by Richardson's voracious expansion. The "persistent Whig"'s public service competed with his devotion to personal finance, but Richardson single-mindedly pursued his private fortune. Another prominent figure, Greenwood Leflore of the eastern Delta, paralleled Richardson's consolidation of cotton planting, processing, and transportation. Indeed, Leflore went even further than Richardson in trying to make an urban center of his plantation headquarters. He spent $75,000 constructing a road into Point Leflore, his settlement near present-day Greenwood, as a way to funnel freight and migrants through his town. At one time farmers brought cotton from sixty miles away for transshipping from Point Leflore. The eponymous town builder also owned the settlement's sawmill, brickyard, and hotel. Leflore's rich plantations produced hundreds of bales of cotton each year, and he lowered costs and increased profits by processing the fiber in his own gin. But Leflore attempted to build his empire on a weak bank of the Yazoo, and floodwaters swept away his protourban complex.[4] Neither Alcorn nor Leflore, despite their great energy and diverse enterprises, could match the scale of Richardson's success.

Just as Richardson's multiplicity of operations was not unique during the Delta's frontier period, neither was his absentee plantation management. Inexorably, towns replaced steamboat landings as the focus of commerce and society, and many planter families abandoned rural life in the decades following the Civil War. Greenville, then and now the principal city of the Delta, attracted many of Washington County's wealthy planter families. Some were probably drawn to the variety of life available in the river town: showboats stopped at Greenville's landing, touring theater companies filled its opera house, and parties were more conveniently given and attended there than at dispersed plantation homes.[5] But it was the business and professional opportunities supported by the urban aggregate that motivated most planters' relocation to town. Many Washington County planters owned mercantile establishments in Greenville, more were lawyers or doctors there, and juggling their professional obligations and plantation roles became second nature. W. A. Percy and William G. Yerger, two leaders in the drive to connect Greenville with the Delta interior by rail, were law partners, and each owned dispersed property. When Henry T. Ireys relocated to Greenville to oversee operations of the Greenville, Columbus and Birmingham Railroad in 1878, he supervised his plantation lands from town. After 1882, when the railroad was sold, Ireys stayed in Greenville to organize a bank. He later operated a cotton factorage in the city and continued to manage his landed holdings from afar. This pattern of absentee ownership, which often fostered dual careers, was replicated by dozens of Washington County planters before the 1880s and endured beyond the turn of the century.[6] Like Richardson, who lived in Jackson much of the year, many of the region's white farming elite discovered that property in the plantation district could be profitably, and more enjoyably, managed from a distance.

The central problem facing Richardson and his fellow planters involved neither the distractions of diverse enterprises nor the distance to their properties. Their greatest challenge was to procure, direct, and sustain a dependable supply of labor for their plantations. Conflict over the rights and obligations of former masters and ex-slaves clouded labor negotiations for several years after emancipation. Consequently, the plantation districts' labor system evolved in fits and starts: a plantation rented by an enterprising freedman might be surrounded by sharecroppers' tracts, while down the river convicts toiled without even the ameliorations of paternalism. Sharecropping quickly spread along the riverside in the late 1860s, but some planters employed the squad labor system from antebellum days well into the 1870s. The plantation districts were thus a heterogeneous mix of wage labor, tenancy, and compulsory labor for decades. Yet one aspect remained constant amid this changeable scene: the planters' perception of a chronic shortage of workers. It was their fear of idle fields that motivated white elites to seek innovative labor arrangements, for they found any agreement preferable to losing a year's income. Thus, while some freedmen labored under conditions akin to slavery, others were able to rent entire plantations for a reasonable sum.

Ambitious for wealth and control over labor, some planters turned to a supply of bound workers who could be dominated more thoroughly than slaves ever were: convicts. Planters accustomed to managing slaves were attracted to the convicts' marginal status. Because almost all of Mississippi's convicts were black in this era, their prison sentences and skin color combined to place them beneath the level of full humanity in whites' eyes. The percentage of blacks among the convict population rose steadily after emancipation, a result of the freedmen's new economic insecurity and increasingly draconian laws against petty theft. Passage by conservative Redeemers of statutes like the "pig law" — which made stealing one hog an imprisonable offense—was largely responsible for swelling Mississippi's convict population from 272 in 1874 to 1,072 in 1877. In the 1880s the proportion of blacks among the prisoners hovered around 90 percent. Planters expected to hear few complaints if a black thief was beaten for insolence or failure to obey instructions. As one recent student of the convict lease has pointed out, "it stood as a system of forced labor in an age of emancipation." Convicts could be set to work without the interminable bargaining that many ex-slaves now seemed fixed upon; prisoners could be threatened with physical abuse rather than tantalized with incentives; and if a convict died from mistreatment, the planter could simply rent a replacement. Unlike slavery, the convict lease removed a planter's interest in prolonging the life of his charge and obviated his need to weigh labor needs against the laborer's health. Because lessees were only tangentially accountable for the health of their laborers, the convict lease system presented far more opportunities for abuse than had slavery.[7]

Nor was the treatment of prisoners the only difference between the convict lease and slavery. The southern convict lease system evolved in the same era that witnessed the region's fascination with railroads, that saw myriad schemes for rebuilding the personal and regional fortunes of the defeated Confederacy, that heard Henry Grady's clarion call for a New South where manufacturing joined agriculture. True, most convicts labored in cotton cultivation, but they also toiled in factories and mines, built railroads, and raised levees. The convict lease system was neither simply slavery reborn nor heedless capitalism, although it had something in common with each.[8] It offered enterprising capitalists a cheap and pliable workforce, a captive supply of unskilled laborers whose use (and possible abuse) was tolerated by white society. Not surprisingly, Edmund Richardson had an insatiable appetite for convict labor.

Richardson began working convicts in 1868. In that year General Alvan C. Gillem, military commander of occupied Mississippi, agreed to give Richardson control of the state's convicts for three years—without charge. In fact, the state promised to pay Richardson $18,000 each year to maintain the penitentiary in Jackson and appropriated almost $12,000 to transport prisoners to distant work sites. Richardson soon had almost all of the state's 194 convicts at work on his Delta plantations.[9]

Upon his election to the governorship in 1870, James L. Alcorn, Richardson's fellow Delta planter, initiated an investigation of the state's leasing system. Republican Alcorn may have privately resented Democrat Richardson's state-subsidized workforce, which gave the latter a clear advantage in the Delta's labor-scarce environment. But Alcorn publicly proclaimed that he was motivated by concerns for the convicts' welfare, and he appointed a commission to investigate the treatment of prisoners held at the Jackson penitentiary and at Refuge plantation. To Alcorn's amazement his hand-picked committee actually praised Richardson's stewardship. It pointed out that the previously high mortality rate among prisoners fell during Richardson's term as lessee and reported that confidential interviews revealed the convicts preferred working at Refuge to incarceration in the cramped Jackson penitentiary. The commissioners found the convicts well cared for, suitably clothed, and amply fed and recommended that Richardson be allowed to continue his control over the state's prison population.[10]

Alcorn's biographer suggests that he read and was persuaded by the commission's report, and that he no longer opposed Richardson's lease on humanitarian grounds. Indeed, before he relinquished the governor's office to assume his seat in the United States Senate, Alcorn gave tacit approval to Richardson's controlling the convicts even beyond the period of his 1868 contract. But Alcorn pocket vetoed a bill granting Richardson a lucrative fifteen-year lease of the state's convicts—a contract that Richardson had dispensed $20,000 in bribes to secure and that would have brought him an estimated $67,500 each year.[11] Alcorn, it seems, was reconciled to Richardson's treatment of prisoners but unwilling to subsidize his rival's wealth for the long term.

Richardson found Alcorn's successor, Ridgley C. Powers, even less cooperative. When the legislature revived the question of granting a fifteen-year lease to Richardson in its next session, Powers promptly vetoed the measure for its "extravagant demands upon the public treasury." In 1872 Powers used reports of increased illness and death of convicts at Refuge to justify awarding the convict contract to Nathan Bedford Forrest instead of Richardson. The former Confederate general and most notable leader of the Ku Klux Klan was then building the Selma, Marion, and Memphis Railroad through northeast Mississippi, and Powers suggested that tracklaying in the foothills would be more healthful than cotton cultivation in the Delta. Powers was correct. Ex-slave trader Forrest's treatment of the black convicts was far better than the conditions they experienced in Washington County, and their health improved dramatically.[12]

But Richardson was not yet out of the convict-leasing business. As the prison population continued to increase, and other lessees were unable to absorb the added convicts, Richardson moved to replenish his Delta labor force. By late 1872 convicts were adding to Richardson's private levee in front of Refuge and constructing his railroad. Even the penitentiary law of 1875, which required private contractors to dole out convict laborers among applicant sublessees, could not remove forced labor from Richardson's plans. He simply persuaded the state's first contractors, O. C. French and Charles S. Jobes, to sublease the majority of convicts to him.[13]

As a sublessee, Richardson was further removed from state scrutiny of prisoners' treatment, and the conditions endured by his convicts soon worsened. Prisoners no longer preferred working at Refuge to alternative incarceration. Escapes increased, and Richardson's reputation among his Delta neighbors, already strained by his brusque manner and conspicuous success, deteriorated further. In April 1875 twenty-three convicts escaped from two of Richardson's plantations. While at large, they attacked a trapper and added his boat and guns to goods they had earlier stolen from Richardson's plantation store. "The community," wrote *Greenville Times* editor J. S. McNeily, "is justly indignant at the loose discipline which enabled so many convicts to escape." A Washington County planter described the aftermath of this escape as a "reign of terror." No gentleman, he explained, now "feels safe in leaving his wife and family alone at night, and widows are in a constant State of fear." Neighboring planters complained that groups of six or eight of Richardson's convicts were sometimes allowed to work without armed supervision, and that it was not uncommon to find only one guard assigned to as many as forty prisoners. In late June a black woman was raped and killed by a gang of three escaped convicts. By midsummer 1875 nineteen Richardson convicts were abroad among the population of southwest Washington County, as were forty-three convicts who had escaped from the plantations of two other sublessees. One planter claiming to own a plantation near Refuge (but declining to reveal his name in the newspaper) called for vigilante action. "If the county officials have not the authority to make Mr. Richardson keep adequate guard," he exclaimed, "I suggest that the Tax Payer's League [a Democratic Party pseudonym during Redemption] take immediate action." Editor McNeily concurred. "This grievance is assuming formidable proportions," he warned, "and unless checked will assuredly lead to a forcible suppression by the people."[14]

In an unusual breach of racial solidarity, the conservative *Greenville Times* began publishing accounts of the mistreatment of convicts. It even reprinted an escaped convict's condemnation of forced plantation labor from the *Vicksburg Monitor*. "The negro," the article concluded, "does not want to go back to the plantation. He gives a bad account of the treatment of convicts on that place." And despite Richardson's Democratic fealties, the Washington County Redeemers denounced the convict lease system. In an editorial in the *Greenville Times,* McNeily likened the county to a penal colony and lamented a system that allowed the "settling upon us [of] hundreds of the most depraved and desperate of human beings, all convicted of crimes, some of whom are escaping almost daily." He accused Richardson of not abiding by the terms of the state's convict lease contract, cried out at the physical danger posed by escaped wrongdoers, and warned that competition from convict laborers would soon confront small farmers with a situation where "fully one half of you will have to leave the county, or get in the penitentiary to secure employment." When Washington County planter W. A. Percy joined the state legislature the following January, he introduced a bill to end the leasing of convicts, but it failed. None of these public fissures restricted Richardson's ability to lease and work convicts on his Delta properties. By September 1876 his Delta detractors were reduced to strewing his path with small inconveniences. In that month the state's convict-leasing agents were persuaded to sunder Richardson's contract abruptly and take possession of his entire allotment of convicts. Greenville officials chose this moment to offer the city's jail yard for their temporary quarters. Meanwhile, Richardson's cotton waited in the fields. "It is pretty tight on the Colonel," McNeily sniped, "to lose his striped brigade at this particular season." Richardson had the last laugh, however, for his convicts were restored to Refuge within a week.[15]

Although Percy's 1876 legislative effort failed, evidence of convicts' poor treatment on Richardson's plantations and on the property of other sublessees eventually brought legislative investigation. Convicts fleeing Delta plantations, it emerged, literally ran for their lives. The average death rate among Mississippi's leased convicts from 1881 through 1885 approached 12 percent. Over 15 percent of the prisoners died in one year, 1882. Black men, whose death rate surpassed 17 percent in 1882, were in particular danger. The percentage of deaths among black convicts was, on average, more than twice that suffered by white prisoners.[16]

Yet convict leasing "left its trail of dishonor and of death" until Mississippi's 1890 constitutional convention. A clause in the new constitution prohibited the leasing of any state convicts after 31 December 1894. But with some multiyear leases negotiated as late as 1894, and the continued availability of county prisoners for forced labor, the stain of convict leasing receded slowly from the state. In addition, the Delta prison farm established by reforming legislators to end the cruelties of convict leasing—Parchman Penitentiary—actually elevated prison brutality to new heights.[17]

Most of Mississippi's convicts were leased to clear and cultivate Delta plantations or to construct the new railroads crisscrossing Mississippi in the postbellum era. Ironically, Edmund Richardson's voracious appetite for convict labor probably restricted the number of Delta planters who could work prisoners in their fields. The institution was justifiably abhorred, but it touched relatively few Delta plantations and included a mere fraction of the region's labor force. The desire to compel labor in the Delta, however, was not limited to the lessees of convicts.

Many whites employed legal maneuvers to bind their former slaves to the plantation. Among the first of the "Black Codes" passed by Mississippi's reconstituted legislature was a bill designed to restrain young blacks from leaving their masters. Justified as a humanitarian measure to protect black orphans and youthful indigents, the apprentice law provoked suspicions soon after being signed into law by Governor Benjamin G. Humphreys on 22 November 1865. Under the provisions of this legislation, black children and their parents operated under disadvantages not imposed upon whites. The apprentice law applied only to black youths, allowing courts to bind them out despite parental opposition and providing the ex-slave's former owner with the first option on their apprenticeship.[18] With this apprentice law, many feared, the courtrooms of Mississippi would be transformed into slave auction blocks.

Planters in the Delta's plantation districts were particularly eager to restrain young blacks from leaving their fields. After Probate Judge J. F. Harris of Yazoo County proved eager to apprentice black children to their former owners, ex-slaves in the eastern Delta grew desperate to hide their children. Harris routinely ignored the vigorous protests of black parents and consigned young freed people to their former masters; his probate court in Yazoo City apprenticed 220 black youths in one term. One of the objecting parents, Laura Taylor of Yazoo County, complained to an agent of the Freedmen's Bureau in July 1866. Taylor and her two children, Mary and Joseph, had remained on the plantation of their former owner, identified as Mr. Allen, until Christmas 1865. When they tried to leave, Allen refused to give up the children, announcing that they were duly bound to him by Judge Harris and would remain on the plantation. When Taylor protested, Allen had her driven off the property. She returned, however, and "stole" the children. The sheriff was summoned; he captured the family and returned Mary and Joseph Taylor to the plantation of their former owner. At this point Laura Taylor approached Judge Harris and begged to have her children restored to her. But he refused to hear the mother's pleas, stating that the children would remain bound to Allen regardless of her wishes. He threatened to jail her for contempt if she complained again. Both Allen and Judge Harris acted within the provisions of the state's apprentice law, and the Freedmen's Bureau could offer Laura Taylor only its moral support.[19]

Complaints against forced apprenticeship rose throughout the Delta's plantation districts. Captain William L. Tidball, the Freedmen's Bureau agent in Greenville, conveyed the story of a Washington County man who had been banished from a plantation but was prevented from taking his grandchildren with him. The agent could not persuade the planter to reinstate the freedman, nor could he pry the apprenticed youths away from the planter. Captain Tidball was similarly powerless to aid a woman whose stepchild was seized; the planter had owned child, mother, and stepmother before the Civil War, and the courts deemed his privilege to hold an apprentice beyond legal challenge. In the absence of incontrovertible evidence proving abuse or neglect, judges ignored parental complaints against planter prerogatives. Other Freedmen's Bureau agents wrote to headquarters for instructions on how to deal with these patent outrages, but the Bureau had no authority to dissolve legal apprenticeships.[20]

The complaints of parents and the objections of Freedmen's Bureau agents, though consistently overturned, eventually had a cumulative effect. Delta judges might browbeat aggrieved parents by threatening to hold them in contempt and avoid hearing their stories out of court, but the region's dockets became swollen with cases contesting apprentice contracts. Judge J. M. Henderson of Coahoma County finally wrote the director of Mississippi's Freedmen's Bureau, General Alvan Gillem, describing his dilemma. Henderson reported a deluge of applications from planters eager to apprentice black youths, yet he could not escape the anger of parents whose children were already trapped in compulsory labor. The apprentice law was a facade, he conceded, for few black parents were "willing to bind their children whether they can support them or not." He was desperate to prevent "double trials" and escape "having every freedman in the county annoying me by explanation." Henderson vowed that in the future he would not approve apprentice arrangements without asking black parents why their children "should not be bound out[,] & if they are unable to do that, then to consult their wishes as to whom they desire them bound to."[21] What should have been the normal, evenhanded procedure came only as the concession of a weary jurist.

Judge Henderson was not alone in his frustration with the impracticalities of the apprentice law. Even Mississippi's conservative legislature could not ignore the flood of complaints. It passed an act repealing the apprentice law, and as of 21 February 1867 black and white orphans were promised equal rights under the laws of Mississippi. But these lofty deliberations were not immediately applied in the Delta, for the new law was vague regarding the fates of those indentured before its passage. Many children apprenticed before the repeal remained trapped in compulsory labor. General Gillem, whose response to the obvious inequities of apprenticing had thus far been glacial, finally swung the official weight of the Freedmen's Bureau against forced indentures. After the legislature repealed the apprenticing law, he issued a general order instructing judges to release black children whose parents could support them and those capable of supporting themselves. Significantly, Gillem's order did not define what level of support judges should consider sufficient. Nor did Gillem cite the new Mississippi law as precedent for his action. Instead, he claimed to act in response to "complaints of hardship in the needless apprenticing of minors, particularly in pursuance of the preference given to the former owner[,] . . . having become almost incessant" — complaints he had ignored before the legislature's action.[22]

The practical effects of Gillem's action were mixed. One of his subordinates claimed that "the probate judges have respected General Order No. 3 [to end apprenticeships], and indentures have been revoked upon all application by the parents of apprenticed children." Agent J. R. Webster reported returning an improperly apprenticed child to his mother in Bolivar County. But the question of what constituted an appropriate level of support for black children was left to each judge's assessment, and planters determined to hold children in unwanted apprenticeships often found they could manipulate the law's vagueness and Gillem's order to their advantage. Captain Tidball in Greenville reported many such cases. In one, a white Washington County planter named Moseby apprenticed a freedwoman's grandchild and then died. Even though the grandmother disputed the indenture, the court ruled that Moseby's heirs could continue the apprenticeship because she was deemed incapable of supporting the child. Despite the new law and the aid of Freedmen's Bureau agents, many indentures remained in force beyond 1867. White planters and conservative officeholders were only dissuaded from maintaining the facade of apprenticing by the continued objections of black parents, the election of Republicans to state and local offices in 1868, and the tightening grip of Congressional Reconstruction.[23]

When sham apprenticeship failed, some planters in the plantation districts looked abroad for laborers. Attention soon focused on the Chinese. Rumors of mass importations of Chinese laborers were heard throughout Mississippi within a few months of emancipation—perhaps circulated by whites as a threat to obstreperous freedmen. The *Vicksburg Times* heralded the arrival of a steamboat said to contain 500 Chinese laborers by inviting whites and blacks to attend the landing for a view of the men whose efficiency would soon render ex-slaves' labor superfluous. But the steamboat docked without a single Asian laborer on board. Similarly, the ballyhooed flood of 500,000 Chinese workers never materialized.[24]

Despite their frustrations with emancipation, the complexities of establishing free labor, and ex-slaves' behavior, most employers refrained from engaging Chinese workers for financial reasons. Planters quickly discovered that the cost of Chinese labor made the wages paid to blacks appear cheap. Indeed, it is a wonder that any Chinese immigrants made their way to the Delta's cotton fields. First, the planter had to pay $300 for each worker's passage from China. Then, would-be employers discovered that the Chinese would not contract for less than ten to fifteen dollars per month—significantly more than the going wage for freedmen. Finally, labor agents would not begin recruiting Asian workers until planters deposited the full amount of transportation costs and five years' wages with New York bankers. The combination of large cash down payments and long-term contracts for untried workers dissuaded most planters from the experiment.[25]

But Frederick Metcalfe was willing to gamble. He had arrived in the Delta before the Civil War and cultivated property northeast of Greenville, a few miles from the Mississippi River yet firmly within the belt of prewar settlement defining the plantation district in 1865. By the early 1870s the Washington

County planter was losing money on his plantations and feared bankruptcy. Somehow he procured several Chinese laborers and installed them at Newstead plantation in 1873.[26] The Chinese lived together in a house across a creek from the dwellings of Metcalfe's freedmen and attempted to maintain their culture by eating their native foods, taking a holiday to celebrate the Chinese New Year, and the like. Their sojourn at Newstead even prompted tentative cross-cultural exchanges. The Chinese developed a taste for cigars, and in 1874 Metcalfe paid one of them seventy-five cents to prepare his family's Christmas dinner. They were eager to earn extra money doing chores for cash, and in 1873 several picked cotton for a neighboring planter after gathering their crops on Metcalfe's property.[27]

Yet ill feelings arose quickly between the Chinese and the freedmen who had been warned they would be replaced by "coolie labor." One of Metcalfe's black employees refused to haul the Chinese squad's cotton to the gin in November 1873, and friction between the two groups soon charged the air. Freedmen broke into the Chinese workers' house repeatedly, stealing even their cigars, and Metcalfe was eventually reduced to calling the constable to restore order. Worse, the black workers provoked fights with the outnumbered Chinese. The Chinese eventually fell to quarreling and fighting among themselves, and one "had a difficulty" with Metcalfe's overseer. Finally, they began deserting Metcalfe's plantation: five slipped away one night, sacrificing the cotton and corn crops they had just planted. By 1875 only black workers remained at Newstead.[28]

Metcalfe's experiences with Chinese laborers were not unique. Racial tensions mitigated whatever superior efficiency the imported workers may have offered, and by the late 1870s most of the first wave of Chinese workers had dispersed. Planters discovered that they could live with black labor, even profit by it, and soon lost interest in importing Chinese workers at great expense. Enumerators of the 1880 census could find only fifty-one Asians in the entire region.[29] Until the turn of the century, Delta planters focused on finding laborers among southern blacks.

Most plantation district proprietors found convict labor expensive and difficult to obtain, apprenticeship full of legal headaches, and labor importation costly and disruptive. To save trouble and expense, many planters hoped to continue using men and women who had been their slaves. Indeed, some successfully maintained their workforce beyond emancipation, despite the incursions of Federal troops and the temptations of freedom. All of the laborers on a Mr. Wynn's plantation in 1867 had once been his slaves. Nearby, a plantation employing over 100 hands was largely staffed by former slaves of the owner, a planter named Harrison. And a Virginian named Goochland, who brought twenty-four slaves to property in the same neighborhood during the war, planned to return to the Old Dominion with his employees after gathering the year's crops. How did these planters persuade former slaves to forsake their full freedom? We know these blacks were aware of their legal freedom: a Freedmen's Bureau agent, made suspicious by such large concentrations of ex-slaves toiling for their former masters, questioned the workers about their legal standing. Most of Wynn's workers were able to explain their rights and obligations as citizens; and although many of Harrison's employees seemed less astute, all were registered to vote, and "they appeared perfectly contented." They, like Goochland's soon-to-be repatriated Virginians, chose to continue working for the men who had once held them as chattel rather than risk finding a worse employer or less amenable situation.[30]

But many ex-slaves were eager to escape their former owners. For generations they had been held against their will, compelled to labor for another's profit, and scarred by someone else's definition of discipline: it was time to shake off the dust of the old plantation and begin working for themselves. Most had been farming all their lives—why not disappear into the Delta's interior, find a suitable clearing, and fill their needs hunting game in the teeming forest and cultivating the region's fabled soil? Or they might leave the region altogether. Few had been born there, most knew of other places, all had relatives in other sections of the South—why not get as far away from the Delta as possible?[31]

Ex-slaves soon discovered, however, that some whites still intended to circumscribe their freedom. Freedmen's Bureau agent Captain W. F. Griffin revealed one former slaveholder's desperate hegemony. A freedwoman named Chasy decided to leave C. P. Atkins's isolated plantation in the summer of 1865. Like many ex-slaves in rural areas, she was attracted to the city; and Vicksburg—with its vibrant economy, large population of freed people, and reputation for racial leniency—was her goal. But Atkins heard of her plans and surprised her before she could leave the plantation. He stripped Chasy, lashed her thumbs together, stretched her arms above her head, and beat her until she fainted from the pain. Word of the act reached Captain Griffin, twelve miles away in Greenwood. He knew that many ex-slaveholders tried to discourage their former slaves from leaving, but even he was surprised by Atkins's extreme behavior. Upon questioning, the planter confirmed Chasy's beating but reminded the Freedmen's Bureau agent that she was his slave. Captain Griffin asked if Atkins knew that slavery had ended. Pressed, Atkins admitted that the incident occurred after emancipation, but he insisted that he still had the right to discipline his former slaves as he chose. Captain Griffin was uncertain of his authority to reprimand Atkins but wrote his superiors that the planter "does not seem to be a well-disposed citizen" and recommended severe punishment. If the Bureau hoped to prevent similar outrages in the Delta's plantation districts, he warned, Atkins must be made "an example in this section of the country."[32]

Planters along the banks of the Mississippi River also abused African-American workers. Lieutenant O. B. Foster reported that Issaquena County whites displayed a "cautiousness" with him when they discovered he was an agent of the Freedmen's Bureau. Yet many planters could not conceal a "deep-rooted feeling of hate, and a desire to show enmity . . . towards the black people. . . . Freedmen have come to me with cheeks pounded, eyes badly inflamed, teeth knocked out, and other evidences of maltreatment." Although blacks outnumbered whites by more than eight to one in Issaquena County, it was ex-slaves who were the consistent targets of violence. Nor did some whites limit demands and abuse to their own laborers. Two days before, Foster reported, "a negro was pursued past my office by a [white] citizen with a pistol who searched long for the fugitive after he had disappeared, with the avowed object of shooting him because he would not, although not in his employ, do some compulsory labor." Local justices of the peace condoned this behavior, and blacks' complaints of assault and battery were routinely "thrown aside by the county court." Plantation district whites organized to prevent blacks from taking the law in their own hands. Foster described the "wholesale disarming of negroes" in Issaquena County in 1865. "Freedmen who have just purchased shotguns, and those who owned them before, have their weapons rudely taken from them. Their trunks and houses are freely . . . broken open for the purpose." The same confiscation methods were still being employed by planters along the Yazoo River as late as August 1867.[33]

Many blacks reported difficulty gaining equitable labor contracts in this environment. In December 1865 Foster explained that ex-slaves in Issaquena County's plantation belt "refuse to enter into contracts with native planters for the ensuing year, but express entire willingness to do so with northerners. For this I think the former owners are in great measure to blame, they having begotten by treachery and otherwise a wide distrust among [the] employed." In the first year of free labor in the plantation district, he found, "the greatest call upon my time is now made in compelling strict justice to be done to Freedmen in the matter of contracts." Many former slaveholders regarded these unprecedented actions on blacks' behalf as intrusions on their contractual purview. In

January 1866 one planter's son summed up this perspective, noting "today the darkies contracted—Yankee approving." Even where no force or intimidation was involved, planters frequently exploited black illiteracy and inexperience to gain unfair advantage. Confronted with much smaller profits than anticipated at the end of 1865, "the black people claim[ed] that in a great many instances their ignorance was imposed upon and they induced to sign writings the force of which they were not fully cognizant of." Similar complaints were still being heard in 1867, as Major George W. Corliss explained from Coahoma County, for unschooled ex-slaves were disadvantaged before the civil law as a result of "their ignorance and their black skins." Some white merchants, planters, and professionals in the plantation district found the allure of fraud difficult to resist when dealing with illiterate blacks.[34]

Despite these handicaps, former slaves quickly learned how to manipulate the Delta's labor shortage to their benefit. They grew comfortable bargaining with ex-masters and other whites, and planters soon found themselves competing for laborers. One Tunica County planter found his black laborers "sharper every year" and was aghast that they might seek to be "independent of me and each other." Not infrequently, planters reacted with indignation to news that a dependable employee or tenant was leaving to join a competitor's operation. Sometimes they accused the freedman of disloyalty, but more often they blamed the enticing employer. "Most of [the departing black laborers] I have built up," a befuddled—and chronically labor-short—paternalist explained, "but others offer them inducements and now and then one of them leaves." Consider Henry St. John Dixon's account of labor disputes in Washington County. He reported that the late George Percy's "negroes have all gone, acting outrageously save 4 house-servants," after their employer's death. Dixon feared Percy's widow and children would suffer without workers to grow and harvest their crops. Even worse was the fact that the ex-slaves had gone to work for a scalawag, one Dr. Blanton, and "his Yankee partner," William H. Bolton. Dixon had no doubt that Bolton and Blanton were at the bottom of the labor defection from the widow's fields, and he accused the two of transporting the freedmen away. Dixon, it turns out, was expressing more than a neighbor's sympathies: the carpetbagger and scalawag had also hired away many of his family's employees. Bolton and Blanton "are a set of scoundrels," he fumed, and "have enticed off one of the best hands on the place, who had signed a contract to stay." Although Henry Dixon's father was a judge and he himself was reading the law, the family preferred to settle the matter privately. Judge Dixon wrote the northerner Bolton requesting that the disputed worker be allowed "to use his own option." Significantly, legal action against the former slave was not considered, despite his contract to serve the Dixons. He was regarded as a pawn by the ex-slaveholding jurist and his son, for the Dixons were slow to adjust to dealing with former slaves as their contractual equals. They were far more comfortable demonizing competitors as Yankees and traitors to the South.[35]

Some planters chose to deal honestly with their black employees. They drafted fair contracts, explained the provisions to their potential employees and tenants, and abided by the terms of agreements. These men were rare in the Delta's plantation district in the 1860s, but they did exist, and their honesty was appreciated by the freedmen. Indeed, these plantation owners probably hoped to attract a dependable supply of labor by their good behavior. Freedmen's Bureau agent Captain Tidball believed these planters "appreciate the relations they sustain to the freedmen, and [understand] that humane treatment and honest dealing are the only means by which to secure [the ex-slaves'] confidence and services." Word of mouth revealed which planters were fair and which would cheat and abuse blacks for a little extra profit. The former soon found themselves with plenty of workers, while the latter pushed their dwindling labor supply ever harder in resentment.[36]

Disparities in labor supply and production were apparent by 1866. Planters who condemned color-blind honesty as racial disloyalty banded together to dissuade their fair-dealing neighbors. Along the Yazoo "an organization of men whose avowed purpose is to discourage freedmen and moderate planters" attempted to resurrect slaveholders' hegemony. Their tactics: "a concerted system of persecution by murdering negroes at work upon the plantations" of honest planters. These activities were not confined to Yazoo County. The Ku Klux Klan torched several buildings on the plantation of a planter who had the audacity to rent land to blacks near Friars Point in Coahoma County.[37] In the plantation districts freedmen and the scrupulous whites who dealt fairly with them faced opposition ranging from fraud to murder.

The Freedmen's Bureau was a potential ally in blacks' search for justice. Many Bureau agents were officers in the army that had recently freed the slaves, and the freedmen often sought their advice and assistance. Although some of the agents serving in the Delta wrote condescendingly of the ex-slaves, most expressed concern for their safety, welfare, and success. Yet the Freedmen's Bureau was not omnipotent. Its agents could advise freedmen and notify authorities of abuses and often drew accuser and accused together to settle disputes out of court, but it did not render summary judgments. Criminal complaints, and most civil issues, still found adjudication in courts staffed by locally elected or appointed officials. Although the Bureau's representatives frequently regarded these bodies as racist and partial to planter interests—especially in 1865 and 1866—the local courts were preeminent by law. Thus, the Freedmen's Bureau agents could help an ex-slave bring his case to trial and might even offer advice in civil matters, but the judgments were rendered by local whites.[38]

Several recent histories of the post–Civil War South allege that Freedmen's Bureau agents were largely racist, easily manipulated by planters, and dilatory in their offices. William S. McFeely led criticism of the Freedmen's Bureau's leadership with his *Yankee Stepfather: General O. O. Howard and the Freedmen,* and a number of subsequent studies have belittled the efforts and sincerity of agents in the field. But zealousness, like beauty, is in the eye of the beholder; even examinations of the same area have produced divergent appraisals of the effectiveness of Freedmen's Bureau agents. Consider how their separate foci led Michael W. Fitzgerald and Ronald L. F. Davis to propound significantly different conclusions regarding Bureau agents in Mississippi. Fitzgerald's concern for the development of black political efficacy convinced him that "in Natchez, as in other localities throughout Mississippi, the Bureau represented a hindrance, rather than an aid, to freedmen's political activity through the [pro-Republican Union] League." Yet in his study of Natchez District agriculture, Davis found that, never "fully able to take the steps necessary for securing the former slave's social and economic independence, the bureau instead worked to at least protect the rights of blacks as free wage laborers." Delta planters did not dismiss the Freedmen's Bureau agents as accommodationist, nor does examination of the agents' reports suggest that any more than one-quarter of their number were overtly sympathetic to the region's white elites. Indeed, Henry St. John Dixon's diary includes several passages denouncing Freedmen's Bureau agents in Washington County not only for their insistent social climbing among local whites but for their thorough advocacy of the freedmen's interests. In his autobiography New Jersey–born planter Samuel French emphasized marked differences among the Freedmen's Bureau agents of Washington County.[39] In the Delta, it seems, the Freedmen's Bureau was no monolith. More likely, local whites and blacks regarded the agents as unpredictable.

Unable to prosecute, judge, or sentence, Freedmen's Bureau agents did keep records of the complaints of ex-slaves and ex-masters. Both races aired their grievances before Bureau agents (graph 1). Black males registered most of the complaints, and white males were the group they most often accused of offenses. Black complaints of white misconduct usually centered on fraud. Fully two-thirds of the freedmen's charges against whites involved breach of contract,

Graph 1. Complaints lodged with the Freedmen's Bureau, October 1867

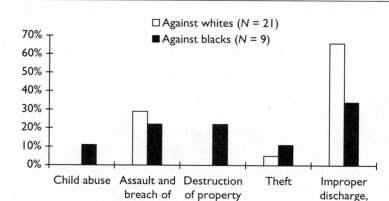

Source: Captain William L. Tidball, 31 Oct. 1867, Narrative Reports, M-826, BRFAL.

improper discharge from employment, or refusal to pay wages or debts. Although blacks sometimes charged black fraud (in 34 percent of complaints) and cited white violence in 29 percent of charges, the separation of crimes by race was fairly consistent. Blacks usually accused fellow freedmen of crimes of violence—assault, child abuse, and destruction of property accounted for 55 percent of blacks' accusations against other blacks—while focusing on whites' financial improprieties.[40]

Just as freedmen and whites both brought their complaints to the Freedmen's Bureau, so too did both races attempt to mislead the agents. Freedmen often told Bureau agents they had been wrongfully denied their wages or share of crops, sometimes omitting crucial details to improve their case. One freedwoman's charge of nonpayment of shares was dismissed after she admitted that she had abandoned the crop of her own volition and without duress. Another freedman's complaint backfired when his landlord demonstrated that the ex-slave was still indebted $58 for supplies after confiscation of his full crop. On the other side, landlords and employers produced receipts for full payment of wages or equitable division of crops with suspicious regularity. We will never know how many of the complaints lodged with the Freedmen's Bureau were spurious, but one official went so far as to claim that "a large proportion of the complaints which have come before me have proved on investigation to be frivolous & without foundation."[41] Notably, he did not single out either race for particular virtue.

The Freedmen's Bureau agents were attuned to class, however, and believed that the poorer members of both races were predisposed to crime. "Among the better class of [white] people" along the Yazoo, agent Allen P. Huggins reported, "the disposition shown towards the freedmen is kind and generous." He noted few complaints about the large plantations of wealthy planters. "But there is a lower class of the whites consisting of men that were formerly overseers," he warned, "ignorant men" who, because "they have got nothing that can be got hold of," are "not [held] responsible before the law for their actions." These poor whites "treat the freedmen badly, and public opinion permits it." Again, the same was true along the Mississippi River. Agent Charles Walden claimed that in Coahoma County "there seems to be much prejudice to the advancement and enlightenment of the Colored people, but this is principally confined to the ignorant and narrow-minded of the whites." Captain E. E. Platt in Vicksburg may have been referring to either or both races when he stated that the majority of false complaints originated in "the more indigent & shiftless class." The agents' reports also reveal that planters, like ex-slaves, often asked favors of the Freedmen's Bureau agents. Despite his anger at the Confederate defeat and irritation at the presence of uniformed officers from the conquering army advising his former slaves, Henry Dixon was not above seeking the invaders' aid. After the death of a neighbor, he asked the Freedmen's Bureau agent to "do all he could to prevent the negroes leaving the place." By late 1867 Yazoo County planters had grown accustomed to the Bureau's quasi-judicial function regarding labor contracts and requested that agent D. M. White be present when they settled their accounts with tenants. Words and deeds of this sort doubtless reduced the effectiveness of the Bureau's agents among freed people and opened its agents to the disparaging comments of reform-minded contemporaries and historians.[42]

Just as many whites were unwilling to lose the laborers who had been their slaves, so too did planters resist changing their system of plantation work. They were particularly reluctant to abandon the large work gangs they had employed as slaveholders. Under pressure from the freedmen, however, many planters agreed to smaller crews, usually called "squads" and comprised of three to a dozen ex-slaves. Blacks still labored in groups, but they now determined the membership of their squads. Although planters agreed to replace work gangs with squads, many balked at further decentralization and refused to rent land to family units in the first postbellum years.[43]

Frederick Metcalfe was one such planter. His workers organized into squads of seven or eight, usually grouping families with a few single friends, and Metcalfe contracted with each squad's self-appointed spokesman. The squad leader, like the obsolete slave driver, was responsible for directing the group's efforts. Metcalfe paid the leader for the squad's work and held him accountable for any debts incurred by his subordinates. The squad leader was expected to motivate his workers and practice good agricultural methods, and there is no evidence that Metcalfe intruded into their management. The planter frequently recorded his complaints in the journal but never mentioned reproving his workers or instructing them to alter their husbandry. Nor did Metcalfe record any acts of physical punishment inflicted on workers by himself, his overseer, or any squad leader. Unproductive or intractable workers were simply discharged and paid off.[44]

But Metcalfe's fortunes were in a perilous state by the mid-1870s. He had been losing money for some time: the price of cotton was falling steadily, and he had undertaken numerous expensive repairs on his property. In February 1875 he estimated that "I'm in a worse condition than I was last year by $1,200." Less than one month later, the sheriff of Washington County auctioned off his share of Newstead plantation to the highest bidder to recover unpaid taxes. The following day Metcalfe journeyed, hat in hand, to persuade Edmund Richardson to cover some of his debts and help him reclaim Newstead.[45]

Even with Richardson's financial aid, however, Metcalfe was driven to change his plantation organization. Ex-slaves were increasingly uneasy with squad labor, and Metcalfe's pool of workers gradually diminished. Many blacks understandably associated the squad with their recently escaped bondage and demanded more autonomy.

After the cotton was gathered in 1874, Metcalfe sent black squad leader Giles Robinson to Alabama to recruit additional workers. Robinson probably was dispatched because Metcalfe now realized that his experiment with Chinese squad laborers was drawing to an unprofitable—and disruptive—conclusion, and that he must add workers for 1875 or abandon the squad system. Robinson proved persuasive as a recruiter, and Metcalfe paid $9 per worker for the new-found laborers' railroad transport from Selma to Vicksburg. But their arrival did not solve all of Metcalfe's problems. The hands' lack of autonomy in their work and possible mismanagement by squad leaders created friction on the plantation. Soon several squads were questioning their putative leaders, and work was disrupted. By the time they had planted all of the corn and most of the cotton, the squads were clearly disintegrating. At one point in March, Metcalfe discovered his workers were "all quarreling & wanting to break up squads." He did what he could to calm the tensions and even fired one entire squad, but his hopes for harmony were soon lost. Worse still, after the discharged group left Newstead the planter discovered that their squad leader had contracted over $100 in debts with a nearby merchant in Metcalfe's name. "I am damned anxious to get rid of the damned plantation business," he proclaimed in April 1875. In debt, his workers fractious, and the cotton market in decline, Metcalfe muddled through 1875.[46]

An ex-slaveholder denied the expedient of physical punishment, Metcalfe at first blamed his labor troubles on a "want of discipline in former years." But the days when planters in the labor-scarce Delta could abuse nonconvict workers in the name of discipline were long gone. He considered more creative changes; his laborers had frequently demanded more autonomy, and Metcalfe tired of mediating between the old order and the new. "A fellow does all he can to please, & parties are still expecting more & not satisfied with what he has done," the aggrieved employer wrote. Finally, in January 1876 Metcalfe resolved to abandon the squad system. He entered a new era tersely, recording simply: "Contracted with two freemen, named Williams, on the half share for 1876." It was the first such agreement made on his lands, but not the last. At the end of the year, he consulted other planters on his rights as landlord and "settled up" with the full plantation.[47]

Metcalfe was motivated to abandon squad labor by a number of considerations. Workers' complaints, their declining productivity in the arrangement, and his financial distress and inability to pay the cash wages that would have assuaged workers' irritations all weighed on his mind. Like many other planters, he could not afford competitive weekly or monthly cash wages: the collapsed state of postwar southern banking and credit mechanisms, the unpredictable nature of the international cotton market in the late 1860s, new scourges of insect infestation, and their own near bankruptcy encouraged planters to compromise with laborers. Throughout the South planters sought some middle way between the squad labor ex-slaves despised and the autonomous production by blacks that would have deprived whites of their full property interest.

Still, sharecropping brought new uncertainties to plantation management, and these unfamiliar challenges sometimes led Metcalfe to the brink of despair. Procuring and preserving dependable sharecroppers became a constant worry. Before, he had been able to consult his squad leaders to determine whether new laborers need be sought. Now, every worker or family acted independently, and Metcalfe watched uneasily as they weighed sharecropping his lands against the offers made by neighboring planters. He second-guessed his tenants' every move and tried to discern their intentions from gossip. "Hands show no disposition to contract," he wrote at the end of his first year's experience as an employer of sharecroppers. "They seem to be unsettled, Bob Marshall is going to

Andrew Jackson's [plantation], so says report." Some of his sharecroppers threatened to leave, perhaps for bargaining leverage, and Metcalfe simply paid them off. He was unaccustomed to negotiating with ex-slaves as his equals and realized his plantation might suffer a labor shortage as a result. He remained pessimistic of his ability to lure tenants to his fields. "Mose Webb made application to work with me this year: doubt his coming." Metcalfe survived his reluctant abandonment of the squad system, but he was never easy in this new role.[48]

Frederick Metcalfe was not the only plantation district landlord to abandon squad labor.[49] In the plantation districts along Deer Creek and the Mississippi, Yazoo, and Sunflower Rivers, old slaveholding domains were being carved into sharecroppers' tracts. Sharecropping—where the landlord furnished land, seed, draft animals, and some implements to the laborer and paid for his work with half the crop—was attractive for several reasons. First, it removed the planter from direct supervision of the men and women who worked his land, the people whose thwarted ambitions in the squad system had driven Metcalfe to the brink of financial ruin. Because freedmen now had the financial incentive to grow the largest crops possible, they would require less direct supervision and encouragement in their labors. Sharecroppers would escape the autocracy many had endured, and fought against, under squad leaders. Thus, many planters looked forward to removing the strains of cotton growing and encouraging black initiative in a mutually beneficial arrangement. Sharecropping also split the financial risk of planting between landlords and workers, a second major factor in the switch. Sharecroppers would bear the major burdens of a short crop or declines in the staple's price, just as they would profit from a large crop or a rising cotton market. Planters would no longer face the dread of harvest and sale alone, for workers were now interested in gathering the crop quickly and thoroughly. The new arrangement also eased credit needs. Unlike squads, which might agitate for full or partial wages throughout the long (and cash-short) growing season, sharecroppers' recompense was delayed until harvest and was payable in the commodity. Planters would not need to negotiate loans to pay workers during the months between planting and picking, they would not be forced to haggle with laborers over the size and timing of wage payments, and they were not locked into paying a set wage while the price of cotton declined. Thus, many planters soon converted their plantation workforces and enjoyed their escape from constant labor supervision, solitary risk, and credit constrictions.

Freedmen, who had endured the postwar squad system in return for wages, were pleased with sharecropping's improvements over earlier arrangements. Although forfeiting a predictable wage income, they gained incentive with the prospect of earning a share of the production from the plot assigned to their use. Even newcomers knew that the soil of the riverside plantation districts yielded large crops, and that they could make far more money sharecropping than working for wages. In fact, sharecroppers in this area were able to earn money and avoid debt with tracts as small as fifteen acres.[50] Although they had to endure the risks of farmers everywhere—weather, pests, and falling commodity prices—the potential returns from sharecropping Delta land were unparalleled in the rest of the South. For many, the reduced supervision and potential for large returns far outweighed the increased risk.

Scholars have spent decades disputing whether the rise of postbellum sharecropping reflected planter hegemony or the evolution of market forces. It probably partook of both, and more. Gavin Wright reminds us that the spread of sharecropping "was a process prolonged by political uncertainties and by inexperience and genuine ignorance about the reactions and priorities of the freedmen, but it was nonetheless a market process." Although less sanguine regarding the beneficial effects of sharecropping's expansion, Harold Woodman shows that the landlord's lien that proved so critical to a planter's profits in tenancy arrangements was not secure in Mississippi until the 1880s. Despite continued debate on the subject, some patterns are clear: that sharecropping was present in the plantation districts of the South within a few years of war's end, that it afforded more autonomy to the worker and less power to the landlord, and that landowners contracted with workers and tenants through a variety of other mechanisms for years to come. This was certainly true of the Delta, where planters' goals and methods varied widely, freedmen were active participants in postbellum agricultural development, and sharecropping was not synonymous with inescapable poverty until after 1900.[51]

By autumn 1867 much of the Delta's plantation district—but little of the backcountry—was organized for sharecropping. In the southeastern Delta, along the lower Yazoo, two-thirds of the freedmen now worked for a share of the crop. Only about one-eighth still worked for wages. In the eastern reaches of the central Delta, 75 percent of the ex-slaves were sharecropping. Freedmen's Bureau officials along the Mississippi River reported that the majority of blacks were working for a share of their crop in the plantation districts of Washington and Coahoma Counties. Significantly, half of the sharecroppers in Washington County already owned livestock, implements, and seed in 1867, and they would keep a larger share of the crop than workers without these items. Sharecroppers with their own mules, seed, and plows escaped further dependence on landlords—an important consideration, for many "furnishing" landlords charged exorbitant prices for these items.[52] Thus, within two years of slavery's formal demise, most freedmen were working separate farmsteads, and many had accumulated enough personal property to increase substantially their share of the crop produced.[53]

But sharecropping, they soon discovered, was not the perfect path for their ambitions. The price of cotton fell each year after 1865. Thus, each crop had to be larger than its predecessor if the farmer was merely to stay even. Moreover, 1867 was a particularly unpropitious year for first-time sharecroppers. A Freedmen's Bureau agent foretold the disaster that summer when he noted that "when the crops are short they will of course have very little money at the end of the year." As a result of bollworm infestations and a cool spring, the 1867 crop was considerably smaller than usual. Many planters panicked when they saw the diminished yields. They suspected the ex-slaves of failing to cultivate the crop properly, thereby causing the pitiful yields. Unwilling to share the crop with blacks whom they now blamed for bad farming, some planters had share-croppers driven off the land. Others insisted that the sharecroppers do additional labor on the property — without compensation — in the weeks between weeding the furrows and picking the lint. When the tenants refused to do work not connected with the cultivation of their crops, believing their sharecropping agreement allowed them to manage their own work and avoid compulsory labor, some planters used this as a pretext to have them evicted and their full crop seized. Blacks often responded to eviction by calling in the Freedmen's Bureau agent (who usually tried to negotiate a settlement), but many freedmen must have rued leaving the security of wage labor behind in that first season of sharecropping. The sharecroppers of 1867 were exposed to the many dangers of cultivating for a percentage: low yields, falling prices, and vague contractual obligations all imperiled a farmer's independence. One Freedmen's Bureau official observed in 1867 that "the proper system of free labor has not yet been arrived at."[54] Most Deltans, white and black, doubtless shared this view.

Sharecropping was not, however, the only option available to recently emancipated farmers without land. They could also rent, paying a fixed amount of money or cotton or offering a share of the crop in return for use of the land. Regardless of whether the renter paid his fee in cash or cotton, he had to convey the stipulated amount by the end of the season. No matter how bad the weather, how pesky the insects, or how unpredictable the cotton market, a renter's payment or share must be paid in November or December. Moreover, those who rented for a fixed fee stood to lose money on the falling cotton market and were hemmed into a price regardless of crop size.

Why, then, would anyone want to rent for a specified amount when they could share the risk of crop failure with the landlord via share renting or sharecropping? The answer, simply enough, was that landlords charged fixed-fee renters a much smaller price to use their land. From a landlord's perspective the fixed-fee renter required the least supervision and returned the most dependable amount per acre. Sharecroppers, by contrast, needed more attention to ensure maximum production, and this oversight came at a price. Land worked by sharecroppers returned an average of over 13 percent of its value to the owner each year. But planters often were willing to rent acreage for less than half that amount if the tenant paid a fixed sum. Landlords with fixed-fee tenants sacrificed sharecropping's additional return because renting made their income more predictable and required less intervention in the production process. And this income could be substantial, even for owners of backcountry property: in the 1880s rental fees for his land near latter-day Arcola brought absentee planter Alfred C. Downs more money than he earned in his Chattanooga, Tennessee, law practice. Although landlords usually earned less for rented land than sharecropped acres, renters stood to make more money in this arrangement. Many tenants must have expected to use the greater profit from renting to buy their own property.[55]

Many landlords, smarting from their unexpected losses on 1867's small crop, considered renting out their property. "Some of the largest planters" in the eastern Delta informed Lieutenant White of the Freedmen's Bureau "that they intend next year to rent out their Plantations, in small lots to freedmen at a nominal rent, the freedmen to have the exclusive control and management" of the property. This arrangement, the planters hoped, would further increase the ex-slaves' incentive to careful cultivation and regularize the owners' income from agriculture. To guarantee that the rent was paid, these planters planned to take a lien (giving them first rights to as much of the crop as needed to pay the leasing fee) "as security for the rent."[56] Generally, rents ranged from five to ten dollars per acre in the decade or so after the Civil War. There was no predictable discount for renting a larger tract. Many other factors—soil fertility, drainage, level of improvements, access to transportation, and the percentage of cleared land—affected the price charged. Thus, "cheap" land often abutted "expensive" acreage. One renter might negotiate a cash rental of eight dollars per acre for a fifty-acre portion of cleared land while another discovered a landlord willing to rent as few as three acres (or as many as thirty) for six or seven dollars an acre.[57]

Even in the plantation districts, tenants encountered a range of conditions and expectations. Some gained free access to the landlord's cotton gin; others were required to pay a portion of the engineer's salary for ginning. Many could rent mules for a fixed monthly rate, yet the tenants of absentee planters often were called on to furnish their own supplies, implements, and livestock. Renters of highly improved acreage—particularly tenants on the most highly developed plantations—frequently were forbidden to cut down any of the remaining woodlands on the property, the fuel being reserved for the owner or protected for aesthetic reasons. Tenants at more wooded locations were encouraged to clear and use—and sometimes allowed to sell—a landlord's timber. Many renters agreed to plant a specific field or number of acres in cotton, and others were required to augment the property's fencing. Thus, in the first decade after the Civil War, the contractual obligations of landlord and tenant fluctuated from farm to farm, and prospective renters could find great diversity in the conditions offered by neighboring planters.[58]

Despite the fluidity of tenancy in this period, many ex-slaves grew discouraged with their prospects. Freedom had not ushered in prosperity. Blacks had escaped slavery and extricated themselves from its stepchild, the squad system, only to discover that the relative independence of sharecropping and tenancy entailed numerous risks. The short crop of 1867 and the bollworm's menace brought home the insecurity of farming, and their share obligations or fixed-fee renting contracts were nagging reminders of the uncertainties of independent production. Natural obstacles and systemic disadvantages were exacerbated by many whites' undiminished recalcitrance: freedom's allure faded with every short crop, every tenant's growing debt, every act of fraud or intimidation. Was the rich soil of the Delta's plantation district worth being ground slowly into peonage? Many thought not, and a steady stream of freedmen left the area in 1867 and 1868. Some abandoned the Delta altogether, while others disappeared into the backcountry. Planters grew worried for their investments, fearful that the chronically low supply of labor would make landowning and cultivation unprofitable.

Many of these ex-slaves were not simply disillusioned with the Delta, they were discontented with freedom's demands. Their erstwhile allies, the agents of the Freedmen's Bureau, documented ex-slaves' increasing restiveness in late 1867. John Hynes reported from Sunflower County that the former slaves refused to discipline themselves to regular work. "I try to impress on [freedmen] the strict necessity of all their duties as good citizens by refraining from all lawless practices[,] adhering strictly to their contracts[,] & not wast[ing] their time in roaming over the county." Another agent identified a growing group of intentionally underemployed blacks who had not entered into tenancy and refused to accept wage labor. "Many of them will not go on plantations to work, but congregate in towns and villages without a visible means of support." Some ex-slaves chose to exercise a basic freedom—the right to quit a job—with a frequency that dismayed the Freedmen's Bureau agents. A confused agent wrote that "it is to be regretted that many of them leave their master just at the time their services are most needed." Unable to explain ex-slaves' assertion of their new privilege, the agents often regarded purposeful idleness as evidence of black inferiority. Freedmen "seem to lack the judgment or ambition necessary to carry them through," one agent hypothesized, and "so neglect their work."[59]

Yet the stereotype was only selectively applicable, as some Freedmen's Bureau agents admitted. Captain Tidball in Greenville reported that some ex-slaves were already renting and cultivating entire plantations in Washington County. The "industrious and economical," he explained, "are prospering." But in late September 1867, he too emphasized the "many instances of extravagance and profligacy," fearing "cases of destitution" before the next spring. By the end of October, the threat to black farmers had grown sharper, and its causes were less susceptible to stereotyped dismissal. At cotton-picking time it was clear that no one would become rich on the diminutive 1867 crop. The sharecropping arrangements that many freedmen entered with visions of large Delta yields now became a burden rather than a boon. Lieutenant White concurred in Tidball's fears of widespread suffering for the winter of 1867–68 but pointed to a different cause. "The system of working for a share of the crop is a failure," he wrote his superiors. "The condition of the colored people is not encouraging, they will make nothing the present year, and many of them will be in debt." The system was flawed, it did not always reward hard work with profits, and in years as bad as 1867 those toiling for shares of a small crop inevitably found themselves mired in debt. Sharecroppers had realized the futility of their efforts late in the summer. "The freedmen," he conceded, "are getting careless and indifferent." Rather than ascribe blacks' difficulties to congenital laziness, White found the sharecropping system to blame.[60]

Large plantations, compulsory labor, and white supremacy all survived the demise of slavery in the Delta's plantation districts. Small farms, the type most accessible to recent slaves, were nearly absent from the riverside areas. Twenty years after the end of slavery, these swaths of antebellum settlement remained the plantation's Delta stronghold. In 1885 fully 93 percent of the farms along the Mississippi River were large plantations of several hundred acres each (graph 2). White elites retained ownership of the much-prized riverside acreage, and its cultivation accrued much more to their advantage than to the benefit of the freedmen who planted, chopped, and gathered the crops of valuable lint.[61]

True, there was a great range in the attitudes and methods of white planters. The fabulously successful Edmund Richardson stood at the pinnacle of planter aspirations and at the edge of their consciences. He commanded large capital

Graph 2. Estimated farm sizes in Mississippi River counties, 1881–85

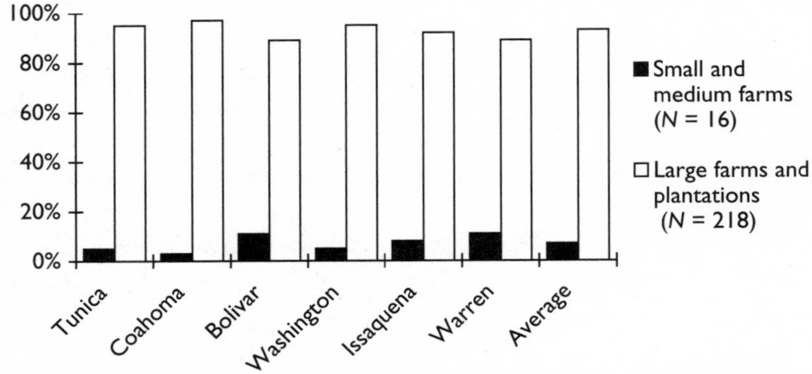

Source: Mississippi River Commission, *Preliminary Map of the Lower Mississippi, from the Mouth of the Ohio to the Head of the Passes* (1881–85; reissued, 1900).

reserves, eagerly explored new (if morally dubious) avenues to circumvent the region's labor shortage, was undeterred by negative opinions, marshaled political pressure against his opponents, and became the Delta's preeminent postbellum planter. A figure of action and accomplishment, Edmund Richardson exuded confidence in his goals and contempt for his critics. But many ex-slaveholders were aghast at Richardson's methods. Frederick Metcalfe—a planter of dwindling resources and limited business acumen, a man who could not stifle the bickering on his own plantation without a constable's aid, a member of the county's social and political elite who witnessed one plantation auctioned off to pay his taxes and another transformed into a patchwork of tenantry—seems to have been more fully representative of the Delta's former masters.[62] Unlike Richardson, most planters struggled into the postbellum era in confusion, their better natures hostage to a heritage of misplaced hegemony.

As for the region's black majority, some remained subject to physical abuse, and now all had to contend with threats of fraud, systematic debt peonage, and competition from imported laborers; their durable allies were few. Those whites who attempted to deal fairly with ex-slaves were subject to physical violence and destruction of their property, and those blacks who achieved success one year might suffer poverty the next. No one had been able to predict the future of Delta society at the close of the Civil War, but by the 1870s one fact shone clear: the plantation districts held little dependable promise for freed people.

3

Away from the Riverside

Even as planters struggled to hold together plantations along the Mississippi River, the Delta's backcountry beckoned to freedmen eager to buy their own property. The Delta frontier's unique combination of fertile soil, high cotton yields, desperate landlords, and timber to supplement cotton income underwrote black farmers' purchase of tens of thousands of acres. A generation of ex-slaves found and grasped prosperity in the Delta's interior during the 1870s and 1880s, and their wealth helped establish diversified communities of black farmers and businessmen. Word of their success spread across the cotton states, and thousands of ambitious agrarians chose this New South frontier as their destination in the final third of the nineteenth century.

Although no frontier was ever settled with ease, the Delta's thick forests and murky swamps made pioneers' tasks especially challenging. One early inhabitant of Bolivar County recalled that the Delta "was almost a complete wilderness from the settlement on the west [along the Mississippi River] to the Sunflower River." The plantation district where a few of the antebellum settlers had erected imposing mansions was merely a "narrow, struggling strip" after the war, and vast forests mocked wealthy settlers' pretensions.[1]

In the wild interior—"primeval forest," according to another settler's account—all the hazards of frontier life were magnified by isolation. Panthers posed a particular menace to settlers and livestock. One panther killed in the late 1850s measured ten feet from the tip of its nose to the end of its tail; Coahoma County takes its name from the Choctaw word for "red panther." Gray and black timber wolves also prowled beneath the green canopy, and bears proved particularly fond of farmers' swine and cornfields. Swamps might hold even greater danger than did forests, for standing water sheltered poisonous snakes and alligators. A white woman who arrived in an unsettled area in the early 1870s recalled that the alligators living near her property often left the water when hungry. "They would come up into the quarter lot for pigs and would not have declined a little pickaninny; but the mothers had such a horror of them that they would not allow the children to play on the bank of the lake alone." Homes and fences would not always deter carnivores' explorations, pioneers found, for predatory animals remained "natural trespassers in what had been their paradise."[2]

The Delta backcountry's wild state was not always a disadvantage. Even among the dense forest and wild animals, pioneers found that "the land was very fertile and mellow. After getting the cane cut off and cleared a little, the settler could stick a hole in the ground, drop corn in the hole, and make fine corn without the ground being ploughed at all." One enterprising newcomer turned the verdant forest's rapid growth to his advantage, lining his entire property with walnut saplings that soon grew sturdy enough to be joined with fence wire.[3]

Even as life could sometimes turn dangerous, conditions were more often simply plain and unappealing. A planter's wife described how she was entertained at the home of a relatively prosperous frontier settler in 1872. Dinner consisted of "bacon floating in grease, biscuit the size of an orange with hard blue centers, a small bit of brown sugar in a broken tumbler, and a small cake of butter in a large vegetable dish, with a very worn piece of oilcloth serving as a tablecloth." At this point, she later confessed, "my appetite failed me, and but for consideration of my husband, I should have indulged in a good cry."[4] She never seems to have understood that the home and meal she disparaged were the hard-won fruits of another's labor. Someone had to slaughter a hog and cure its flesh for the greasy bacon; plant, harvest, and grind the corn that comprised the biscuit; churn the milk to make her small cake of butter; and pay a high frontier price for the brown sugar, crockery, and oilcloth that failed to impress her. Existence was arduous enough; high society would have to wait.

Frontier homes, stores, and churches were crudely built—Cleveland, a railroad town and one of the seats of Bolivar County by the turn of the century, boasted only three houses with glass windows in 1886. Backcountry neighbors were often separated by miles of standing water, forest, and canebrake, roads were few and never in good repair, and traveling was a hazardous undertaking. Most inhabitants walked, rode horseback, or drove a farm wagon to their destinations; even after the railroad linked central Bolivar County with the outside world, there were only two surreys outside the county's riverside plantation district. Nor did rail connections immediately attract a surplus of doctors to the backcountry. Dr. Sparkman of central Bolivar County was kept so busy that he needed two saddle horses to ride on his rounds.[5]

Settlers' isolation elevated issues of road construction and repair, school construction, and other governmental responsibilities to political significance. Washington County farmer D. A. Love complained to the *Greenville Times* in 1888 that remote settlers felt neglected by their elected officials. His precinct northeast of Greenville contained "no railroad facilities, no public roads, or school houses except [those] built by private parties." Yet settlers were assessed, and paid, taxes on their real and personal property. He recounted his neighbors' difficulties in persuading the county Board of Supervisors to construct a school in their area. Two years after promising to build schools in the vicinity, the supervisors had still not initiated construction. Citizens complained, and the supervisors sought a compromise. The board offered to loan settlers funds to build a school (repayable, plus 10 percent interest, in five years) if "five solvent men" in the district would sign a note promising repayment. Washington County's backcountry settlers did not, however, find this prospect appealing. "Mr. Editor," Love wrote, "we do not feel that we should have to borrow our own money and pay interest on the same." Backcountry taxpayers, he declared, were growing tired of "taxation without compensation."[6]

Contrary to myth, isolation and a lack of amenities did not foster good-neighborliness among remote settlers. A Freedmen's Bureau official confirmed the backcountry's rough character in the late 1860s. Writing from Minter's Landing in Sunflower County, John Hynes described the individualism that had already replaced notions of slave community and paternalism by 1867: "Few of the whites do any thing more for [destitute freedmen] than keep them from actual starvation, and even their own race show no sympathy" for ex-slaves. An early settler recalled merchant Pat Dean, "who early established himself as a one-man law and elected himself as Merigold's first justice of the peace." The storekeeper styled himself "Squire Dean" and bristled at any slight. He did not deem murder a serious offense, especially if the victim was black. After Merigold's white railroad depot agent killed a black man in the early 1890s, Dean fined the murderer only $5, and let it be known that he would not press for collection. Not surprisingly, "every man carried his own weapons and was his own peace-or trouble-maker."[7] Still, even the most fractious agriculturist spent little time disturbing the urban peace, such as it was, of tiny Merigold. Farming was the chief occupation of the backcountry, and furrows could not be plowed from a saloon stool.

Farmers arriving in the Delta backcountry found that the best available land straddled silt ridges. These elevated silt soils had been raised above swamp level by eons of unrestricted flood activity, and land there was fertile, free of rocks and boulders, and less threatened by overflow and standing water than were lowland acres. Dogwood Ridge, which rose above the floodplains of the Yazoo and Sunflower Rivers, was the region's most substantial elevation.[8] Originating in Coahoma County, the black, sandy loam of Dogwood Ridge reached its greatest width (six to nine miles) in Leflore County and extended into Holmes County. A second inland ridge rose along Deer Creek's winding banks in Washington and Sharkey Counties. Although narrower than Dogwood Ridge, the elevated lands beside Deer Creek were rich in plant food, and steamboats found much of the stream navigable for several months each year. Other smaller backcountry ridges—like Egypt Ridge in southern Bolivar and northern Washington Counties—also provided good land to early postbellum arrivals.[9]

Riverside planters had not overlooked these flood-safe, fertile ridges before the war. Planters began clearing parts of Egypt Ridge in the late 1840s, several plantations stood beside Deer Creek in the antebellum period, and Dogwood Ridge's broad expanse hosted dozens of settlers before 1865. Indeed, many riverside planters speculated heavily in backcountry lands on these ridges. Absentee speculators bought thousands of acres in the interior, confident that development would soon swell the value of their wilderness lands. By 1860 most of the Delta's land was privately owned, although little of it had been improved.[10]

The Civil War and its aftermath eroded ownership of these backcountry lands, as fledgling backcountry plantations and speculative tracts lost much of their appeal. Inland planters faced all of the problems that bedeviled riverside plantation owners—labor shortages, confusion over how and whether labor should be supervised, and an uncertain cotton market—without riverside estates' proximity to transportation. Contrary to the boom-time expectations of the 1850s, the plantation districts had not grown quickly inland, and postbellum backcountry cultivators now had to contend with isolation from the flow of laborers, as well as distance from supplies and difficulty in getting cotton to market. Speculators, moreover, found that few of the cash-poor planters already established in the region were eager to buy interior land and assume the added difficulties of its remoteness.

The increased financial burdens of Reconstruction dwarfed these difficulties. New revenues were needed as Mississippi's state and county governments assumed greater responsibilities for black citizens after emancipation. Most revenue proposals focused on increasing real property taxes, and levies on privately held land skyrocketed.[11]

By 1874 Delta landowners faced state and county land tax rates that were at least 750 percent higher than in 1866. In some counties land tax rates rose 1200 percent between 1866 and 1874. In 1866 Bolivar County landowners paid county and state taxes totaling 3 mills; in 1874 the rate stood at 30 mills. In Issaquena County the combined state and county tax rate rose from 2.5 to 30 mills in the same period, and the basic tax burden in Washington County increased from 5 to 37.5 mills. Moreover, these Delta landowners were accountable to a third taxing authority, the Mississippi Board of Levee Commissioners. Thus, in addition to state and county taxes, a typical property owner in the region paid $4.15 per acre in levee taxes in 1874. At that time the Delta's most expensive riverside land seldom sold for more than $15 per acre, and most improved land along the Mississippi River could be purchased for $10 to $13.[12]

Tax costs were no longer an afterthought for any Delta landowner. The *Greenville Times* reported on 7 November 1874 that Washington County plantations assessed at $20,000 (the value of a large operation) would incur state, county, and levee taxes totaling at least $3,000, and perhaps as much as $4,000. The same issue of the *Times* described Greenville's related financial woes—the city's debt had grown so large that aldermen considered discharging the entire police force to save money. Not surprisingly, Democrats and other conservatives latched onto the tax issue as a way to overthrow Republican political rule and end Reconstruction. Beginning in November 1874, and until the Delta was fully "redeemed" from Republican leadership in 1876, the region's Democrats organized Taxpayers' Leagues, held meetings to denounce the high costs and low returns of Republican office holding, and canvassed white and black voters to turn them against the party of Lincoln. Delta Democrats William A. Percy and William G. Yerger of Washington County were especially influential in swelling the plaintive chorus of the Taxpayers' League and installing more frugal Democratic rule.[13]

Many landowners could not afford to wait for a change in government policies; tax bills were due, and they lacked the cash or credit to pay them. Owners of extensive acreage faced a dilemma: should they immerse themselves in debt to hold distant and uncleared lands, or should they forfeit nonessential property? Leflore County planter C. E. Holmes, for example, paid taxes on his plantation along the Yazoo River but forfeited less desirable wilderness land. Many other planters followed suit. By 1871 most of Leflore County's delinquent taxes had been levied on wilderness property in the six townships within the Delta's interior. In one month the sheriff attempted to auction over 20,000 acres of Leflore County land to pay tax arrears. Leflore County's burgeoning tax delinquency was not unique. The year before, over 35 percent of Washington County's land area had been seized by either the state or the Delta's Board of Mississippi Levee Commissioners. There too, almost all of the forfeited property was unimproved land lying away from the plantation district (graph 3). In more than one-third of Washington County's townships—all in the backcountry—the amount of seized land exceeded 50 percent of the total acreage.[14] By 1871 over 1.3 million acres were listed as forfeited in the Delta's seven counties.[15]

Forfeitures mounted as tax burdens increased. By October 1874 the *Greenville Times* was publishing long lists of Bolivar, Issaquena, and Washington County property held for delinquent taxes and offered for sale.[16] By January 1875 the list of seized lands stretched across two pages: the small type described thousands of acres. Significantly, the owners of many of these tracts were unknown, and title to the lands was confused: Deep South land speculators, like other male citizens of the region, suffered a high death rate during the Civil War, and the survival of absentee landowners (or their probate dispositions) could not be verified. Titles were so entangled and money was so scarce that over two-thirds of Washington County's land was presented for tax auction in February 1875. Similar predicaments visited other Delta counties. Leflore County, where C. E. Holmes and his fellow planters forfeited tens of thousands of wilderness acres in 1871, saw its list of delinquent lands stretch ever longer. Between 1871 and 1876 the number of state-seized acres in Leflore County rose over 45 percent.[17] A vicious circle resulted, for with fewer acres in the hands of private owners, each county's tax base shrank and tax income diminished

Graph 3. A comparison of land values, Washington County, 1870

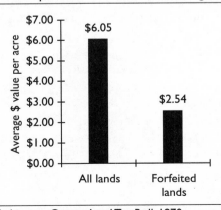

Source: Washington County Land Tax Roll, 1870.

Graph 4. Privately held acreage in three Delta counties, 1869–73

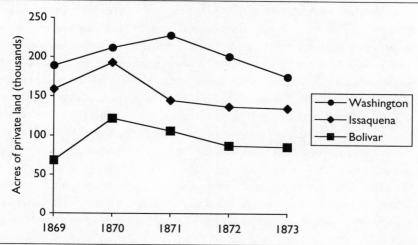

Source: Greenville Times, 2 Jan. 1875.

(graph 4). This increased pressure to raise tax rates, which led to additional delinquencies and forfeitures.

The large number of tax seizures did not wrest all economic power from the hands of prominent planters. State law allowed previously delinquent landowners to reclaim land if they paid their back taxes within two years of seizure. Of course, this sullied the attractions of public-auction land titles. Why would anyone go to the trouble of purchasing a tract at auction, paying to have the deed entered into the county records, and then work the land or attempt to re-sell the property when its previous owner might reclaim his lapsed acres? The prospect of reclamation injected a great uncertainty into seized-land auctions, and few bidders stepped forward, despite low prices.[18]

A clear trend soon emerged from this welter of debt, delinquency, and polit-ical machination: owners of backcountry property began leasing and selling lands cheaply to escape rising taxes and to avoid seizure of their property. They could not hold fast to speculative acreage, blithely confident that long-term price increases would return large profits to compensate for their patience, for they could not count on being able to pay the next year's taxes. Nor could they afford to lure wage laborers into the backcountry to clear and work the prop-erty. Workers would demand high wages for remote labor, and wooded lands must be cleared before cotton could be grown to ease a landlord's debts. Because they could neither maintain the property for future speculations nor work the land to offset its tax burdens, many landowners grew open to tenants, purchasers, and terms they had previously scorned. Rather than lose their backcountry lands forever, these men and women gave up control of the property temporarily by renting their land to freedmen. Prospective tenants were eager to pay cash or crops for use of fertile land, and these rental fees allowed landowners to pay their taxes and retain title to the property. Renters, not sharecroppers, were usually the tenants on these backcountry farms. Landlords found sharecropping most profitable on fully cleared fields under the eyes of an overseer—the sort of conditions best met in the riverside plantation districts. The difficulties arising from supervising sharecroppers at a distance led most planters to favor renting their backcountry land in this period. The same backcountry that speculators now regarded as a poor risk for investment became a poor man's promised land.

Tracts of land containing some cleared acreage and decent transportation prospects were the likeliest spots for settlement. Potential tenants and purchasers alike preferred tillable acres over land that had to be cleared before a cotton crop could be planted, and cheap, nearby transportation appealed to every farmer engaged in production for the international cotton market.

Farmers eager to lease or purchase found no shortage of local landowners ready to deal. In fact, there was a pronounced shortage of tenants and farm buyers. Many of the workers emancipated from Delta plantations had left the region for the urban delights of Vicksburg or Jackson, and experiments with convict labor and apprenticing freed youths did not augment the Delta's appeal to migrants. The region was increasingly short of laborers by the late 1860s, and this was the group from which tenants and land purchasers must be drawn.[19] Even in the plantation district—where proximity to transportation, an established population of black agriculturists, and more settled conditions combined to provide planters with greater access to tenants and laborers—workers were in short supply. "Labor is in demand," one Freedmen's Bureau agent reported in 1867, "and some of the planters are fearful that they will not be able to procure sufficient hands to gather the crop." Landowners' labor worries continued into the 1870s, despite the migration of thousands of freedmen to the region.[20]

The sudden appeal of emigration to Kansas in 1879 and 1880 further depleted the Delta's stock of farmhands and tenants. Landlords worked themselves into a frenzy at the sight of laborers and tenants abandoning the fields. The *Greenville Times* reported that 150 blacks from Edmund Richardson's Peru plantation (which was worked with wage laborers), along with those from neighboring enterprises, had assembled at Leota Landing on the Mississippi and were attempting to hail steamboats to take them to Kansas. Boats were reluctant to stop for the large group, however, especially after county sheriff William Hunt telegraphed for an armed posse to protect Leota from the depredations of frustrated emigrants. Significantly, the *Times*—long an organ for planter interests—did not urge retaliation against departed laborers. Instead, the editor counseled patience and reminded readers that violence would only exacerbate fragile labor relations. "The only policy for the planters," the *Times* proclaimed, "is to abstain from all efforts at repression; it is hard upon all, ruin to many, to lose this year's crop, but there is no cure for it except time." The newspaper advised landlords against restraining Kansas-bound workers and reminded them that the partial loss of one crop was preferable to permanently sullying the region's reputation, driving off other workers, and turning potential settlers away from the Delta. The newspaper's appeal was successful. The region survived the "Kansas Fever" without permanent damage or violent attack, and soon migrants were again making the Delta their destination of choice rather than a point of departure. Eager to avoid another mass exodus, capitalists in the region formed the Mississippi Delta Agricultural and Immigration Company and pledged to "introduce immigrants [and] assist them in acquiring desirable tracts" of land.[21] Yet, if labor was in such short supply in the plantation district, how bad must the situation have been in the distant interior?

Landowners hoping to stave off financial disaster by selling or leasing their acreage could not wait for potential purchasers or tenants to seek them out; these threatened speculators must actively encourage migration to their fields. It was soon apparent that owners of land along Deer Creek and similar areas—where ridged banks left crops immune from all but the worst overflows, fertile soil nourished cotton bushes standing ten to fifteen feet tall, and seasonal navigability aided the movement of crops and supplies—held the advantage in drawing settlers. Moreover, Deer Creek's antebellum plantation development had cleared many acres along and near the watercourse, and the section contained resident landowners willing to sacrifice some property for their continued livelihood. By the early 1870s Deer Creek plantations were being surveyed for sale or lease, and tracts were laid out in forty- and eighty-acre lots. Similarly attractive sections along the Sunflower and Yazoo Rivers were also surveyed for sale or lease.[22]

Tenancy on these backcountry tracts was characterized by a variety of contractual obligations. Terms such as *sharecropper* or *renter* barely begin to describe the range of factors involved in tenants' lease arrangements. Tenants paid for their use of the land with crops, cash, fencing, industrial labor, and by clearing wilderness acres.[23] The most striking aspect of tenancy on these tracts was the paucity of sharecropping arrangements. The majority of Delta farms continued to be worked by their owners or by renters until 1910, when the number of farms cultivated by sharecroppers first surpassed 50 percent of the total.[24]

Instead of sharecropping, most backcountry tenants paid a prearranged amount of cotton or cash for use of the land. Local experience and demography conspired together for this outcome. The rapid growth in sharecropping described by Freedmen's Bureau agents in 1866 and 1867 was abruptly halted by the small 1867 crop. Landlords blamed sharecropping (and sharecroppers) for the unusually short harvest, and many were turned against working their land on shares. Freedmen grew similarly wary of sharecropping after 1867, when low cotton yields made it difficult to pay off their expenses. Most ex-slaves also disliked the supervision that, after 1867, often accompanied a sharecropping arrangement. Overseers, sometimes the same men who had whipped them during slavery, were now employed to guarantee that croppers cultivated for the maximum yield, and these men frequently threatened physical harm if disobeyed. Small wonder that freedmen after 1867 took advantage of the labor shortage and, where possible, negotiated cash or commodity rental contracts instead of sharecropping.[25] Riverside plantations, where laborers were more accessible and supervision was more easily accomplished, pursued more restrictive sharecropping arrangements, but most backcountry lands were rented for cotton or cash.[26]

Although Delta farmers usually aspired to economic independence, it was not uncommon for unmarried freedmen to rent backcountry lands in partnership. The rigors of frontier life — from the physical danger of predators, disease, and mishap to the need to clear as much land as possible for a larger crop — encouraged farmers' cooperation. Partners found that two men working together could accomplish more than twice what they could separately, and the fact that few ex-slaves owned all the implements, wagons, and livestock necessary for farming further encouraged combination. Landlords of frontier property realized that partners had a better chance of surviving to fulfill their lease agreement, and partners thus enjoyed a negotiating advantage over solitary tenants.[27]

Most backcountry tenants in the 1870s paid for the land they rented with cotton. The amount of cotton charged for each acre of land varied widely, however, and a host of factors influenced the fee demanded of each tenant. Consider the situation confronting Samuel French's tenants in 1873. In February of that year, French negotiated four commodity rental contracts with freedmen eager to plant cotton on his Matilda plantation on Deer Creek in Washington County. But that was the limit of their similarity.[28]

Most aspects of the frontier rental agreement, it appears, were negotiable. The four Matilda leases exhibit no firm tendency on French's part to limit farmers to twenty or forty acres, and the planter was as amenable to renting land to groups of farmers as to solitary freedmen. One contract applied to three men planting sixty acres, another bound two men with fifty acres, a third applied to one individual farming forty acres, and the last governed one man's lease of sixteen acres. The price paid per acre also varied widely. While the tenants on the three larger tracts were charged 75 pounds of cotton per acre, French demanded 130 pounds per acre from the farmer of the sixteen-acre plot. This 73 percent difference in the rental price reveals the biggest factor governing frontier land rental: the higher price was charged for cleared land— which would produce more cotton per acre—while partly wooded tracts were available for a smaller fee.[29]

The rental contracts negotiated by landlords like French and their prospective tenants were not, however, limited to the fees charged for land use. Myriad other provisions, restrictions, and obligations were set forth in these documents. It was in these aspects of the contract that the power—or desperation—of backcountry landlords was revealed.

French required tenants on Matilda plantation to deliver their entire cotton crop to him; he would attend to its ginning and marketing and would remove his rent portion at that time. Should their crop fail to cover the lease obligation, French held a lien on the tenants' other crops, their livestock, farm implements, and wagons. This lien authorized French to have sold at public auction as much of the tenants' personal property as was needed to pay off their lease obligation. The landlord also had the option of carrying any unpaid rent into the next year as a debt and adding this remaining amount to the tenant's subsequent lease. If the tenant and his family thriftily avoided accumulating other obligations, produced a large crop of high-quality lint, and commodity prices did not fall too far, he might pay off his full debt in the following year. Too often, however, a tenant's carried-over debts became an inescapable millstone. The price of cotton fell annually for much of the last third of the nineteenth century, and farmers needed a bumper yield to offset this decline. Otherwise, they would be trapped in an ever-expanding cycle of debt, with their unpaid obligations growing larger each year. Eventually, even the most compassionate landlord might have tenants' belongings sold to pay off what was owed him.[30] Not that Samuel French was primarily motivated by compassion in his dealings with tenants. If all tenants met their leases' terms, the planter's annual return on these four tracts probably would have surpassed the lands' value. At a time when an acre of cleared backcountry land sold for between $5 and $10 (and uncleared property for less than $5), French charged his tenants an average of $9.64 per acre.[31]

Samuel French's fee of over $9 per acre for mixed acreage was not uncommon along Deer Creek. R. G. and G. G. Sims charged the same rate for similar land on their nearby Sligo plantation in 1872, and the extra duties required of their tenants made French's terms seem cheap. Freedman George H. Brown rented seventy-five Sligo acres in 1872 in partnership with three other black men and one black woman, all illiterate. Brown not only was responsible for paying his rental fee but also was required to operate the plantation's cotton gin. He was not compensated for his work as gin engineer, and Brown and his partners received no ginning discount for this labor.[32]

Renters along the Yazoo River encountered similarly demanding clauses in their lease contracts. William Campbell, who rented fifty acres of Belzoni plantation in present-day Humphreys County, agreed to pay landlord Edward A. Fisk a cash rent of $5 per acre in 1873. Compared to the charges borne by other backcountry renters, this was a small price for rich land. His willingness to pay cash and his landlord's eagerness for a predictable return (one not dependent on the fluctuations of the cotton market) worked in Campbell's favor. But his landlord made other demands, despite the small fee. In what may have been an attempt to guarantee control over the use of his land, Fisk specifically denied Campbell the right to sublease any of the acreage. Fisk applied the same restriction to the five other tenants who rented his land that year.[33]

Cash-paying tenants along Deer Creek also encountered a mixed bag of lower rental fees and restrictive leases. In one example from 1873, landowner Camille Bourges agreed to lease 130 acres of her Camelia plantation to black farmers John Rucks and Adolph Smith in exchange for a cash fee of $7 per acre. Although her plantation was surrounded by forest, Bourges looked to the long-term value of her property's timber and limited tenants' access to its woodlands. Their use of her timber was confined to cooking and heating their house, powering the steam gin when processing their cotton, and fashioning fence rails to protect crops. They were not allowed to remove or sell any lumber from the property. Rucks and Smith also were charged a fee for use of the plantation's cotton gin and cotton press.[34]

Renters, like landlords, also negotiated contracts to their advantage through attention to the details of an agreement. Offering to pay their rent in cash was only one stratagem. The primitive nature of backcountry farms gave tenants another bargaining option—by offering to build and repair houses and fences on unamenable farmsteads, tenants could reduce their rent cost. The extra work saved money for renters and heightened the value of landlords' property. Farmer John Rucks, whom Camille Bourges had denied full access to her forests, soon saw a way to turn landlords' desire for improvements to his advantage. In return for building a house on D. L. Stone's Deer Creek plantation, Rucks gained rent-free use of the dwelling for twelve years. Nearby, R. A. Willshire convinced his Deer Creek landlord to discount his rent in exchange for a cash payment and went on to pursue other benefits in the relationship. By the terms of his 1872 lease, Willshire was responsible for $500 rent at the end of the year, but his landlord agreed to reduce the fee to $200 in exchange for reasonable improvements to the farm's fencing and house. Willshire emerged with a cheap rent in exchange for work he probably would have performed anyway.[35] Rucks, Willshire, and many other tenants found landlords eager to make concessions that would improve backcountry property.

Although not all landlords gave rent reductions or rebates in exchange for labor on fences and buildings, many substantial landowners paid cash to tenants who cut cordwood, carved gates and pickets, hauled wood, or erected fences on backcountry property. Planter Frederick Metcalfe paid tenants to fashion and erect both picket and worm fences on Newstead plantation. In the mid-1870s Metcalfe paid his tenants 5 cents per fence post, 10 cents for every picket-fence panel constructed, and $1 for each gatepost. Between crops and when the cotton did not require their attention, he also paid his tenants to cut cordwood and haul felled lumber.[36] Although these tenants' labor did not directly reduce their rent, cash payments helped them avoid debt and buy goods that might otherwise have been beyond their means.

Tenants' improvements were not limited to fences and buildings. Planters knew that a high proportion of cultivable acres heightened the rental and sale value of their property, and unlike Camille Bourges, many landlords offered incentives to tenants who cleared their woodlands. Delta renters were frequently offered three years' free use of any land they cleared. This incentive of free use was a crucial method for bringing land into cultivation in the 1870s and 1880s and was common for decades thereafter. The practice of free rent for clearing was still employed in the Delta as late as the 1930s.[37]

Many backcountry farmers—both landowners and tenants—pursued what amounted to second careers as woodsmen. By the 1870s many backcountry farmers were finding distant markets for the trees they felled in clearing interior lands. Settlers along the Sunflower and Quiver Rivers had supplied logs to sawmills in Vicksburg and New Orleans in the 1850s, and this commerce was revived and expanded after the Civil War as pioneers encountered a variety of valuable hardwoods in the Delta's interior. The linty cottonwood was especially suited for use in constructing wagons, buggies, and caskets; the region's native gum was fashioned into high-grade furniture; and few applications eluded the ubiquitous oak. But the most prized lumber was drawn from the cypress. Antebellum settlers had dismissed the graceful, moss-draped trees that canopied the swamps as "a worthless sort of pine," but builders after the war increasingly sought out cypress lumber. The cypress's dense, termite-resistant hardwood was the perfect timber from which to construct a lasting structure. One Issaquena County storekeeper paid $5,000 for the cypress boards, joists, and beams that formed his two-and-a-half-story mercantile establishment in the late 1860s. As the region's urban places grew from mere hamlets to cities, home builders came to demand cypress lumber, and budding sawmills advertised "Cypress Lumber always on hand."[38]

The lumber companies of Greenville, Greenwood, Yazoo City, and other burgeoning towns had cypress and other hardwoods "on hand" because inland settlers were bringing logs to town sawmills. Frontier farmers fastened together several tree trunks using chains, rope, or spikes and guided the resulting raft to the nearest sawmill downstream, where they received cash for their wood. Others, like Metcalfe's tenants, shaped the wood to specific forms before selling it. Black farmers and wage hands in Bolivar County's interior cut railroad crossties, wagon-wheel spokes, barrel staves, and other products from wood on their land and hauled the goods to the nearest railroad station in farm wagons. The money earned from these activities could underwrite purchase of farmland.[39]

The part-time timber earnings of farmers encouraged some settlers to specialize in lumber. Small operators—both black and white—bought portable, steam-driven sawmills and soon were combing the countryside hiring out their services or denuding the forests of unwitting owners. Their work could be highly remunerative: one planter paid a sawmill operator $800 for a single month's service in 1875. The portable sawmills were so busy that one environmentally minded Delta editor predicted that "although twenty years ago there was no seeing the end of the timber, now with the modern mills . . . we are beginning to learn [of a] time when the 'wooden age' will be a thing of the past."

This "dire certainty" was, however, slow in coming. Large stands of lumber were profitably harvested in the Delta for decades beyond the turn of the century.[40]

In fact, the Delta forests were so immense, and their depletion so profitable, that large lumber companies from the Midwest and abroad began to invest in the land and relocate permanent sawmills to the region. At one point in 1878, lumber production by farmers, small sawmill operators, and large timber companies combined to place an estimated 2.5 million feet of logs in the Yazoo River. By 1880 logs containing 1 million feet of lumber floated in the Yazoo at Greenwood. A Peruvian timber merchant lived year-round in Greenville, and the editors of Delta newspapers reported daily inquiries about land and timber. "Rafts" comprised of 600 logs were common. Within five years lumber companies in Michigan, Iowa, Illinois, Wisconsin, and England had dispatched agents to examine and purchase large sections of the Delta's forests. Eager to corner the market, these agents threw money at grateful Delta land speculators. In 1884 the *Greenville Times* reported landowners receiving payments for timber rights that exceeded their property's assessed value. Timber rights to land near the region's recently constructed railroads brought a premium, and companies soon were shipping massive loads of lumber out of the Delta by rail. One sawmill in Leflore County disgorged 1 million feet of quartered oak for shipment to Europe.[41]

Communities sprang up in the interior, towns devoted to leveling and processing the forests. Most squatted beside railroads; if no existing rail line connected with a targeted stand of timber, lumber companies frequently constructed a narrow-gauge spur from the timberhead to the nearest railway.[42] These towns were small, ugly, and exuded an air of unmistakable impermanence. Their inhabitants ignored the rich land under their feet to concentrate on the deciduous growth it supported. When surrounding forests were stripped of all desirable timber, many workers moved along to the next doomed woodland, and the temporary communities they had created shriveled or vanished. "Here and there," around the denuded community at Merigold in Bolivar County, "small parcels of land were settled by people who were unable to get away and go to some other place." The temporary lumber towns competed with roving groups of axmen. Colonies of European sawyers disappeared into the forests for months at a time, axes, adzes, and other implements poised to shape oak barrel staves. Bolivar County resident Mary Hamilton reported 450 Slavonian woodsmen chopping away near Black Bayou late in the century. Despite the efforts of logging companies and European stave makers, farmers who sold wood in slack agricultural seasons and small operators with their portable sawmills continued to find markets for their timber through the end of the century. The competition these less capitalized lumbermen offered to fixed, capital-intensive industry seems to have irritated the pro-development sensibilities of some. Greenville's J. S. McNeily proclaimed in 1883 that "one good effect of the building of the M[emphis] & V[icksburg Railroad] will be the extinction of the raftsmen in the Bogue Phalia and Sunflower; as the bridges over those streams will not admit of the passage of rafts." Perhaps it was not small operators' log rafts that the *Greenville Times* editor resented so much as their race and economic mobility. For most of the black farmers who moved from tenant to independent cultivator in the Delta worked and purchased land in the interior, where these crude rafts originated, and many of the craft probably were piloted by new or future landowners.[43]

The massive clearing wrought in the 1880s and 1890s did not, however, contribute to the number of yeoman farmers owning fully improved acreage. Although the proportion of Delta land under forest declined abruptly in this period, the cleared acres were not placed for competitive sale. Lumber companies had often purchased the land from the Louisville, New Orleans and Texas and other railroad companies, which had themselves obtained the property for only pennies per acre after it was forfeited for nonpayment of taxes. Although farmers might appreciate the open land ready for plow and seed, few purchasers were forthcoming before the turn of the century. Farmers owning these acres would not, for example, be able to supplement their cotton income with cash sales of timber, for none remained to sell. Worse from the farmer's perspective was the seller's valuation of the property. Having leveled the land of trees, lumber companies considered the property improved and asked a higher price from potential purchasers. But most buyers did not regard the lumbermen's improvements as completely beneficial. As the price of cotton declined, and more emphasis was placed on other sources of income, bare acres offered at a premium price by lumber companies went unsold.[44]

Just as the environmental structures of the Delta—the land, water, and trees—endured a revolution heralded by the piercing whine of the sawmill's blades, so too were other foundations of life transformed. In the days of rapidly escalating land taxes, planters and speculators came to view underdeveloped and isolated real property less as a testimony to their status and acumen and more as a means of keeping their imperiled fortunes above a tide of debt. Better to sacrifice some distant acres, many seemed to believe, than lose the most developed fields. Others found that by renting those distant lands to freedmen, they could maintain ownership of their interior lands and use renters' payments to meet tax levies. Even after Redemption greatly reduced tax burdens, many of these landlords continued to offer attractive lease arrangements in order to induce good tenants—who were ever in short supply before the turn of the century—to keep their backcountry acreage in production. These individual acts of self-preservation by landlords, it turned out, brought far-reaching consequences. Tenants hoping to gain property of their own brought forth bounteous crops of cotton on the new fields, cleared the land of valuable hardwoods (opening additional acreage and receiving much-needed cash for their efforts), and bargained for and redeemed a number of advantageous rental provisions. By their labors these men and women, most of whom had once been someone's chattel property, accumulated cash and credit to buy their own land, investing the purchase with their hopes of attaining some economic independence with which to make their legal freedom ring true. Even as the sawmill blades screamed out the destruction of stately forests, former slaves labored nearby in the deep, rich loam to build their dreams upon a cushion of pale lint.

4

The Rise of the Backcountry Farmer

Despite myriad obstacles, African-American farmers of humble means frequently purchased Delta land in the decades during and after Reconstruction. By the mid-1880s the economic rise of these backcountry farmers—and their accompanying political strength—had transformed the Delta's interior into a promised land for poor but hopeful farmers and an implicit challenge to riverside planters. The majority of these new farm owners were freedmen, and their diverse and unpredictable paths from slave to property holder can be traced in the lives of three men: Bohlen Lucas, Lewis Spearman, and William Toler.

Bohlen Lucas found that many of the habits learned in slavery served him well as a free man. A slave driver on a Delta plantation since age sixteen, Lucas was reluctant to pursue an independent course immediately after emancipation. He continued to work supervising other blacks' agricultural labors, assisting white overseer James Collier in the first years after the Civil War. Even when Lucas began farming on his own behalf, he continued to express implicit fealty to his former masters—the first land he rented belonged to the widow of his former owner.[1]

Lucas was a good farmer. He drove himself hard, worked long hours in backcountry clearings near Deer Creek, saved his money, and looked about for a likely plot of land to purchase. By the end of 1870, Lucas had tucked away enough money to buy his own property. He paid James Collier, his former employer, $1,000 cash as the down payment on a 200-acre farm just off Deer Creek and promised to pay another $1,120 by 1 January 1873. Perhaps as a token of their extended relationship, Collier did not charge Lucas interest on the outstanding amount. Lucas's hard work in the fields and his ability to maintain profitable relations with former superiors had paid off. He now had a farm of his own.[2]

Owning 200 acres was not enough for the politely ambitious Lucas, however, and he soon moved to expand his operations. He rented nearby property, again from the widow of his former owner, and bought livestock and implements. This expansion left him heavily indebted, but he owned twenty-five mules and horses by the beginning of the 1872 crop season. Of course, Lucas could not plow twenty-five furrows at once; he needed laborers. Rather than employ wage laborers, the former slave driver took on tenants, leasing his own land and sub-leasing the property he had rented. Again, his efforts were rewarded with success. He paid off his note to Collier and now owned the 200 acres free and clear. He entered into another lease agreement with his former mistress in the spring of 1873, this time renting almost all of her Hermitage plantation and swelling his livestock corral with thirteen of her horses and oxen. By now Lucas was playing for large stakes. He owned or leased several hundred acres under cultivation and supervised numerous tenants. His risk was also substantial: the Hermitage lease cost Lucas $4,000 per year, and he had liened his own property to merchant C. W. Lewis in return for debt consolidation and advances of up to $2,000. Still, his hard work and good connections had always paid off, and Lucas must have expected further success.[3]

Like other backcountry renters, Lucas's lease agreement detailed more than a simple exchange of money for using another's land. First, he negotiated conditions that rewarded his improvement of the property: Lucas was authorized to deduct $3 from his rental fee for every 100 oak rails he placed in fencing around the leased land. The lease contracts also suggested a continued paternalism in his relationship with the widow of his former owner, Mrs. E. A. Fall. In both his 1872 and 1873 agreements, Lucas was obliged to supply the widow's household with ground corn.[4]

But Lucas was approaching the limits of patronage in the early 1870s. In 1871 he apparently rented land in partnership with a white man, one Mr. Dingy. Dingy died that same year, and Lucas sought the executorship of a farm owned by the estate of his deceased partner. With the support of neighboring white planters, Lucas convinced the court to accept his bond as estate administrator. He then took possession of the property and installed tenants. Yet the Dingy estate was much more complicated than Lucas or his white allies had expected, and a bereaved but contentious widow soon surfaced to contest their fleet administration. Mrs. Dingy demanded immediate return and control of the property. Lucas's white supporters were placed in a peculiar dilemma: they could continue to aid their faithful black confederate against this woman whom none of them knew, or they could follow the simple dictates of white supremacy and retract their support for the former slave. Lucas offered them a way out. Dingy had never mentioned any wife to him, Lucas reported, and he doubted that anyone else in the area could substantiate the late farmer's marriage. Nor had any of Lucas's planter friends ever heard Mr. Dingy speak of having a wife. Moreover, this alleged widow was from New York. It appeared more and more likely that the woman claiming Dingy's estate was just an alert fortune hunter from the North, and Lucas's allies remained firm. Lucas disputed the claim of marriage in court, and a local magistrate found the planters' testimony convincing. The ex-slave, aided by white planters, maintained executorship of the deceased white man's farm by sullying the veracity of a white woman.[5] Perhaps, in a peculiarly paternalistic fashion, Mississippi was being reconstructed in the early 1870s.

But the spurned New York woman proved persistent. She appealed the ruling all the way to the Mississippi Supreme Court. Meanwhile, certain of Lucas's supporters were beginning to doubt his ability to prevail. His adversary presented numerous circumstantial proofs that she had known Dingy and eventually convinced the high court that they had indeed been husband and wife. The reason no one in Washington County had ever heard of her or the marriage was simple: the wedding had taken place in Issaquena County, and the new bride had quickly departed the malarial region to preserve her health. Moreover, she could provide witnesses to the vows. Not surprisingly, the appellate court awarded her the estate. It ordered Lucas to vacate the property forthwith and pay the widow $1,500 (plus interest) for his use of the land while claiming executorship. He borrowed more money from his creditors and abandoned the farm, even though crops had been planted by his tenants.[6]

Bohlen Lucas's financial problems were not over. The cost of paying off Mrs. Dingy and the money lost in abandoning cultivation drove him too far into debt. His former patrons, embarrassed at having supported his exaggerated claim to a white woman's land, now fell away from him. Jim Collier, his former boss and the man who had sold him his farm, was among them. Although Lucas's purchase of the 200 acres was long concluded, he had subsequently borrowed money from Collier and pledged the farm against its repayment. Now that Lucas could not repay all of his debts, Collier refused to lengthen the term of the loan. In accordance with their deed of trust, the property was offered at public auction after Lucas could not make his payment.[7] Another creditor (and former ally) C. W. Lewis registered the highest bid; for only $500 he acquired the same 200 acres that Lucas had paid $2,120 to purchase less than five years before.[8] Lucas rented other land and resumed his practice of supervising sub-lessees in cotton cultivation.

His fickle white friends were soon back, however, for they needed Lucas's help. White conservatives chafing at Reconstruction under biracial Republican rule were organizing to seize office. Blacks, who voted heavily Republican, far outnumbered whites in the county, and Democrats knew that they could not return to office solely through intimidation and electoral abuse. They must add black votes to their tally, even if it required splitting offices with freedmen. Lucas, a prominent freedman with a record of loyalty to powerful whites, was the perfect candidate to present their case to the county's black population. He accordingly was welcomed into their counsel and soon took his place among those selected to present the view of the conservative Taxpayers' League to the black electorate. Lucas's on-again, off-again ally (and frequent creditor) C. W. Lewis was president of the Taxpayers' League. Another black landowner, the house-building John Rucks, was also selected to stump for the league. Rucks's patron, D. L. Stone, was secretary of the organization.[9]

Lucas was so vigorous in his support that his white allies congratulated them-selves on overlooking his indiscretions in the Dingy case and made him one of only two black delegates to the Democratic Party's 1875 county nominating committee. Again, the fervor of Lucas's fealty justified recognition and reward: his name was placed in nomination for the crucial office of county treasurer, and Lucas soon found himself on the ballot.[10]

Bohlen Lucas and the Redeemers won the local elections of 1875, breaking the power of the Republican Party and lowering the curtain on Reconstruction in the Delta. Lucas's role in bringing black voters to the Democratic column was crucial. He even organized his subleasing tenants and marched them to the polls, probably instructing them in the delicate relationship between political loyalty and personal fortune. But not everyone was impressed by Lucas's devotion to his conservative patrons: the candidate was attacked on his way home from the polls, presumably by freedmen unhappy with his political alliances, and left severely injured.[11]

Lucas recovered to assume office as county treasurer, but his impact in the position was negligible: he was illiterate, and his white patrons took advantage of this condition. Just after he took office, his confederates prevailed upon Lucas to appoint assistants who could read and interpret contracts for a pend-ing sale of county bonds. Convinced that his inability to read the documents jeopardized individual transactions and the county's fiscal security, Lucas agreed to deputize two white Democrats (W. W. Stone and C. L. Farrar) as his assistants. The record of their appointment cites Lucas's illiteracy as the only reason for the action. The former slave driver could not sign his name to the documents but confirmed the act by making his mark. From that point on, Stone and Farrar apparently performed most of the duties of the office.[12]

Lucas was not uniquely disadvantaged in his illiteracy; most of Mississippi's adult freed people in the last third of the nineteenth century were unable to read or write. Despite the work of volunteer teachers in the late 1860s and the state's constitutional obligation to black education after 1870, decades passed before even half of the Delta's black population gained literacy. Much of this can be attributed to slavery's legacy of denying education to bondsmen. Before emancipation, even valued slaves in supervisory positions like Lucas were denied education, their owners prohibited by state law from teaching bondsmen to read. After the war Mississippi's ambivalent support for black schools hampered formal learning, and older freedmen and their children often judged the sacrifices required for schooling (long distances to travel for instruction, fees levied, and the like) to be too great. In 1900, thirty-five years after gaining their freedom from slavery, over half of the Delta's black population remained shackled by illiteracy.[13]

Bohlen Lucas's success in gaining his own farm suggests that illiteracy was not an insurmountable handicap. In fact, most of the blacks who purchased Delta land in the 1870s could neither read nor write their name. In 1880 only 38 percent of the region's black male farm owners were literate, a figure barely distinguishable from the 34 percent of black male farm tenants who were similarly educated. Although literacy might help a farmer negotiate the pitfalls of credit, it did not guarantee a freedman the ability to gain land. Like Lucas, most black farm purchasers in the late 1860s and 1870s found that hard work and ambition more than compensated for their lack of schooling.[14]

The great flaw in Bohlen Lucas's career was not illiteracy but patronage and the uncertainty and dependence it engendered. Although his connections brought status, wealth, support, and the chance for financial security, they also compromised his independence. After his term as treasurer ended, Lucas found that his patrons, now safely ensconced in a courthouse "redeemed" from Republican competition, did not need his assistance and withdrew their support. Lucas was abandoned to obscurity. By 1880 the onetime slave, slave driver, entrepreneurial farm renter, landowner, political candidate, and county treasurer was reduced to cultivating a twenty-acre plot.[15] In the end, eagerness to harness his ambitions to the wishes of white patrons became Bohlen Lucas's curse.

Lewis Spearman purposefully avoided the conflicting demands of patronage. In January 1873 he leased John Burton's entire Ridgeland plantation in present-day Humphreys County for $900. It was a good place for an energetic farmer to get his start: the soil was fertile, he was able to ship cotton from Burtonia Landing on the Yazoo River, and few white settlers had ventured this far into the Delta's interior. Although much of the nation was soon thrown into an economic panic, Spearman prospered. His 1873 crop was good, he was thrifty, and he discharged his rent obligation to Burton on time. Spearman fared so well that he determined to buy his own land in 1874. A nearby tract owned by a white planter-speculator caught Spearman's eye, and he purchased the property, 130 acres of good land (most of it wooded), for $1,050 cash.[16]

Spearman improved his holdings and carefully avoided debt. His land was convenient to the Yazoo River, so it was easy to float timber off the property. For fourteen years the Spearman family enlarged their cultivable acres, sold what they produced there, and escaped debt. Spearman added a second mule and a horse to their corral, and perhaps to broaden the family's diet and diversify the household economy, he also procured thirty head of cattle. This last acquisition was unusual, for Delta farmers, whether black or white, seldom owned large droves of beef cattle. Meat protein was most commonly derived from pork, chicken, fish, and venison. The latter two sources were to be found in the streams and forests of the region well beyond the turn of the century. The average black male farm owner in 1880 kept sixteen pigs, four dairy cattle, three mules, and one or two horses on his 160 acres. White male farm owners, whose landholdings averaged almost 700 acres, kept proportionately larger stocks of beasts: thirty-eight pigs, ten dairy cattle, thirteen mules, and four or five horses.[17] Later, Lewis Spearman added an additional 119 acres to his holdings. Although their backcountry farm was not totally self-sufficient, the family was self-supporting.[18]

Spearman did not work alone. Like most of the Delta's farmers of small and medium-sized plots, he turned to his own family for labor. Eldest son Lewis Spearman, Jr., was old enough to help in the fields and forest. Although twenty-two years old in 1870, the farmer's namesake remained with his parents to help improve their land and gather its harvest. Family ties held Lewis Spearman, Jr., nearby even after marriage. In 1880, married and a father to three children, he and his family lived next door, and he continued to work on his father's property. Two other sons (then eighteen and sixteen years old) added their labor on the farm, as did three daughters (aged twenty, fifteen, and fourteen). Only one child, a twelve-year-old son, attended school.[19] This reliance on family labor, and its concomitant reduction of the time children spent in school, was not unique to the Spearman family. Many illiterate farm owners might understandably consider anything more than basic instruction wasted on children and count as lost the days spent inside a schoolhouse instead of out on the farm.

As late as 1900, the school-age children of black farm owners passed more than twice as many months laboring on the farm as they spent inside a classroom. These children, aged ten to eighteen, attended classes an average of 3.48 months each year in 1900. These same children performed field labor an average of 9 months each year (apparently spending some weeks engaged in both school attendance and farmwork). The offspring of black female farm owners, most of them widowed, spent an even larger percentage of their time in farm labor. These adolescents were in school for 3.57 months each year and working in the fields for 9.3 months. By contrast, the school-age children of white male farm owners spent an average of 5.3 months in school each year and in many cases did little or no field work.[20] Part of the discrepancy between white and black school attendance likely resulted from the greater availability of schools in the plantation districts and towns where most whites lived, compared to the shortage of facilities in the frontier areas most heavily populated by black settlers. But part of the difference also sprang from black parents' need for farmworkers. As the example of the Spearman family reveals, the availability of a school and parental willingness to have their sons and daughters educated did not guarantee that children would continue instruction into their teen years. Every household had to mediate between its immediate needs for labor and the younger generation's long-term needs for education.

A householder might shelter extended family members, take on boarders, or engage hired help to lessen the burden on his or her children. Indeed, the shortage of housing on the Delta frontier encouraged extranuclear households.[21] More than a fifth of black male farm owners were host to relatives or boarders in 1880, and another 14 percent housed field laborers or domestic servants in their home. Black female farm owners seldom hired long-term workers (only 3 percent of their households included servants or laborers), but approximately one-third housed relatives or boarders.[22] In 1880 the household of Lewis Spearman, Sr., included a farm laborer and his family (six persons) and a fourteen-year-old boarder who worked on the farm and attended school part-time.[23] Thus, the need for labor and housing in the backcountry often led to augmented households.

But Spearman's large labor force could not fully shelter him from the decline of the international cotton market. The price of cotton dropped year after year, falling near the cost of its production by the late 1880s. After fourteen debt-free years, Spearman could no longer support himself and his family, and in 1888 he conveyed a deed of trust on his 130 acres to Herman and Nathan Wilczinski, two Prussia-born merchants living in Greenville. Spearman had fallen $325 into the Wilczinskis' debt during the winter of 1887–88, and like most Delta merchants they would not extend further credit to indebted landowners without first receiving a deed of trust for real property. Spearman agreed to their terms: in return for up to $500 in additional credit for purchases and cash advances, he must repay the total debt plus 10 percent flat interest. He also agreed to pay credit prices—customarily advertised as 2 percent above what was charged for cash sales—for all goods he received from the Wilczinskis. If he failed to make timely payment against his arrears, their deed of trust authorized the merchants to reimburse themselves by having his land, crops, two mules, one horse, and thirty cattle sold at public auction. Spearman essentially bet his livelihood and the family's future prosperity on the prospect that cotton prices would improve in 1888.[24]

But cotton prices continued to fall, and the black farmer became increasingly uneasy in his relationship with the Wilczinskis. He pursued other credit options the next spring. Because he owned a substantial farm on good soil near a navigable river, Spearman could attract a broad range of potential lenders, even during the agricultural depression. He wanted to avoid doing business with the local merchants and eventually took a $1,000 loan from a Memphis firm with international mortgage connections. He was charged the same 10 percent interest he would have paid for a local loan, but with $1,000 cash Spearman could pay off the Wilczinskis and reserve enough money to buy supplies until his cotton was gathered.[25]

Again, Spearman had bet that the cotton market would improve enough before 1892 (when his note fell due) to enable him to retire his loan and avoid further debt. Again, like hundreds of thousands of farmers across the nation during this agricultural depression, he bet wrong. Cotton prices did not improve; they declined. By 1891 Spearman faced difficulty getting the supplies he needed to plant and live until his cotton was sold. In time-honored Delta tradition, he temporarily solved his debt problem by taking out another loan. In January 1891 he borrowed $1,000 from Delta merchant G. W. Meek to pay off the balance of his debt to the Memphis group and persuaded Meek to allow him an additional $250 credit toward the purchase of supplies. The terms of their agreement were identical to Spearman's loan from the Wilczinskis.[26]

Spearman's debts to Meek piled up as the agricultural depression deepened. Meek and Spearman updated their original deed of trust agreement several times in the following years to reflect the latter's increasing debt and to keep his line of credit open. Despite his farming experience and the thrift he demonstrated in the 1870s and 1880s, Spearman was unable to profit during cotton's protracted slump. After gathering the 1893 crop, he realized that he could no longer hold his head above the rising wave of debt, and Spearman sacrificed the 119-acre tract he had purchased to augment his farm. The deed of trust was activated and the property sold at auction in the spring of 1894. This desperate action did not end Spearman's debt problem. His home farm was also hostage to a deed of trust agreement, and his 1894 crop must be very large (and the price of cotton must improve) if he was to maintain ownership. But commodity prices did not rise, and G. W. Meek activated that deed of trust. Spearman lost the farm he had toiled to buy and scrimped to keep, the land he and his family had cleared and brought into cultivation, and the economic foundation of his standing in the community. In accord with the deed of trust, the 130 acres were sold at public auction in March 1895.[27]

As Lewis Spearman's experience demonstrates, even talented, thrifty farmers eager to diversify their operations and seek creative credit sources could fail. Like Spearman, many black farmers who had battled for solvency all their lives lost the fight in their later years and were unable to stave off crushing debt. The Delta's rich soil was no sure guarantee of success, especially when the cotton market was in free fall, and a lifetime of hard work might yield only bitterness in the end. Backcountry pioneer Lewis Spearman, Sr., died within a few years of losing his farm in 1895. His son never attained landownership despite a lifetime of farming in the Delta.[28]

But debt did not always spell disaster. William Toler, another black farmer who purchased Delta land in the 1870s, walked a tightrope of conditional solvency for decades, never falling into the threatening lake of red ink. Unlike Spearman and Lucas, Toler proved that debt need not foreclose a black farmer's financial or political options.

Toler bought eighty acres of Washington County's most fertile land in 1875. He obtained the farm, located just over one mile southeast of the present town of Arcola, for $250 cash and the promise of another $150 due in January of the following year. As a harbinger of his coming prowess in debt negotiations, Toler dissuaded the speculators who sold him the property from charging interest on the unpaid balance. Their faith in his dependability was justified; Toler retired his obligation on time and purchased an additional eighty acres.[29] Toler paid only $5 per acre for his original tract, and the low price for such fertile land suggests that most of the property was not yet cleared. But Toler's improvements — clearing, fencing, commencing cultivation — soon improved the property's value dramatically. Toler's propensity for debt made increasing the value of his real assets vital, for by 1878 he owed Greenville cotton merchants Weiss and Goldstein $800. Within five years Toler's arrears to the merchants had more than doubled, and he signed a deed of trust to his property for $1,654.06 in 1883.[30]

Seven crops later, Toler's position had worsened. In 1890 his debt to Weiss and Goldstein approached $2,000, and the merchants feared for their repayment. Consequently, the deed of trust they presented to Toler in 1890 included a host of fees and requirements, all designed to increase their return on the loan even if Toler was driven to bankruptcy in the process. As usual, Toler was required to sell his entire cotton crop through Weiss and Goldstein and to pay 10 percent interest on his debt. And the merchants held a lien on his land, crops, and seven mules as guarantee of payment. But Toler now encountered a new requirement. If the cotton crop he sent to the factors was less than seventy-five bales, he would be charged $1.25 for each bale under the quota. It was a small matter and not a major problem for a farmer with significant arable land, but it signaled a change in the lenders' relationship with Toler. Now the debtor's obligation extended beyond the money loaned to him.[31] Toler's debts to Weiss and Goldstein fluctuated between $1,500 and $2,000 for the next three years. The bale requirement was continued, and another stipulation was added. Beginning in 1893, Toler was charged an extra 2.5 percent interest for all purchases he made through the merchants. But Weiss and Goldstein had lost faith in Toler's ability to repay his arrears. The farmer seemed unable to keep ahead of his debts, and the agricultural depression that devalued his cotton showed no sign of ending. In February 1894 the creditors activated their deed of trust, and Toler's land and six mules were auctioned off to the First National Bank of Greenville for $2,000.[32]

Now the farmer's talent for negotiating emerged. Rather than seek wage labor or a sharecropping position, Toler convinced the bank to sell the property back to him. He agreed to pay $285 over the auction price for the property and livestock and to add 10 percent interest to the full amount. Moreover, he persuaded the bank to extend up to $300 in additional cash to pay for his supplies.[33]

Toler chiseled away at his debt for the next several years. Luckily, the price of cotton began to increase in the last half of the decade, and he was able to make more money than he spent. Yet Toler never fully retired the debt. When the bank pressured him to pay off his note in 1899, Toler persuaded a Greenville merchant to loan him the money. When the merchant became eager for his money six years later, Toler found another moneylender. By this time Toler had refined his cycle of negotiating, borrowing, and partially retiring his debts to a fine art. He kept his farm, paid only the interest on his debt each year, and replaced his creditors when they demanded he decrease his principal obligation. In a sense, Toler simply took on new investors every six or seven years, paid them an annual 10 percent dividend on their investment, and found other investors to buy them out once they became dissatisfied.[34]

But William Toler was more than a clever debtor. Unlike Bohlen Lucas, who reconciled himself to the petty degradations of patronage in his pursuit of financial gain, Toler prized his independence. He bought his land from real estate brokers, not nearby planters; he borrowed money from factors, merchants, and bankers, not former owners and overseers. Occupational distinctions were blurred and intermingled in the Delta's frontier period, but as far as possible Toler narrowed his financial dealings with whites to persons who had no other interest in his affairs and limited his relationships with these men to business. Nor did Toler countenance political co-option. Unlike the Redeemers' ally Bohlen Lucas, Toler was a faithful member of the party of Lincoln. His fellow Republicans expressed their admiration for Toler in 1900, when he was made a census enumerator, charged with ferreting out and tallying the vital statistics of a large section of Washington County. His service as census enumerator reveals another difference between Lucas and Toler, for the census manuscripts left by the latter are written in a fine, clear hand. Toler had been illiterate upon emancipation, too, but he learned to read and write before 1880. And there was one final, important difference between William Toler and both Bohlen Lucas and Lewis Spearman: only Toler succeeded in passing along property to his descendants.[35]

Black Delta farmers' movement from tenancy to landowning suggests that something like an "agricultural ladder" functioned in the region during the 1870s and 1880s. Not only do the deed records in the Delta's courthouses reveal numerous farmers, like Lucas, Spearman, and Toler, who worked their way from renters to property owners, broad demographic data support these individual accounts. Despite high rental fees and complicated contracts, many renters prospered in the backcountry. George Brown, for example, purchased a

55-acre farm one year after completing the contract requiring him to labor at his landlord's steam gin without pay. One year after his landlord denied him the right to sublease, renter William Campbell and a partner paid cash for an 80-acre tract. Deer Creek renter Aaron Cole worked land owned by LeRoy and William A. Percy in 1878. His lease demanded cotton worth approximately $7.46 per acre for a 45-acre tract of mixed land. Cole was very successful, earning enough money from his crops for a $675 cash down payment on a 139-acre farm. This large down payment, half the property's price, reduced the farmer's future mortgage payments and saved him money on interest. These are only a few of the black farmers who moved from tenancy to landowning in the generation after emancipation.[36]

If a broad group of Delta farmers worked their way from sharecropping to renting to landowning, one should find an incremental increase in the average age of each group. Had nothing like an agricultural ladder existed, however, farmers in the various tenure groups would have shared an average age.[37] The Delta's black and white farmers revealed a clear relationship between increasing age and greater economic standing.[38] In 1880 the average age of black male sharecroppers, tenants, and landowners stood at 40.4, 43.7, 46.4, respectively. The pattern among black male farmers continued to the end of the century. In 1900 the average age of Delta sharecroppers was 34.3, the average age of tenants stood at 37.8, and the average farm owner was just over 46 years old. Among white farmers a similar pattern was evident. While white male sharecroppers and tenants shared an average age of just under 37 years in 1880, white male farm owners averaged 40 years. But the pattern among white male farmers grew much more striking by 1900. In that year the average age of sharecroppers, tenants, and landowners was 27, 37.9, and 44.4, respectively.[39] Years of work on Delta farms enhanced one's chances for renting or owning fertile land; sharecroppers and tenants could hope to emulate the good fortune of more experienced, older farmers in the last third of the nineteenth century.

Not all of the backcountry's farmland was worked by individuals or isolated households. Several groups of settlers—numbering hundreds of households in one case—worked and lived together at farming colonies in the Delta's interior. Their incentives for cooperative effort were diverse, ranging from financial necessity to religious community to secular utopianism, but all brought their communal experiments to the Delta's inland frontier in the 1870s and 1880s.

The first such colony, and the only one organized by whites, came about by accident. When brothers Jesse H. and John Barefield both died in the early 1870s, their numerous heirs and relatives confronted a dilemma: whether to try to save the pair's struggling backcountry farms or quit the isolated endeavor. Although the property was situated on Deer Creek's fertile and elevated ridge, miles of swamp, canebrake, and forest separated the site from the nearest town. Had the Barefields' descendants been able to find a buyer for the entire property, approximately one square mile in size, they probably would have sold the land, divided the proceeds, and drifted off to their individual pursuits. But there were few purchasers for large tracts of Delta land in that era, so the descendants settled in to clear and farm the overgrown estate, dubbing the place Barefield Colony.[40]

Leadership and property followed the lines of patriarchy in the Colony. Samuel Barefield, surviving brother of John and Jesse, and John's oldest son, Steven T. Barefield, played prominent roles in the group's affairs. Samuel already owned land by the 1870s, and Steven was his father's principal heir. Despite the communal implications of its name, landownership in the Colony was controlled by senior males, not shared equally among family members. Samuel and Steven T. Barefield were probably at the head of the group of Colony voters who cast solidly Democratic votes in the 1875 election that overthrew local Republican Reconstruction.[41]

Significantly, the small farmers of the Colony did not limit their efforts to cotton cultivation. They were herdsmen as well, keeping and selling large numbers of cattle. Steven T. Barefield, for example, sold a drove of seventy-five beeves in 1875. Multifaceted agriculture eventually brought a measure of wealth to numerous members of the Colony. The census takers listed four landowning Barefields in 1900, and upon Samuel Barefield's death in that same year, he left several hundred acres to his three less successful offspring. Close ties of blood and kinship bound members of the Barefield Colony, an unquestioning patriarchy led them, and they prospered by diversifying their agricultural efforts in the remote but fertile backcountry.[42]

Whereas the Barefield Colony was begun from necessity and sustained by family ties, the next group experiment in the Delta backcountry was born of concerns for religious community. Little is known about the Reverend H. K. Solomon. Whether he was free or enslaved before 1865 cannot be determined, and even his place of birth is a mystery. Despite his elusive background, those who met the charismatic Solomon after his arrival in the 1880s must have found him difficult to forget. A religious entrepreneur, Solomon founded his own church. In 1884 he established the Solomon Chapel, African Methodist Episcopal, at Catfish Point near the Mississippi River in Bolivar County's plantation district. Like many pastors of poor congregations, Solomon was obliged to pursue a secular vocation: he farmed. Specifically, he rented rich land near Catfish Point that he then subleased to black farmers of lesser means. Indeed, many of the adherents of Solomon Chapel were his tenants.[43]

We will never know why the Reverend Solomon left Catfish Point—whether he was forced out by neighboring white planters who feared his economic and spiritual influence among area freedmen, whether he thought his financial prospects would be improved by relocating to the backcountry, or if he and his congregation thought to make "a city upon a hill" deep in Bolivar County— but the group left the plantation district only one year after forming Solomon Chapel. Solomon, his tenants, and other members of the congregation traveled east into the backcountry, eventually settling near present-day Cleveland just as that town was becoming established in 1885. The area they chose had some obvious advantages. Settling there was a much less daunting task than hacking out a home in the wilderness they had to pass through on their trek from the riverside. Too, the village they joined was located along the tracks of the recently completed Louisville, New Orleans and Texas Railroad (LNO&T), and work and society would accompany the hamlet's likely growth. In 1887 the congregation built the first church constructed in the just-incorporated town.[44]

After gathering together as a church in the plantation district, trekking through sloughs and canebrake to a tiny inland settlement, and building a house of worship, Solomon's band inexplicably dispersed. Some probably experimented in clearing and farming wilderness land nearby; the railroad was then selling uncleared Bolivar County tracts for as little as $5 per acre. Others doubtless left the Delta as the agricultural depression squeezed the cotton economy into debt. In any case, the Reverend Solomon disappeared, leaving no more evidence of his destination than he had earlier revealed of his roots. A lumber company later took over the lot where his Cleveland church had been erected.[45]

Bolivar County's second communal experiment was much more successful, perhaps because its founder, Isaiah T. Montgomery, was experienced in organizing and leading large numbers of freed people before arriving in the Delta. Montgomery was born the slave of Joseph E. Davis in 1847, learned to read and write while in bondage, and observed his father Benjamin T. Montgomery's skilled management of Davis's Warren County plantation. After the war the Montgomery family purchased the Davis holdings, some 4,000 acres, and annually gathered up to 3,000 bales of cotton on the property for the next decade. Although they lost the plantation in the 1870s, Isaiah Montgomery maintained his interest in running a large cotton-growing operation.[46]

In 1887 Montgomery found another opportunity. The LNO&T railroad was offering large tracts of land for cheap prices in the Delta, and Montgomery made several trips to the alluvial basin searching for a site suited to his next undertaking. He settled on a spot alongside the railroad line in central Bolivar County, fifteen miles east of the Mississippi and four miles west of one of its tributaries, the Sunflower River. Two bayous converged near his land of choice, and a large Indian mound rose between their banks. He dubbed the place Mound Bayou and persuaded his cousin Ben Green to join him in buying 840 acres there. By midsummer, Montgomery and Green had persuaded a small group of friends and relatives, most of them also former slaves of the Davis brothers, to join them in settling the area the next year.[47]

Montgomery and his early followers regarded Mound Bayou as a utopian experiment, founded on notions of self-help and independence from white interference. Upon reaching the site of their hopes in early 1888, Isaiah Montgomery made a speech in which he told his followers "they might as well buy land and own it and do for themselves what they had been doing for other folks for two hundred and fifty years." Heeding his advice, the few colonists purchased more than 700 acres that same year.[48]

Within three years Mound Bayou showed prospects for success. Even though the thick hardwood forest was a detriment to cotton cultivation, colonists turned what could have been a problem to their advantage. They erected a sawmill and began cutting down the oak, cypress, and ash trees surrounding their little settlement. Timber agents were eager to purchase all the wood they could fell, and the nearby railroad served as both a customer for crossties and a vehicle for transporting other wood products. By 1891 the colony had earned almost $9,000 from timber sales, and the 655 acres cleared in the process already yielded crops. Colonists gathered 379 bales of cotton and harvested 3,045 bushels of corn in the first three years of settlement. Life was not easy—food was occasionally in short supply even though some of the women and children worked as hired hands on plantations ten miles away to earn cash wages—but the colony had found a toehold for survival, and Montgomery's dream of a black utopia in the Delta backcountry was gradually becoming a reality.[49]

In 1907, twenty years after Mound Bayou's founding, the colony was a clear success. In that year 800 families (about 4,000 persons) made their homes in and around Mound Bayou, and colonists owned 30,000 acres of land. Over 5,000 acres were cultivated each year, yielding an average cotton crop of 3,000 bales as well as providing much of the settlement's corn and fodder needs. The town was greatly expanded, now encompassing 96 acres and boasting a population of 500. Inhabitants had their choice of thirteen stores and six churches (with four more in the town's environs), and farmers could use any of three cotton gins. The sawmill remained active and had been joined by a bank, a telephone exchange, and a weekly newspaper, the *Demonstrator*. And the community was preparing to embark upon a campaign to build their own cottonseed oil mill, valued at $100,000.[50]

But Mound Bayou was more than a thriving village. For Isaiah Montgomery, it was proof that blacks were capable of honest, unsupervised industry and worthy of self-government.[51] For other black businessmen in the Delta, like Clarksdale's Charles Banks, who arrived to organize the Bank of Mound Bayou in 1904, the town was a place where African Americans' commercial success would not call down the wrath of envious whites. For young blacks growing up in Mound Bayou, the town was a model of their own potential. One native son, who later took a law degree at Harvard University, recalled that "everything here was Negro, from the symbols of law and authority and the man who ran the bank down to the fellow who drove the road scraper. That gave us kids a sense of security and power and pride that colored kids don't get anywhere else." For harassed blacks across Jim Crow Mississippi, Mound Bayou was a constant refuge from persecution. Montgomery frequently sponsored the resettlement of blacks fleeing from "the white cap districts" of Mississippi to the Delta.[52] Mound Bayou never became a perfect utopia, but the colony thrived for two decades.[53]

Mound Bayou's success spawned imitation. Joseph E. Ousley, another former slave of Joseph E. Davis, attempted to form a similar black colony at Renova, also in Bolivar County.[54] By that time Ousley was well established in the region. He had begun a public career in the Delta in the twilight of Reconstruction. In 1874–75 he held the potentially explosive position of tax assessor of Bolivar County. Yet white and black voters were so satisfied with his service that he was elected county sheriff for 1876–77. Then Ousley settled into an even more prestigious office, serving as clerk of Bolivar County's probate and circuit courts from 1880 through 1895.[55]

But Ousley's colony soon failed. Although he and his brother Gabe attempted to take advantage of the same cheap railroad land that Montgomery and his followers were clearing in the late 1880s and 1890s—Renova is about six miles southeast of Mound Bayou on the railroad line—the settlement foundered. Indeed, Renova suffered from many disadvantages. Unlike Montgomery, the Ousleys did not recruit a core group of dependable colonists from among people they had grown up with, farmers whose abilities and weaknesses they already knew. Moreover, in the crucial early period of settlement, Joseph Ousley could not devote his full time to the project. His duties as county clerk kept him at the courthouse in Rosedale along the Mississippi River; he probably spent more time there than in his fledgling colony. The biggest problem, though, was Gabe Ousley, upon whom leadership devolved in Joseph's absence. Gabe was a spendthrift, frequently broke, and habitually relied on white planters to aid him in times of financial embarrassment. Joseph indulged his brother, which only made the problem worse. Whereas Isaiah Montgomery was sometimes accused of running Mound Bayou dictatorially, Joseph Ousley's loose hand (and his brother's mismanagement) doomed the Renova colony.[56]

Despite their apparent diversity, the experiences of the Delta's frontier colonists—at the Barefield Colony, with H. K. Solomon, in Mound Bayou, and at Renova—provoke two general conclusions. First, the backcountry was a place where groups of farmers, both white and black, could work together for economic and social goals. Moreover, these endeavors were most profitably commenced in the 1870s and 1880s, when the backcountry was largely unsettled and land could be purchased cheaply.

The two enduring efforts, at Barefield Colony and Mound Bayou, reveal the three attributes any backcountry colony had to incorporate for success. Most importantly, the settlers must share prior connections. The family relations that bound the Barefields and their married kin were paralleled at Mound Bayou by an original group of pioneers who had known one another since their shared bondage on Joseph Davis's plantation. These links informed the colonists' efforts, made them sensitive to the goals, predilections, strengths, and weaknesses of their fellows, and provided a bond on which they could rely in difficult times. Second, the Mound Bayou and Barefield Colony experiences reveal the importance in the community's emotional investment in the endeavor. While Solomon's followers might have been coerced into following him by his leverage as their landlord, and the Ousleys never put forward a unifying vision for Renova, the successful colonists had extra incentive for prevailing. At Barefield Colony the extended family's welfare required success. At Mound Bayou the settlement's avowed mission as a model community for southern blacks spurred them on through sacrifice. Finally, clear lines of authority were needed if a colony was to live, as well as work, together. The patriarchal leadership at Barefield Colony was nearly replicated by Isaiah Montgomery at Mound Bayou. By contrast, the Ousleys' settlers never knew which brother was in charge (if either was present). Similarly, the divided pursuits of preacher-landlord Solomon may have left his flock wondering whether their leader was more interested in their souls or the rental fees they paid to him. Groups of farming pioneers could successfully unite for common good in the Delta's backcountry, even pursue utopian goals, but long-standing connections among participants, full commitment to the shared enterprise, and unclouded leadership were crucial to their long-term prosperity.

The Delta backcountry—despite its carnivores, danger from flood and disease, and tree-choked acreage—offered struggling farmers who arrived alone, with their families, or in colonies of several hundred households the opportunity to attain a modicum of financial independence. But the Delta's frontier stage would not last forever. With every new settler, every new isolated store, and every new line of transportation and communication, the distance between the plantation districts and the backcountry was effectively narrowed. This joining of town and country not only ended farmers' isolation, it also ended their immunity from planters' competition. In retrospect it would be a cruel paradox: left relatively free to improve the region's interior, they succeeded so well that the area became attractive to the very individuals and interests who had earlier deemed the interior expendable. As planters, speculators, and other developers moved into the backcountry, they pulled closed behind them the door to middling farmers' opportunity.

Washington County tenant farmer Glover Webb on his calico pony about 1900

Young African Americans outside a segregated Delta school

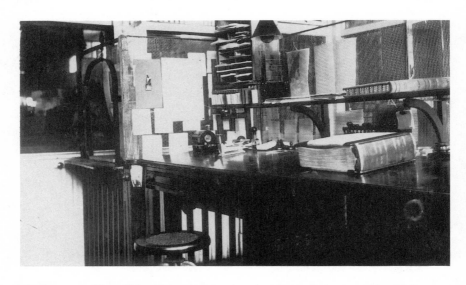

The business office of the Chism Brothers' store at Friars Point; note the thick account ledger in the foreground

The *Kate Adams* approaching a Coahoma County landing

Loading the steamer *James Lee* just after 1900

Washington County cotton pickers in 1909

5

Joining Town and Country

Near his life's end, Greenville's William Alexander Percy recalled the long-past heyday of the steamboat, when

> the *Pargo* landed regularly on Sunday, usually between eleven o'clock and noon. Everybody would be at church, but when she blew, the male members of the congregation to a man would rise and, in spite of indignant glares from their wives and giggles from the choir, make their exits, with a severe air of business just remembered. With the *Pargo* came the week's mail and gossip of the river-front from St. Louis to New Orleans and rumors from the very distant outside world. If the occasion was propitious a little round of poker might be started and a few toddies drunk. They were a fine fleet, those old sidewheelers which plied between St. Louis and New Orleans and stopped on signal at the various plantations and river settlements.[1]

Percy's recollection probably dated from the late 1890s, when a dwindling steamboat armada, diminished in competition with cinder-spouting locomotives, still patrolled the Mississippi. Today, more than a century later, the steamboat landings that were the frontier Delta's strongest link with the news and goods of the larger world are almost forgotten. In the first decades after the Civil War, however, these muddy embankments dotted with storekeepers' hastily erected shanties—the crude outposts of America's industrial revolution—were barometers of local society as well as places of exchange for goods, gossip, and ideas. Imagine yourself at a landing and consider the curiosities descending the packet boat's gangplank: travelers and new settlers entering the region, friends returning from obscure and celebrated journeys, lawyers and judges making the circuit of dusty courthouses, the latest consumer goods, and metropolitan newspapers full of political and economic portents. Of course, ginned cotton's autumnal ascent of these same well-worn boards was also a matter of local concern and weighty spectacle. Well into the 1880s, the steamboat landing was the focal point of a Delta community's economic, political, and social life.

Small wonder that landings often expanded to bring forth hamlets and towns. From initial settlement, Delta merchants realized the commercial potential of access to river landings, and most set up their stores at choice points along the Mississippi River and its tributaries. There, shopkeepers were convenient both to their waterborne supply line and to the bored, news-starved, and itinerant folks who might spend time and money in a merchant's establishment. One merchant's success then attracted a second and a third shopkeeper to the landing, persons offering services (blacksmiths, doctors, and lawyers) soon followed, and before long the district's prominent planters moved to the little city to enjoy proximity to goods, services, and diversion.

But the same access to transport that underwrote a landing's commercial viability also brought disadvantages, for just as people might easily come to the landing store for goods, they might also commit depredations and be quickly gone from the scene of their perfidy. One merchant, elected mayor of a riverside town, bemoaned his duty of keeping order in a place crowded with footloose river folk. After pushing a vagrancy ordinance into law, the mayor conceded that the town was still "overrun with dangerous and vicious characters," a "bad class" who openly threatened his life. White merchants and local officials were not the only persons preyed on by rootless occupants of river towns, for freed people were also robbed and assaulted.[2] River towns and landings thus suffered from, as well as profited by, their proximity to river traffic.

While vagrants might threaten an individual's peace of mind, far greater tumult threatened the Delta's cotton-based economy after the Civil War. The chief institution of the antebellum plantation economy, the cotton factorage, faced extinction after years of war and the emancipation of plantation slaves.

Cotton factors had long guided Deep South commerce. These men functioned as a planter's credit source, commodity broker, purchasing agent, and general factotum. They loaned money to a plantation owner in the long months between crops, sold his cotton for the highest possible price, found and shipped the goods he ordered for his family and slaves, and attended to a variety of petty errands. Although factors frequently complained of the excessive demands made by cotton snobs upon their time, patience, and credit, few of these merchants were willing to abandon the lucrative field. For each bale of cotton the factor sold, he deducted a commission from the planter's earnings.

For each loan, he assessed interest. For goods purchased and shipped to the distant plantation, he attached a handling charge. Although their role placed them at the beck and call of arrogant nabobs, antebellum factors found comfortable livings in that dim zone between an agent's obligations to his patron and the capitalist's ability to charge what the market would bear. Some factors grew rich in those years before slavery's collapse, and a few parlayed trading acumen into large estates of their own.[3]

Much of the factor's prewar prominence and wealth was accrued at the expense of smaller local businessmen. The local storekeeper labored under pronounced disadvantages, for his wealthiest customers, plantation owners, had little incentive to trade with him. Unless faced with an emergency shortfall of some necessary item, why would a planter choose to patronize the dusty, thin-stocked shelves of a frontier shop? True, he might enjoy the social role of patron and calculate that the storekeeper's vote would prove important at the next local election. But planters could purchase a greater variety of goods at lower cost by trading through their factors. The local storekeeper—distant from the paths of commerce and lacking strong connections to the international cotton market—expected occasional small purchases from nearby planters but would never wrest away the lion's share of their business as long as cotton factors controlled plantation credit and cotton marketing. Indeed, storekeepers—who also purchased goods and marketed cotton through factors—were frequently beholden to these competitors.[4]

Still, merchants found a niche in the Delta's antebellum economy. Except for the luxury items that planters would rather buy locally (even at a higher price) than do without—especially spirituous liquids—storekeepers focused on humbler segments of the market. For the fur trappers, axmen, pioneering yeoman farmers, and rivermen who comprised the obscure majority of free antebellum settlers, shopkeepers stocked knives, axes, farm implements, and other items for daily use. Enterprising shopmen also sold livestock—especially mules and oxen bred in the upper South's more salubrious climate—and traded with slaves.[5] Local merchants were able to piece together sufficient trade from sales to slaves, lesser whites, and planters to survive and sometimes prosper, but they never controlled the Delta's cotton-based economy before the Civil War.

In the 1860s, however, the dominant commercial position of factors was severely eroded. The Confederacy's unofficial policy of discouraging cotton exports was a large part of the problem. Factors hoping to concentrate on some other aspect of the supply trade found the exchange of commodities and consumer goods choked off by the Federal naval blockade of southern ports. War-related deaths and the financial ruin of many Deep South planters during the conflict further weakened the trade and client base of cotton factors. And the collapse of many southern banks, upon which traders had relied for the operating capital they extended to planters as credit, brought bankruptcy to many overextended factorages. Their import-export trade destroyed, their patrons dead or bankrupt, and their credit evaporating, many factorages closed their doors before the end of the war.[6] Although cotton factors continued to supply some Delta plantations into the twentieth century, their influence was greatly diminished, the range of services they could offer was restricted, and they lost their grip on the Delta trade.[7]

Local merchants moved to fill the trade and credit vacuum created by the factors' decline. Just as the factor's control over the Delta trade had been broken by Federal armies and navies, now northern manufacturers and wholesalers succored his rising competitor. Northern firms dispatched salesmen to the South as soon as the guns of Appomattox cooled. Their mission: to regain southern markets for northern goods. By contacting Delta storekeepers directly, northern factories and supply companies eliminated the factor's role as commercial middleman. The credit terms offered by these interlopers were even more significant, for Delta merchants purchasing goods from these northern companies were now allowed several months to settle their accounts. Instead of paying for goods on or soon after delivery at their stores, merchants could wait until the cotton crop was gathered to settle accounts with their suppliers.[8]

Shopkeepers needed the extra time to pay their bills. Emancipation dramatically increased the number of poor farmers needing implements, supplies, and other items, yet most ex-slaves had little savings with which to purchase necessary items. Using northern suppliers' lenient credit terms, small storekeepers could extend credit to freed people for the crop year, accept payment after the cotton was gathered and sold, and still have time to pay off their own bills. Thus, the ex-slaves' initial relationship with local merchants served many interests: farmers got supplies while growing their crops, merchants won new customers, planters were not burdened with supplying the needs of all of their tenants, and factories and wholesalers strengthened their southern trade. Although many Delta farmers later became mired in debt to "furnishing merchants," as the revitalized storekeepers were increasingly described, their first relationship was mutually beneficial.[9]

Just as the opportunities open to Delta blacks suddenly expanded with freedom, local merchants' role in the region's economy also swelled at war's end. Their stores, once repositories of incidental merchandise—traps for woodsmen, small items for slaves, and whiskeys favored by estate holders — now became crucial to the new farming economy. Where the shopkeepers had once scurried for the scraps left by the plantation economy, they soon held forth at the main table. In the 1860s local merchants moved from the edge of the plantation economy to a central role in supplying credit and goods for hundreds of small producers. As long as the plantation district remained the center of the Delta's cotton cultivation, storekeepers did not need to worry about finding customers for their goods. Not surprisingly, postbellum migration to the region included many hopeful merchants, eager to supply the Delta's developing economy and duplicate the antebellum wealth and influence, although not the postbellum demise, of the cotton factors.

The arriving shopmen were a diverse lot. Indeed, no single profile captures the variety of origins, business pursuits, and perspectives among these would-be kings of the Delta trade. Yet a few prominent characteristics are worth noting. The fictitious Snopes family, William Faulkner's cunning clan of lowborn but fiercely ambitious traders, had flesh and blood precursors in the Delta. The Snopeses calculated their way from rags to riches but could never scrape the grime of humble origins from beneath their misshapen fingernails.[10] Many of the Delta's merchants were similarly calculating in their drive for money and power, if less memorable.

Like many newcomers to the Delta, George W. Faison did not immediately settle in the area of his eventual prominence. The Virginian arrived in the region in 1858 and first sought his fortune in the Delta's southerly counties, overseeing a plantation and selling goods near Rolling Fork Landing in Issaquena County. Although he found a bride in Issaquena, Faison despaired of financial success there. Selling his stock and trade to George F. Ring, an Alsace-born merchant, Faison relocated to Sunflower County in 1862.[11]

The Faisons were slow to commit to their new home, living for some time in a houseboat on the Sunflower River while George worked as overseer on the property of an absentee landowner, one Mr. Lee. Soon he was also renting land from Lee and farming it for his own profit. He returned to merchandising in 1868, however, opening the first of several stores at steamboat landings along the Sunflower River. Faison remarried the next year, his first wife having died soon after moving to their houseboat. He was eleven years older than his new bride, but her father was a circuit court judge and former member of the state legislature. When Lee died, Faison finally cast his lot with the central Delta, buying over 6,000 acres of rich land along the Sunflower from the estate.[12]

The new landowner styled his property Faisonia and undertook construction of a suitably grand dwelling. By 1873 the Faisons had a four-room house with separate dining room and kitchen but were unsatisfied with the impression it made. Constant additions and modifications to the original structure eventually produced an imposing edifice: a wide-galleried, seventeen-room white house behind a cedar-lined circular drive.[13] Faison's houseboat days were long behind him.

George Faison was not ready to abandon all aspects of river life, however. Realizing waterborne transportation's importance to both agriculture and commerce in those days before railroad service, Faison purchased two steamboats to carry cotton and goods between Faisonia and Vicksburg. One of the craft was called *Fair Play*, the sort of concept any businessman on the make could be expected to stress. The other ship, the *Addie E. Faison*, memorialized a family member, emphasizing the importance of kin in George Faison's growing empire. Relatives were crucial to his success, for they provided trustworthy lieutenants in his mushrooming operations. Reliance on relatives was widespread among frontier entrepreneurs, as was Faison's eagerness to invest in both land and trading goods. Faisons bought property in Sunflower, Bolivar, Leflore, Sharkey, and Washington Counties and kept their complicated farming and trading empire afloat with loans from international mortgage firms, which extended credit at lower rates than were generally found in the Delta. The Faison clan also dominated the government of Sunflower County, exercising particular control over the office of postmaster, a position from which the business affairs of likely competitors could be monitored.[14] George Faison, like Faulkner's Snopeses, attained a diversified business empire through hard bargaining, prescient investment, and his ability to entrust key subordinates (often family members) with complex and important duties.

Whereas Faison's goals and methods may have been common among backcountry entrepreneurs, evidence from Greenville, the region's largest and most influential city from the late nineteenth century to the present, suggests that town merchants were a different sort.[15] Most of the town's merchants confined themselves to their shops. Although they might purchase land for homes or invest in backcountry acres on speculation, few Greenville merchants attempted to control anything like Faison's multiplicity of interests. From one decade to the next, most of these storekeepers remained storekeepers.[16]

An even greater dissimilarity between Faison and the average town merchant lay in their origins.[17] In 1870 half of Greenville's merchants were foreign-born. These shopmen hailed from much greater distances than Faison's Virginia. The greatest number immigrated from Prussia and other German principalities, with the remainder coming to the Delta from Italy, Ireland, Poland, and France. Few had lived in the state long: less than one-quarter of the foreign-born merchants lived in Mississippi before or during the Civil War. Even fewer came directly from the country of their birth to the Delta. Most had passed through, and probably failed to realize their ambitions in, other states. In fact, many had lived in Massachusetts, New York, Illinois, Missouri, Tennessee, and Louisiana long enough to begin families there.[18] Unlike Faison, the large proportion of foreign-born merchants had few ties to the antebellum South and fewer still to the factor-rooted plantation economy that had serviced it.[19]

Greenville's proportion of foreign-born merchants did not decline after the overthrow of Reconstruction; on the contrary, the percentage of foreign-born shopmen was higher in 1880 than it had been a decade before.[20] In 1880 nearly two-thirds were immigrants.[21] Of these, the largest number still cited the German states as their birthplace, but there was an intriguing addition to their ranks. By 1880 over 10 percent of Greenville's immigrant merchants were Chinese.[22] Foreign-born merchants (and their American-born offspring) continued to predominate among Greenville's merchants through the end of the century. In 1900 a majority of the town's nonblack merchants were born outside the United States, and nearly 60 percent of all Greenville storekeepers were either foreign-born or had at least one nonnative parent.[23]

Of course, foreign birth or parentage was not uncommon in the United States in the last third of the nineteenth century. Millions of Europeans journeyed to America in this period, especially to its midwestern and northeastern cities, and thousands of Asians arrived on the Pacific Coast. But the South was not a common destination for either Europeans or Asians, nor did most immigrants to the United States so quickly enter into commerce.

More significant was the fact that most of Greenville's non-Chinese foreign merchants were Jewish.[24] Jews accounted for nearly half (nineteen of forty-one) of Greenville's merchants in 1870. By 1880 their number had increased 37 percent, and they comprised over two-thirds of the town's storekeepers. Passing through Greenville in 1878, Charles Wessolowsky was impressed with the wealth and number of Jews in the frontier town. The associate editor of the weekly regional newspaper the *Jewish South* estimated that Jews comprised one-seventh of Greenville's total population.[25]

Despite the prevalence of anti-Semitism in nineteenth- and early twentieth-century America, Jews found support among powerful figures in Delta society.[26] Greenville whites welcomed Jewish immigrants; in fact, three Jews served as mayor of the town in the 1870s.[27] When the *New York Sun* published an article blaming southern cotton growers' troubles on Jewish merchants and "the Jew Deed of Trust," *Greenville Times* editor J. S. McNeily fired back an angry editorial denouncing the aspersion. "The charge will not stand," he wrote, "for the Deed of Trust has been used by Jew and Gentile, merchant and planter. Laborers and planters who have never dealt with a Jew are 'busted' equally high with those who have. For that matter, the Jews as a class are as bad off as others." Nor was McNeily alone in his opposition to anti-Semitism. In February 1882, at the height of the Russian pogroms, clerics from the local Methodist-Episcopal and Presbyterian congregations joined Rabbi Juny of Greenville's Hebrew Union Congregation in condemning the acts as "contrary to the spirit of Christianity." Taylor Rucks, the scion of a prominent Washington County planting family, went even further in opposition to anti-Semitic brutality. Rucks died defending a Jewish hotel clerk, one Mr. Gottschalk, against the attacks of three assailants armed with pistols. Despite Mississippi's twentieth-century reputation for anti-Semitic demagoguery (who can forget Theodore Bilbo's utterance when charged with anti-Semitism: "I'm for every damned Jew from Jesus Christ on down"), the Delta welcomed Jewish settlers in the late nineteenth century.[28]

The Delta's commercial class was not limited to Snopes-like Faisons, European Jews, and Chinese. Another group, fewer than the Jews and less likely to single-handedly dominate a county than Faison, played the most dramatic role in the Delta's economic development. Indeed, they best understood the region's commercial nexus—transportation—and brought it to life in railroad construction.

This strain of commercialists are easily confused with Faison and his ilk. Like Faison, most were white and southern-born, frequently engaged in more than one vocation, and did not eschew political influence. Unlike the proprietor of Faisonia, however, these men blended pursuit of their individual interests with active promotion of the region's economic development. Indeed, it was partly their strenuous search for personal wealth that led to dual careers as lawyer-merchant, planter-merchant, and the like, and this multiplicity of interests convinced them (unlike the immigrant shopmen) that their fortunes would only advance with the Delta's economic diversification.

The frontier character of Delta society between the Civil War and the 1890s encouraged dual careers among the acquisitive and well connected. In the immediate postwar years, a paucity of merchants and professionals in the riverside settlements of the region prevented job specialization of the sort found in more established locations. Literate men with the slightest training in the law might pass themselves off as barristers. Anyone whose holdings or credit history justified wholesalers' confidence could style himself a merchant, and white landowners frequently used plantation stores to make clients of their tenants. It was difficult to make a living at the law, though, when courts only met at the circuit judge's whim, and the cyclical nature of cotton culture frequently played havoc with a storekeeper's cash flow. While it was relatively easy to enter a vocation, it was difficult to become rich in any single pursuit during the region's early days. Occupational permeability and financial need pressed many into a hyphenated career as lawyer-merchant, merchant-planter, or planter-storekeeper.

Greenville and Washington County are again instructive. Although the county was home to the region's largest antebellum population, a busy commercial center, and two fertile and relatively flood-free agricultural districts along the Mississippi River and Deer Creek, many of its ambitious white citizens found it necessary to pursue gain outside their avowed vocations.[29] Thus, attorney Samuel W. Ferguson not only practiced law and sold insurance from his Greenville office, he also acted as guardian for several war orphans, a position that left him supervising thousands of acres in the early 1870s. The West Point graduate and former Confederate general was also the Winchester firearms company's local agent. General Ferguson, as he preferred to be known, led a tempestuous existence. He was, for example, at the center of conservative efforts to "redeem" Delta government from Republican control in 1875. A United States Senate investigation subsequently called him to testify at length on his activities in that election, where as election judge he prevented hundreds of black voters who were disinclined to support the Democratic Party from casting their ballots. He escaped prosecution for these activities, however, and was highly esteemed by local conservatives. Unfortunately, Ferguson seems to have emerged from the experience with the belief that his actions were above the law, and ensuing improprieties led to his downfall. One gentle chronicler recalled that "in those poverty-stricken years the General was elected by his friends treasurer of the levee board [the Mississippi Board of Levee Commissioners], though he had neither aptitude for nor experience in business or accounting, besides being high-handed and utterly unmethodical. After some years Mr. Everman, secretary of the board and his close friend, checked the books and found him twenty thousand dollars short." Ferguson fled to South America, where he lived out the statute of limitations in mute humiliation. He returned to the Delta in his dotage, proclaiming innocence and vowing to prove he had been unjustly accused.[30]

Although his legal difficulties were uncommon, Ferguson's wide range of activities was shared by numerous ambitious Washington County men in the busy years after war and emancipation. Greenville lawyer William A. Percy owned a Deer Creek plantation that had been partially cleared and cultivated before the war; he now scrambled to tenant the place. Greenville merchant Edward P. Byrnes also had other interests, including ownership of land valued at $30,000. Brothers LeRoy and Frank Valliant, Greenville lawyers, jointly owned over 500 acres of highly improved plantation property near the Mississippi River, and LeRoy held a separate tract (one-half square mile of uncleared wilderness) in the backcountry. Several other merchants and professionals in Greenville owned land in partnership with Kentuckian William A. Haycraft, a self-described real estate broker.[31] Rather than separate into warring coalitions of self-conscious planters and merchants, acquisitive Deltans sought gain by taking on additional occupations, thus combining commerce and agriculture.[32]

Not all Delta landowners successfully bridged the gap between their two (or more) careers. Washington County planter E. A. Fall sought to offset the unpredictable cotton market and the insecurity of slaveless cultivation by selling goods to his laborers. In the late 1860s he ordered a large store of dry goods he believed sure to appeal to his workers—flashy jewelry, red-topped boots, gaudy handkerchiefs, combs, calico gloves, and "perfumes of every odor, all strong." He was not present when the goods were sold, but subordinates reported upon his homecoming that the entire stock had found purchasers. However, his vague instructions on trading the goods had been misunderstood, and many items were exchanged for freedmen's elastic promises of eventual payment. His relative Elisha Greenlee recalled: "Fall was frantic, but finally he said, 'Greenlee, let me see the book.' He read and lamented, 'Old Fosey—$150.00, My God!; Club-fisted Jim—$75.00. Oh God! Old Frank—$94.00, the Lord help us!!!' He read and commented down the line. His strength failed him and as tears came into his eyes he said, 'Cotton gone, money gone, goods gone. Old Lady, we are dead broke.'"[33]

Whether they were merchants owning rural plantations, lawyers juggling Blackstone and cotton price reports, or planters dabbling in dry goods sales, the actions of all of these hyphenated commercialists contradicted a division of town and country. And their ownership of plantations or speculation in unsettled acreage made them acutely aware of the need to develop the Delta backcountry.[34] If more farmers could be enticed to the Delta to rent or purchase backcountry tracts, then labor shortages might cease to bedevil planters, speculative land could be sold for a profit, and storekeepers would have more customers for their goods. Moreover, landowners would not lose their property to tax forfeiture.[35] The hyphenated commercialists soon convinced themselves that railroad construction—linking established riverside stores and settlements with growing inland farm areas—was the key to their future prosperity.

In their desire for rail transportation, Deltans partook of nineteenth-century America's fascination with the prospects of technology. After the Civil War, as dozens of railroad companies laid tracks across the South, locomotives were expected to carry social, as well as economic, benefits. Railroads were considered more than mechanized freight and passenger conduits, for they promised to aid in settlement, speed travel, and deliver enlightenment to the doors of the backward. As one respected commentator predicted, "Build a railroad into a most benighted region where the people are lawless and ignorant, rude and savage, brutal and vicious, and in a few years industry and energy will establish trade, schools will be opened and intelligence will light up the faces of the inhabitants."[36] Ambitious settlers need only add railroads and stir.

Deltans were no less awed by locomotive potential. Indeed, they expressed numerous, specific expectations of railroads' contributions to life in the region. Construction of steam-powered railroads, Washington County resident W. A. Pollock predicted, would "bring us new population, infuse fresh blood into our debilitated social system, add to and fix the value of our real estate, and [add] to the volume of business of all kinds; they will give daily mails, reliable and cheap telegraphy; following the completion of these railroads will come the building of manufactories in our midst, and means afforded for the speedy transmission of diversified products, thus enabling us to cut loose from the policy of raising cotton as our only crop for export."[37] For Pollock and many other Deltans, railroads were more than a sign of progress, they were the engine of its delivery. Population, land values, trade, and manufacturing would automatically increase with the introduction of steam locomotives; and communications, product selections, and occupational opportunities would be noticeably broadened.

Delta residents could not ignore the call for better modes of transit. *Greenville Times* editor McNeily expressed the sympathies of the region's railroad boosters when he addressed Pollock's neighbors, the "brethren of the mercantile profession, and property owners of Greenville," one wet winter. The black farm renters and owners on Deer Creek, he admonished the commercialists, had been "shut off from the delights of Greenville for the past few weeks on account of mud. Thousands of dollars that would be spent in Greenville go down Deer Creek [to trade with Vicksburg and other south-Delta merchants] every winter on account of the impassable condition of six miles of road." Off the roads, east-west travel was even more difficult during Delta winters. An early settler of neighboring Bolivar County recalled that in this period the region was thatched with "evergreen cane and bamboo, through which no rider could pass, and only with difficulty could a man work his way through on foot." Wet weather the next winter brought editor McNeily back to his theme of missed trading opportunities. He explained that Greenville's commercial life was imperiled by dependence on "swamp roads." During winter, freight bound from Greenville to Arcola, only twenty miles to the southeast, had to be shipped hundreds of miles on steamboat "by way of Vicksburg, and up the Sunflower and Bogue Phalia. Lewy Brothers [merchants in Greenville] shipped some $700 worth of groceries for Arcola by this route last Saturday. Who will say this country does not need a railroad?" Other citizens of the county confirmed McNeily's analysis, with one pointing out that even on the better-maintained avenues of Greenville, four mules were required to haul one 450-pound bale of cotton.[38] The trade coveted by Greenville merchants was being siphoned off down the river, and only an all-weather form of land transportation could rectify the situation.

Although dependable, all-season transport was appealing to Deltans with crops to transport, goods to buy and sell, or court dates to keep, wooing railroads to the region proved difficult. The greatest problem was competition. Any railroad that penetrated the Delta would have to compete for through-travelers with an existing line, the Mississippi Central Railroad, which ran from Memphis to Jackson along the bluffs marking the Delta's eastern edge. The Mississippi Central might be convinced to extend branches into the region, but its established presence was a large obstacle to those who hoped for a main line through the Delta.

But steamboat traffic on the region's waterways, not the Mississippi Central, proved to be the greatest deterrent to railroad promotion.[39] Steamboats were the region's established mode of transportation, carrying lawyers, judges, and litigants to riverside courthouses, bearing goods to and from merchants at landing points, and hauling each year's cotton crop to New Orleans factors. Planters knew the packet captains who stopped regularly at their landings; indeed, many steamboat pilots owned land in the Delta. Moreover, the rhythm of regional travel had been dictated by steamboat schedules for decades, and the owners of river craft proved assiduous in cultivating customer loyalty. Hospitality and small acts of thoughtfulness went a long way in impressing settlers of the untamed region. "The steamboat captain was always kind to the children, who hurried to the landing as soon as the whistle was heard," one early inhabitant of Sunflower County recalled. "He brought us all kinds of goodies, sometimes a whole bunch of bananas, and we usually had something nice, a cake or pie, for him. The greatest thrill, though, was his taking us up the river—not too far for us to walk back." This tradition of packet-boat hospitality made the steamboatmen adjunct members of the community, a connection they could tighten with well-directed acts of charity. The *Kate Adams*, a packet that traveled from Memphis to Arkansas City each week, contributed toward the construction of churches and donated Bibles and hymnals to communities in its territory, gaining the lasting thanks (and patronage) of many riverside shippers. A steamboat running on Deer Creek donated a bell for another church. Railroads might be all the rage, but the steamboatmen acted as if God was on their side. Perhaps the rivermen were correct, for the *Kate Adams* (and two successors bearing the same name) plied the Mississippi in profitable competition with railroads for forty-five years. The friendliness exhibited by steamboat captains did not, however, extend to cheap freight rates. In 1880, before the existence of a transregional railroad line, steamboats charged between $1.25 and $1.50 to transport each bale of cotton from the Delta interior to New Orleans. By 1891, with the cotton market in decline and competition from the Louisville, New Orleans and Texas Railroad increasing, rates fell to only 75 cents per bale for the same service.[40]

Good public relations was only part of steamboats' advantage. Settlement patterns also supported waterborne transportation. At the end of the Civil War, most of the Delta's inhabitants lived within a few miles of the Mississippi and its tributaries, all within reach of a steamboat landing. As a result, railroad planners faced a dilemma—should they run their rails near the river's edge in direct competition with the established steamboats, or should they locate a line in the middle of unsettled wilderness? Neither option appealed to most railroad companies.[41] Thus, by the late 1860s railroad-boosting Deltans discovered they could not depend on outside entrepreneurs to undertake construction of rail facilities in the sparsely settled region. In the early 1870s inhabitants of both Coahoma and Washington Counties resolved to build their own rail systems. Significantly, persons manifesting a broadly commercial perspective—those planters who also kept stores, lawyers owning plantation property, and merchants speculating in backcountry acreage—were the guiding spirits in these enterprises. Surprisingly, the more profitable and enduring effort drew upon the enthusiasm (and investments) of both black and white residents.

Persistent Whig James L. Alcorn, who proved so influential in levee construction and elective politics, also dominated Coahoma County rail efforts.

Alcorn owned riverside plantation property but also manifested interest in developing fertile inland tracts, land he feared would be deprived of the plow unless transportation systems were improved. He was, moreover, cognizant of the rewards of expanded mercantile operations: this man who owned so much Coahoma County farmland that he carried one-ninth of the jurisdiction's tax burden was the same individual frequently found behind the counter of his plantation store, the same man who employed his entire family in stocking the business's shelves and taking orders for sale. He embodied the commercial perspective of the Delta's frontier era, when even those who styled themselves planters often engaged in trade—whether from financial necessity or in eagerness to attract every possible dollar. This combination of agricultural and commercial interests made Alcorn a natural railroad booster: his biographer even contends that "Alcorn believed in the power of railroads as a sort of magical growth-and-prosperity stimulant for the areas through which they would go."[42]

Alcorn supported a plan for building a railroad through the length of the Delta and beyond. In 1870 he and a small group of like-minded north-Delta investors incorporated the New Orleans, Baton Rouge, Vicksburg and Memphis Railroad (commonly called the Memphis and Vicksburg Railroad)[43] with the intention of operating a line stretching from the Gulf of Mexico northward beyond the edge of the Delta. Alcorn and his confederates proposed to ignore the competition of steamboats on the Delta's waterways and the Mississippi Central to the east and plunge ahead with a rail line traveling through hundreds of miles of Delta wilderness.[44]

The incorporators of the Memphis and Vicksburg were drawn from Alcorn's family, friends, and political supporters. All were wealthy residents of Coahoma County; most owned extensive tracts of land; and—like planter-merchant-lawyer-politician James L. Alcorn—a hybrid of agricultural, commercial, and professional avocations was not uncommon in their membership. James A. Peace, for example, the second wealthiest incorporator after Alcorn, combined planting with storekeeping and a medical practice. All of the incorporators owned real estate, with the average investor holding more than 1,000 acres of improved land and almost 1,500 acres of wilderness. The value of their real property ranged from Pleasant C. Legg's $25,000 farm to Alcorn's Eagle's Nest appraised at $215,000. The group rested comfortably within the wealthiest 10 percent of Coahoma County society, and they must have expected investment in the Memphis and Vicksburg to increase their prosperity.[45]

The Coahoma countians raised sufficient funds to survey and grade a few miles of roadbed from the Yazoo River north to Valley Park, but work ceased when the company's coffers ran dry. Alcorn's grand railroad plan did not appeal to outside investors, who must have doubted its ability to compete with established rail and steamship lines and wondered who (besides the incorporators) would use a railroad chugging through the Delta wilderness. Nor could the enterprise chase up sufficient dollars within the region to keep its employees at work. Few investors in the Delta or in nearby commercial centers judged the region capable of supporting a major railway in the early 1870s. The line's grading ground to a halt in 1872, and the operation was soon abandoned. Alcorn's scheme to connect Delta cotton fields to the port of New Orleans via rail languished for the next decade.[46]

The failure of the Memphis to New Orleans line forced Alcorn and his supporters to narrow their goals. Rather than strike out across hundreds of unsettled miles merely to connect the commercial centers of the lower Mississippi River valley—cities that were already linked by steamboat service and the Mississippi Central—their new plans called for local rail service. The Coahoma County rail boosters sought to connect a riverside trading center with fertile inland areas where embryonic settlements would spread quickly with the support of reliable transportation. This new east-west orientation allowed railroads to carry goods to and from the river packets, thereby removing them from competition with the steamboat trade. Moreover, approaching the Mississippi Central from the west both reduced the perils of rail competition and held out prospects of an eventual junction with the older line. Finally, by linking existing populations, the entrepreneurs increased the prospects for local investment, because area landowners would be more likely to contribute to an effort promising to bring a railroad near their property.

Alcorn's railroad enthusiasts embraced this new east-west approach and formed a new company. They chose a grandly ambiguous name for their new undertaking, the Mobile and Northwestern Railroad, received a charter from the state of Mississippi, and set out in search of capital. The generous title of their company must have helped seduce investors from outside the region, for a local historian claims the railroad was partly supported by "Alabama and Mississippi moneymen." Nearby counties were unimpressed by the venture, however, and declined participation in or public support for Alcorn's second railroad plan.[47]

The deliberate pace and placement of the Mobile and Northwestern's construction belied the railroad's expansive name. Land was not broken for the roadbed until 1873. Construction finally began, not at Mobile, but at Dowd's Landing in Coahoma County, the property of a state senator and longtime Alcorn ally. Dowd's Landing had more to commend it than the owner's relationship with Alcorn, however, for it lay across the Mississippi River from Helena, Arkansas, a vital river port and trading center. Alcorn and his investors may have hoped to link their railroad with one of the rail lines entering Helena from the Arkansas interior, or they may have simply located their terminus across from the larger city in an effort to guarantee access to its river traffic. From this humble start their railroad began a slow trek inland. After four years only eight miles of narrow-gauge track were in place, but construction quickened in 1877 and 1878, and another ten miles were soon added. With a similar regimen in 1879, the rails reached Clarksdale, a small trading community on the Sunflower River that later became the seat of Coahoma County government.[48]

The path chosen by the railroad's directors reveals the line's essential purposes: to aid area development by enriching its investors. Locating the railhead at Dowd's Landing would both benefit the company's chief financial backers (and political allies) and maximize connections with river packets docking at Helena. The route taken by the railroad as it left the riverside was even more illustrative of the founders' goals. To the casual eye the Mobile and Northwestern snaked randomly across the county—traveling first east, then looping southward, next jogging west, and finally running south again—but its route brought the machine fully into the gardens of its most prominent supporters. Alcorn's Eagle's Nest plantation was the railroad's most prominent stop, and the inland terminus was the hamlet of Clarksdale, named for an English-born planter ally of Alcorn, John Clark. The railroad never made its way to Mobile, nor did it ever proceed on any dependably northwestern course, but the stockholders had their railroad, and their freight transportation difficulties were greatly eased.[49]

Although the Mobile and Northwestern served some of the interests of its wealthy stockholders—carrying goods from merchants to inland farmers and hauling cotton crops from field to steamboat landing—the short line never prospered as an independent business concern, partly because it failed to ignite development along its path. Because much of the railroad's route lay across land held by the company's owners, the line's ability to increase settlement along its path was diluted. Alcorn and other owners of interior land could bring sharecroppers and wage laborers into the backcountry by rail and did not need to rent their lands to attain clearing and cultivation. This simplified labor scheme had adverse consequences for the railroad, however, for poor sharecroppers and wage laborers provided a slim market for consumer goods, and freight shipments on the Mobile and Northwestern were paltry. The Delta's focus on cotton culture exacerbated this dearth of commercial shipments, for the seasonal shipping needs of Delta farmers and merchants varied wildly. Freight cars bounced lightly over the rails for much of the year, hauling what little stock was needed for Clarksdale's few early merchants and provisions for plantations along its route. Then, in fall and early winter, the railroad was crushed under tons of cotton, hard-pressed to find sufficient cars to haul out the county's crop. Its stockholders may have enjoyed the convenience of rail transportation at their front doors, but seasonal fluctuations of the area's freight needs undermined the railroad's long-term viability. The railroad was desperate for shipping traffic because passenger travel was so light; the absence of a connecting line at the railroad's interior terminus limited riders to settlers along or near the road, most of whom were modest farmers and laborers without the need or wherewithal for frequent rail excursions. After a few years of profitless wanderings through Coahoma County, the Mobile and Northwestern was sold to a trans-Delta railroad company, which promptly ceased service along much of its route and scavenged miles of its rails.[50]

Many of the problems encountered by the Mobile and Northwestern would have hampered any Delta railroad venture: the uneven flow of freight, a paucity of travelers, and the lack of private or public capital for investment in large-scale infrastructure projects. That the Mobile and Northwestern was ever built, even on a small scale and with parochial objectives, is testimony to the energy, dedication, and wealth of its stockholders. Railroad construction was simply too expensive, the Delta too sparsely populated, and the freight needs of area businesses too thin to support much more than a short-line railroad bent to the narrow needs of its owners. Yet somehow, among Alcorn's rivals in Washington County, a much different course toward railroad construction was being charted. There, a profitable narrow-gauge railroad that actually spurred back-country development was under construction. The diverse backgrounds of its participants—white and black, native and foreign-born, wealthy and of middling incomes—more accurately reflected the region's broad prospects. As in agriculture, where former slaves became property holders, commercial opportunities were not limited to those who had been born free American citizens.

Washington County residents had attempted to build a railroad much like Alcorn's Mobile and Northwestern in the antebellum period. Incorporated as the Lake Washington and Deer Creek Railroad and Banking Company by the Mississippi legislature in 1836, the venture's charter stockholders aimed to run a line east from the riverside town of Princeton to their plantations along Lake Washington and Deer Creek. Like Alcorn's group, these investors were wealthy (all owned land in the area, and most hailed from Kentucky or South Carolina) and thought a rail link connecting their inland holdings with the steamboat traffic on the Mississippi could only increase their assets. But the antebellum railroaders did not plan on the panic of 1837, which largely destroyed the banking industry from which the company planned to borrow construction funds. The effort succumbed in 1837, leaving behind a few banknotes, a pretentious two-story depot and banking office in Princeton, and a partially graded roadbed.[51]

More than three decades passed before Washington countians' second effort at indigenous railroad construction. At times the postbellum company seemed likely to replicate the antebellum failure. After a company was organized in 1870, four years passed before construction commenced. Then, once a nine-mile roadbed was cleared and graded, the project came to a halt. Where the antebellum effort was thwarted by financial panic, the postwar company was derailed by a recalcitrant bond trustee who felt the railroad was overcharging the county for the value of work completed.[52] As in 1837, Washington countians feared that a much-ballyhooed enterprise had succeeded only in cutting a raw gash into the wilderness. Four more years, new corporate leadership, and a drastically different plan for funding and construction were required actually to place rails and rolling stock on that roadbed. Yet, despite this arduous eight-year campaign to bring a railroad to Washington County, the company not only prospered, it became one of the most profitable railroads in the South. The secrets of its success lay mainly in contrasts to Alcorn's efforts.[53] The Coahoma and Washington County railroad groups were very different in the diversity of their respective memberships, the goals they pursued with rail construction, and their methods for funding the projects.

The most noticeable difference between the Coahoma and Washington County efforts was the latter's inclusive breadth of support. Whereas Alcorn and a narrow group of supporters ran the Mobile and Northwestern, Washington County railroading was much more various. There were, for example, two railroad companies competing to serve Washington County in the early 1870s. The first, formed in 1870, was the Greenville, Deer Creek and Rolling Fork Railroad (GDC&RF). Like its failed antebellum predecessor, the GDC&RF hoped to link riverside settlements with the fertile Deer Creek backcountry. A second company, the Arkansas City and Grenada Railroad (AC&G), had more ambitious goals. Its founders planned to link the Mississippi River with the Mississippi Central Railroad at Grenada on the Delta's eastern edge. By choosing Arkansas City, Arkansas, as its western terminus instead of Greenville, the railroad promised trans-Mississippi travel, which it apparently planned to accomplish by loading rail cars on steamboat ferries to cross the great river. Stockholders of these rival companies realized the area could never support two east-west railroads, and that without cooperation neither stood a good chance for public funding. They merged in 1873 as the Greenville, Columbus and Birmingham Railroad.[54]

These two companies brought diverse members to their union (graph 5). The most shocking example was the AC&G's list of incorporators, which included both Nathan Bedford Forrest (a founder of the Ku Klux Klan) and Blanche K. Bruce (the only ex-slave to serve a full term as United States senator). Although most of the stockholders in both enterprises were white, blacks comprised 14 percent of the AC&G investors, and the GDC&RF included a black state senator among its charter members. The 1873 merger also bespoke political reconciliation, for the AC&G was largely composed of Republicans while its partner featured many prominent Mississippi Democrats. By contrast, all of the stockholders in Alcorn's Memphis and Vicksburg were white, and his political allies figured prominently.[55] Racial and political diversity was accompanied by a variety of national origins in the GDC&RF. Although none of Alcorn's investors hailed from outside the United States, 22 percent of the Greenville company's incorporators were foreign-born.[56] The racial, political, and ethnic variety of the Washington County railroad groups did not merely signal desire for rail-

Graph 5. Railroad entrepreneurs: race, origin, and age

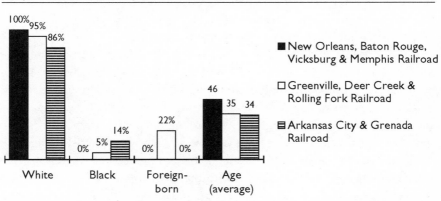

Sources: GDC&RF Railroad papers; AC&G Railroad papers; Ninth Census, Population and Agriculture MSS for Mississippi, Arkansas, and Tennessee; Lillian A. Pereyra, *James Lusk Alcorn: Persistent Whig* (Baton Rouge, La., 1966).

road construction in and around Greenville, it also reflected the breadth of financial support on which the combined Greenville, Columbus and Birmingham company might rely in its prolonged struggle to realize rail transport.[57]

Hyphenated commercialists, usually town dwellers with backcountry holdings, had been the foundation of this support from the beginning of the postbellum railroad effort. Their business pursuits and holdings displayed a multiplicity of interests and revealed the connections between the prosperity of Greenville merchants and professionals and backcountry development. The first president elected to head the Greenville, Deer Creek and Rolling Fork was LeRoy B. Valliant. Valliant was trained in the law and continued to describe himself as a lawyer even after his selection to head the railroad. Yet he and his brother Frank, also a lawyer and a stockholder in the transportation company, pursued business interests beyond the bench and bar, and both invested heavily in Washington County land. In 1870 the Valliants held joint title to 400 highly improved and cultivated acres near Greenville, and another 122 cleared but fallow acres in the same area. LeRoy Valliant owned another tract in his own right, half of a square mile of unimproved land farther away from settled areas that he held in speculation of higher farm prices. In all, railroad president LeRoy Valliant's real estate holdings were valued at $20,000 in 1870.[58] The investments of other railroad entrepreneurs showed a similar diversification.[59] The business interests of Washington County's railroad investors extended well beyond their self-proclaimed occupations, and the company's members stood to gain (or lose) great sums by the whims of the speculative land market.

Although Washington County's railroad stockholders were active in land speculation, relatively few pursued agriculture as a primary or secondary calling. More than two-thirds of Alcorn's investors were listed as farmers, planters, or planter-merchants, but a majority of the Washington County railroaders pursued nonfarm occupations. Among the incorporators of the GDC&RF, 55 percent were merchants, carpenters, office clerks, ministers, industrialists, holders of political office, or landless lawyers in 1870. The group who formed the AC&G was even less directly tied to agriculture: 67 percent held one or more of the above nonfarm occupations in 1870. Most Washington County railroad stockholders, while they frequently speculated in backcountry land, were not personally active in cotton farming. They were not intimately tied to the fate of one plantation, unlike many of Alcorn's investors. Although their speculative holdings made them concerned for the region's settlement and agricultural development, their railroad would not simply meander from one stockholder's plantation to the next.

This loose but important connection of town and country was further exhibited by the railroads' disparate funding sources. Although Alcorn depended mainly on stock sales to wealthy planters and merchants, Washington County railroad construction was largely paid for by bond issues from local governments. Greenville was particularly amenable to financial support for the line's construction, and its citizens voted to approve bond issues for $150,000.[60] But the Washington County railroad group did not depend solely on public funds. They too pursued stockholders among the local residents. Both of the original railroad companies employed stock agents, and the identities of these persons shed further light on the broad support sought by the Washington County enterprise. The first company, the Greenville, Deer Creek and Rolling Fork Railroad, was particularly interested in garnering the support of town-dwelling merchants. By employing a hefty percentage of foreign-born stock agents, many of them merchants in the town, the company clearly hoped for the patronage of Greenville's large immigrant class of shopkeepers. The Arkansas City and Grenada Railroad, its eventual merger partner, pursued a different course for stock sales. A majority of the stock agents commissioned in its support were black (table 1).

Table 1. Stock agents and electioneers selling Washington County's postbellum railroads

	White (%)	Black (%)	Age (avg)	Foreign-born (%)	Nonfarm occupations (%)	Real property (avg)	Personal property (avg)
Greenville, Deer Creek & Rolling Fork Railroad	100	0	34	25	33	$15,646	$7,421
Arkansas City & Grenada Railroad	45	55	35	0	73	$4,053	$1,669

Sources: GDC&RF Railroad papers; AC&G Railroad papers; Ninth Census, Population and agriculture MSS for Mississippi, Arkansas, and Tennessee; Lillian A. Pereyra, *James Lusk Alcorn: Persistent Whig* (Baton Rouge, La., 1966).

Hiring black stock agents was a prescient tactic. Just as foreign-born representatives would have an advantage in dealing with immigrant investors, black agents might sell stock to the upwardly mobile black farmers cultivating land around Deer Creek. The Deer Creek area, partly cleared and worked by slaves before the Civil War, was a magnet for the county's growing class of black farm owners by the 1870s. Ex-slaves were renting and buying land along the creek's banks in increasing numbers, and it was their transportation needs, as much as those of the few plantations still attempting cultivation with closely controlled laborers, that the railroad hoped to serve. Indeed, merchants and professionals in Washington County's seat were anxious to tap this inland market before another railroad, whether from Edmund Richardson's Refuge plantation or another source, helped a competing town supplant Greenville as entrepôt to the central Delta.[61]

Aiming the railroad toward the Deer Creek area proved a wise tactic. The inland farmers needed goods, transport for their crops, and occasional passenger service to Greenville. Unlike Alcorn's Mobile and Northwestern, which languished in simply connecting the plantations of its wealthy owners, the broad base of potential users afforded by the Deer Creek settlement made the GC&B instantly profitable. After the railroad's first segment linked Greenville with Stoneville (nine miles away on upper Deer Creek), the line enjoyed heavy use. The Greenville to Stoneville section brought in over $13,000 in passenger and freight receipts in 1878, and almost $9,000 of that amount (two-thirds of the gross return) was profit. Henry T. Ireys, who was responsible for operating the railroad in its early years, estimated that 8,000 bales of cotton were carried from Deer Creek to Greenville in 1878, and another 10,000 were shipped in 1879. Although the railroad's costs increased as it expanded the line southward parallel to Deer Creek in 1879, profits for its second year of operation approached $10,000. No wonder one Greenville rail booster crowed: "Through Railroads, the king of progress, all . . . enemies will be conquered. We will get out of the old ruts we have been in so long, and with the help of the Railroad enter upon a new departure of progress and enterprise."[62]

In its early years the Greenville, Columbus and Birmingham Railroad brought laborers to Deer Creek plantations, renters and purchasers for speculative lands, increased trade to area merchants, and profits to its stockholders. But the young railroad also encountered its share of problems. In a cost-conscious move the line bought used broad-gauge passenger cars and had them refitted for the road's narrow-gauge tracks. But narrowing the wheelbase encouraged the tall, wide passenger cars to sway and rock around curves, and many patrons complained of acute motion sickness. Ever ingenious, the rail-road responded by utilizing its narrow-gauge flat cars for travel. Seats were built on the level freight platforms and awnings raised to shade riders. This innovation only changed the passengers' complaints, however. Riders were no longer nauseated, but several patrons on the converted flatcars found their clothes suddenly set ablaze by engine sparks from the straining locomotive. Luckily, the slow pace of travel on the GC&B allowed flaming passengers to jump overboard and prevent a general conflagration. Likewise, the energy-efficient snail's pace of the train afforded any gentleman whose hat blew off en route sufficient time to disembark, retrieve his headpiece, and still overtake the train. "Railroads, the king of progress," were not without their drawbacks.

Nor did rail travel lack vocal detractors. One planter opposed the GC&B's extension south along Deer Creek because the innovation threatened the pace and style of rural life. This gentleman preferred the comfort and congeniality he found aboard steamboats, which navigated much of Deer Creek in the wet months, to the sooty efficiency of railroads. "When Captain White lands the 'Pargoud,'" he explained, "you can go aboard and get a good drink of liquor with ice in it, and the captain will take one with you, and he ain't in no hurry, he will talk with you and give you plenty of time for your liquor to cool and to drink it." Railroads, on the other hand, "come like a streak of lightning through your field, scaring your mules, killing your chickens and hogs—stopping about a minute for you to get off or on—[and] nothing to drink aboard." His was not an uninformed complaint, he stressed, for the planter had survived rail travel once and was not eager to test his luck again. He recounted a trip from Vicksburg to Jackson on a railroad employing greater steam pressure than the GC&B. Spying a saloon near the tracks at Edwards, Mississippi, the planter had temporarily disembarked. "I told the cap'en of the train to wait a moment[,] I was going to get a drink of liquor, for I was mighty dry. Well I hadn't more than touched the bar, hadn't even had time to order my liquor, when off the train started. I hollered to stop and ran after it, but the blamed thing kept going faster and faster, and I had to stay in town until the next day." Railroads threatened the leisurely conviviality of his life, and the planter rose to speak in opposition to Washington County subsidizing rail extension down Deer Creek from Stoneville. "There is no [liquor] accommodation in a railroad," he stressed, "and we don't want them things in this country, killing the chickens and hogs and scaring the game."[63]

Other Delta residents found much to welcome in the new railroad. Besides making travel and freight shipment easier, the new mode of travel brought diversion to the region. Groups of white and black Washington countians, often in church congregations, made "excursions" along the line for picnics, sightseeing, and the thrill of modern locomotion. The railroad offered reduced rates for these holidays, and groups sometimes brought along a brass band hired in Greenville. The first train along the LNO&T's riverside branch carried several hundred black Greenville residents on an excursion to Lake Washington. Railroad excursion fares were also offered to travelers bound for Greenville on special occasions, as when "S. H. Barrett's New United Monster Railroad Show" brought a circus to town. And despite the slow pace of the GC&B trains, young Deltans soon found a way to make rail travel more adventurous; they rode in pairs perched on the cowcatcher in front of the locomotive. This mode became quite the rage, and courting couples sometimes experienced the thrill together—until the cowcatcher cast a calf at the feet of one young woman.[64]

Deltans' varied uses of railroads, for shipping, travel, and entertainment, only added to the profits of the Greenville, Columbus and Birmingham. Despite the cost of adding to the line in the late 1870s and early 1880s (the railroad built eastward into Sunflower County in 1881), net returns remained high. The GC&B enjoyed the highest profit margin of Mississippi's sixteen railroad companies in its first year and remained among the state's most profitable concerns in its expansion period.[65] The GC&B's profits brought it to the attention of national railroad magnates, and the line's stockholders were considering overtures for sale of the narrow-gauge system by 1881. Because they had always been more interested in what the railroad would mean for area commerce, freight shipment, and land speculation than in simply becoming railroad tycoons, the line's stockholders were amenable to sale. Moreover, if a national railroad company purchased their small system, additions to the line could link the Delta with the travel and trade of the nation. Convinced that the system being created by former Confederate general John B. Gordon was best able to extend their system and unite Washington County with national markets and manufacturers, the stockholders sold out to a holding company, and their little railroad became part of the Georgia Pacific Railway.[66]

Significantly, the GC&B's purchaser did not scavenge its rails, as had the buyer of Alcorn's railroad. The new owners soon extended the Deer Creek branch an additional 12 miles, and the main line from Greenville to Johnsonville was widened to standard-gauge track before the end of the decade. More importantly, in 1889 the rails east from Greenville stretched 460 unbroken miles to Atlanta, Georgia.[67] The completion of the Georgia Pacific Railway brought Washington County and the rest of the Delta direct rail connections to the southeastern United States. By then, another national rail line already traversed the region from the north.

In the early 1880s the mass and dispersion of Delta settlement attracted the attention of out-of-state railroad magnates eager for new markets and likely routes through the South. This was a period of general railroad expansion and consolidation. Throughout the nation prominent settlers in potentially profitable areas like the Delta played host to visiting railroad entrepreneurs, encouraging rail companies to run a line through their town, county, or region and reap great returns.[68] Although Coahoma County's circuitous Mobile and Northwestern Railroad was in danger of bankruptcy by the early 1880s, the Greenville, Columbus and Birmingham's profits proved that money could be made in Delta rail transportation. Convinced he could increase his fortune where other rail boosters had failed, national railroad impresario Collis P. Huntington began purchasing the franchises of several abandoned or impoverished Mississippi railroads in 1882, among them Alcorn's defunct Memphis and Vicksburg line. Huntington saw the wisdom in Alcorn's vision of connecting Memphis with the Gulf of Mexico by way of a Delta route. By 1884 Huntington's Louisville, New Orleans and Texas Railway (LNO&T) was open for passenger and freight traffic, and much of the line's subsequent earnings came from Delta shipping.[69]

Like Washington County's railroad entrepreneurs, Huntington understood the importance of subsidizing his railroad's construction with funds from municipalities along its path. He masterfully orchestrated the insecurities of small but ambitious settlements; planters in one section reportedly offered to invest $300,000 to steer the LNO&T to their corner of the Delta. Greenville, already the western terminus of the Georgia Pacific Railway, subscribed $25,000 to underwrite LNO&T facilities, including construction of a Mississippi River wharf to handle coal shipments.[70] By 1892 the LNO&T stretched 807 miles, with more than half of its track inside the Delta. Huntington's headlong expansion across the nation (the LNO&T was only one of his railroads) cost money, and he was forced to sell the LNO&T later that year to reduce his debts. Its purchaser, the mammoth Illinois Central Railroad (which already owned the Mississippi Central and other railroads in the state), paid Huntington $25 million for the line. The Chicago-based rail conglomerate then christened its consolidated Delta holdings the Yazoo and Mississippi Valley Railroad (Y&MV).[71]

The Y&MV expanded existing routes within the Delta, laid new track, and purchased railroads operated by local transportation entrepreneurs and lumber companies. One group of Bolivar County entrepreneurs attempted to replicate the success of the Greenville, Columbus and Birmingham by building a narrow-gauge line from the Mississippi River town of Rosedale into the interior in the 1890s. Their company, the Rosedale and Mississippi Central Valley Railroad, was forced into bankruptcy by the unstable cotton market, and the Y&MV acquired it in the late 1890s. Another Bolivar County combination, L. V. Boyle and Company, had better success with its rail venture. The Boyle group built a narrow-gauge line from the Y&MV's main north-south line eastward into the Bolivar and Sunflower County forests. Boyle and his partners cut timber on tracts along the Sunflower River, then used their private railroad to haul wood to the main line for shipment to distant timber users. After a few years of extraction, the surrounding woodlands left barren, Boyle's group sold the railroad to the Y&MV, which refitted the line for passenger traffic and connected it to the previously acquired Rosedale line. Locals came to refer to this circuitous section of the Y&MV—one of its few east-west segments—as "the Pea Vine" in honor of its indirect route. With these acquisitions and its steady expansion program, the Y&MV eventually pulled away from its competitor, the Georgia Pacific. By the turn of the century, the Y&MV enjoyed a firm hold on the Delta's freight transportation. Indeed, the varicose track laying of the two railroads brought 90 percent of the Delta within five miles of a railroad by 1906.[72]

Plantations abutting or bisected by rail lines often established freight and passenger stations. A depot was erected at the turn of the century on Will Dockery's Sunflower County plantation, which sat at the eastern end of the Pea Vine. The area's bounteous cotton production convinced the Y&MV to employ a full-time ticket agent, who lived with his family in a separate section of the station house. In less active locales, where passenger and freight traffic justified erecting a station but did not require an agent's full-time attention, riders and shippers stopped approaching trains by raising a flag. Many times, the train was already slowing to a halt to disgorge riders, for the volume of travelers and migrants coming to the Delta swelled after the transregional railroad began operation. The *Greenville Times,* a dependable organ for planter interests, claimed in 1885 that "since the completion of the Louisville, New Orleans and Texas Railroad both the quantity and quality of labor has been greatly increased." A nearby merchant on Deer Creek concurred, hypothesizing that "three times the amount of land in my neighborhood could have been rented this year to desirable tenants" as a consequence of increased train-borne migration. These arriving farmers not only put existing fields under the plow, they also cleared new acres, augmenting the number of improved acres and dispatching load after load of wood to awaiting sawmills.[73]

Some plantation stops grew into hamlets and towns, and other cities were created anew along the railroad tracks. Competition occasionally arose between rival planters, each eager to place a railroad station on their land and thus control the catalyst of local development. The LNO&T laid tracks along the line dividing the property of Captain E. A. Lindsley and Dr. Van Eaton when it built into Coahoma County in 1884. Because each planter demanded that the station rest on his plantation, the railroad constructed the building so that one-half lay on each man's land. Naming the station proved an equally contentious problem. Local legend has it that place was eventually called Lula after the first child (the daughter of a railroad worker) born at the site. The development of the present-day city of Cleveland shows how important the location of a railroad station might be for local landholders. When the LNO&T construction gang reached William L. Pearman's plantation in central Bolivar County in 1884, they set up a small shack for a depot and called the place Sims. Then they erected a house for themselves and other railroad employees. A small general store and post office sprang up next door, and the embryonic community had its start. The name was changed twice more before the Democratic majority of settlers christened the place Cleveland in 1887, by which time the village sported two stores, one saloon, a two-story frame hotel, and a few residences. Cleveland was well located, the railroad brought new settlers, and the surrounding countryside cried out for cultivation. Within a year the town grew to contain five or six stores, an equal number of saloons, one church, and two hotels. It was no metropolis, but quite a bit had changed since the railroad's arrival four years earlier. Early Cleveland was a child of the railroad and openly acknowledged this relationship in choosing an abandoned freight car for its first city hall.[74]

Leland, in central Washington County on the banks of Deer Creek, was another of the LNO&T's urban offspring. Although farmers and planters lived in the vicinity before the 1880s, the nearest stores were in Stoneville, a couple of miles west toward Greenville. The LNO&T bypassed Stoneville, though, to take advantage of a right-of-way donated by planter J. A. V. Feltus. On the arrival of the first LNO&T train in February 1885, Feltus dedicated Leland (named after a railroad official's sweetheart) and laid off its grid of streets on his plantation. Feltus apparently believed there was more money to be made selling lots to potential merchants and town dwellers than in growing Delta cotton. The town's rapid growth justified his gamble: by 1900 the population stood at

762. Many in the town worked directly for the railroad, and a bustling business district included four doctors, thirteen merchants and grocers, two fruit dealers, one preacher, and five bartenders, among others. Settlers from as far afield as Italy, Germany, Greece, Ireland, Wales, and Denmark called Leland home. The town continued to grow; by 1905 its population had more than doubled to 1,800.[75] The railroad's construction had birthed a town and still provided an umbilical cord of trade and migrants.

Stoneville, however, suffered from its proximity to Leland. When D. L. Stone laid off the town on his plantation at the headwaters of Deer Creek navigation in 1876, several Greenville merchants relocated to Stoneville or established branch stores there. These merchants planned to supply the growing number of farmers along Deer Creek and looked forward to the imminent arrival of rail connections with Greenville. Thus, Stoneville was partly the creation of the Greenville, Columbus and Birmingham railroad. By 1879, one year after the GC&B began running daily trains from Stoneville to Greenville, the Deer Creek village boasted two stores, six saloons, two livery stables, one hotel, and one blacksmith shop. But the growth of Leland squelched Stoneville's expansion, and the latter's population stood at only 150 in 1900.[76]

Many settlers left Stoneville for Leland, correctly appraising the newer village's brighter prospects. One was building contractor John H. Collier, who constructed the homes of many of Leland's wealthier new citizens. Another was B. O. McGee. A native of Anderson, South Carolina, McGee clerked in a Senatobia, Mississippi, store before coming to the Delta in 1886. Hearing that Stoneville was a jumping little town, McGee's employers offered him a partnership in their business if he would open a Delta branch on Deer Creek. McGee realized that Stoneville was doomed to wilt in Leland's shadow, however, and he established the store in the newer town. McGee prospered there, began making loans to small farm owners and renters, and eventually amassed extensive holdings. In 1899 McGee and his brother-in-law C. C. Dean opened the Bank of Leland; their descendants are still prominent in the Delta.[77] Just as Stoneville came to life by one railroad, so did it languish by a second (busier) line.

Other small towns along the LNO&T's path were more fortunate. Like Stoneville, Clarksdale had grown up at the inland head of an indigenous railroad. In contrast to the Washington County village, however, John Clark's trading town successfully lured the LNO&T its way and flourished. Clarksdale grew quickly, counting 781 souls by 1890 and almost 1,800 citizens at the turn of the century.[78] It seems the railroad's choice of paths could break or save a town's future.

Many small Delta towns were made by the railroad's arrival. In the early days of the region's rail boom, the *Greenville Times* gushed forth praise (and self-congratulation) at the urbanizing implications of rail transportation. "The new town of Glen Allen, at the terminus of the Lake Washington branch of the LNO&T, enters the list as a competitor to the many new towns this road has created. As railroads are aiding in the development of the vast resources of the Delta, it is but natural that its most favored localities should attract those on the lookout for new fields of enterprise and investment." Local rail boosters found much to praise in towns as small as Hollandale, which was found to contain "splendid hotels, schools and churches" and conduct "a magnificent business" despite a population of only 250.[79]

Newspaper editors and other parties interested in the region's urban growth were reluctant to criticize the railroads they had been so desperate to entice. The seamier urban offspring of the Delta's rail connections were revealed, however, by papers outside the region. Consider the Bolivar County settlement named for rail magnate C. P. Huntington. The town of Huntington perched where the LNO&T met the Mississippi River; a ferry hauled goods and railcars from the Mississippi side of the river to the Arkansas bank, where they connected with an unrelated rail system. The Arkansas City newspaper took great delight in revealing that Huntington was filled to overflowing with "bunco men, crap shooters, all kinds of gamblers . . . gathered from all parts of the country—Greenville, Vicksburg, Leland, etc." On levee workers' paydays, the Arkansans reported, a crowd of 200 men and women quickly gathered for gambling and drinking, and "in less time than it takes to write this the fights commenced." By contrast, the *Greenville Times* accentuated the positive when reporting on Huntington, as seen in its reassurance that "the train of flat cars which ran in the river at Huntington last week were all got out undamaged."[80]

For some older settlers the railroads brought worse things than bunco men. Railroad transportation cut into the river traffic both along the Mississippi and on its inland tributaries. Many hopeful riverside settlements lapsed into overgrown landing spots for infrequent steamboats, and some hamlets vanished altogether. Thus, the Mississippi riverside town of Concordia was doomed when the Y&MV passed only three miles to its east, and bustling Australia, which contained three stores, a Methodist church, a doctor's office, and a saloon in the early 1880s, expired "with the advent of the railroad." Similarly, inland settlements like Sheppardtown and McNutt in Leflore County were abandoned when railroads passed at an inconvenient distance.[81] Rail-less river towns left to rely on dwindling steamboat traffic would have disputed whether railroads were truly "the king of Progress."

A clear pattern emerged in the 1880s and 1890s: the locus of Delta population shifted from the riverine edges of the region to the rail corridors that cut through its interior forests. A shift of political power accompanied this population transfer.

Friars Point was founded in northwest Coahoma County before the Civil War, and the riverside town maintained its primacy in area commercial and economic affairs for years thereafter. The completion of Alcorn's Mobile and Northwestern Railroad in the late 1870s, despite its own poor financial showing, breathed new life into Friars Point's competitor, John Clark's eponymous inland settlement. Interior agriculture increased, and Clarksdale began to look like a permanent venture—and an explicit challenge to the river town's continued prominence. Clarksdale citizens demanded that the county seat move inland as well, and a referendum was held in 1880 to decide the matter. The upstarts were disappointed, however, for Friars Point still outnumbered Clarksdale's voters, and the courthouse and jail remained by the Mississippi River.[82]

The LNO&T's arrival in central Coahoma County in 1884 reopened the issue, for Clarksdale's population increased quickly. Within three years of transregional rail connections, the county held another referendum on the location of its seat of government. Again the riverside town claimed victory, but Clarksdale residents alleged ballot-box tampering. A group of Clarksdale citizens swarmed to the courthouse to check the Friars Point vote against its list of registered voters, but the documents they sought were concealed by the Friars Pointers. Clarksdale's adherents were vociferous in their disappointment, and claims, charges, and allegations flew back and forth between the neighboring towns for years. By 1890 the dispute had gone from competition to conflict, and local leaders realized a settlement must be reached. Thus, two prominent citizens from each town met in Memphis, a neutral site, to reconcile their differences. There, a Solomonic compromise was fashioned, splitting the county into two judicial districts and appointing one courthouse for Friars Point and a second coequal seat for Clarksdale. Neither town was completely happy with the result, but everyone was relieved to conclude the rivalry. By 1894 claims to civic prominence had been transferred to bricks and mortar, and each Coahoma County town could point to an imposing Victorian edifice—the two structures were ironically similar—as proof of its importance. The county's awkward two-seat government continued until 1930, when Friars Point finally relinquished all claims to civic importance, and Clarksdale took over the county's rule.[83]

Such disputes flared throughout the Delta, as upstart towns along the interior rail corridor demanded relocation of seats of government in accord with the new commercial and agricultural role of the region's inland expanse. In Bolivar County the feud was kicked off by a proposed railroad extension through the riverside plantation district. Interior voters, served by the LNO&T and Y&MV Railroads since the mid-1880s, were reluctant to pay for a bond issue to support a new railroad for rich planters' use. Will Dockery explained that "the eastern part of the county fought it, as they had a railroad themselves, and as there was quite a bit of rivalry between the smaller farmers on the east side of the county and the large landowners on the river." Charles Scott and other riverside planters eventually got their $150,000 railroad bond issue, but the interior settlers got something just as important: like Coahoma, Bolivar County was divided into two judicial districts, and a courthouse to serve the eastern half of the jurisdiction was constructed in Cleveland in 1900–1901. Today Cleveland, like Clarksdale to its north, is the sole seat of Bolivar County government.[84]

Despite Leland's growth, Washington County avoided political division in this period. Greenville's population continued to dwarf all other urban settlements in the county, and the most prominent owners of land in Leland's Deer Creek hinterland actually lived in Greenville. By building the Greenville, Columbus and Birmingham Railroad, the river city won a lasting advantage over future railside competitors.[85]

Although the railroad building of the 1880s and 1890s did not dislodge Greenville's hold on commercial and political affairs in the lower Delta, trains did bring new variety to the town's commerce. In established towns and burgeoning railside urban centers, business increased and diversified as new merchants arrived and new products and services were offered to the growing population. Railroads brought many of the goods sold in these establishments and often carried the proprietors and their customers to the region as immigrants. Although much of the Delta's increased commerce in the 1880s and 1890s was a factor of the region's general economic development and increased population density, much too can be credited to the railroads' influence.

Greenville and Washington County make a good case for the catalytic effects of railroad construction on commerce.[86] In the tax year 1878–79, when the first leg of the GC&B Railroad was completed to Stoneville, the county already contained an impressive number and diversity of commercial establishments, most located in Greenville. There were 122 merchants of various kinds in that year. A pair of dentists called Greenville home, as did 18 lawyers, 7 peddlers, 3 insurance agents, and a photographer. One might find diversion in the four "billiard and ten pin alleys" of the city, or refreshment at its single soda fountain, two hotels, or two restaurants; those with larger thirsts or more demanding views of entertainment might patronize any of the county's six dealers of liquor by the gallon. Greenville had only one bank and housed only one real estate agent, so financial transactions were somewhat simplified.[87] For a frontier county, Washington County was fairly energetic, and those who doubted Greenville's commitment to progress and enterprise need only contact one of the city's ubiquitous boosters to be informed of the town's glittering prospects. The newly constructed railroad was the centerpiece of their faith.

The energizing effects of the railroad were clearly evident two years later. By 1880–81 the total number of merchants in the county had increased 51 percent, from 122 to 184. Most of this commercial growth occurred in Greenville, although the number of stores in Stoneville also expanded. Greenville now had two banks and two real estate agents, and the city's stock of lawyers increased 22 percent. There were now twenty-two hotels instead of only two, and the number of feed and livery stables climbed from three to ten. These all signified a swelling flood of trade and suggested that newcomers were attracted to the region by its agricultural fecundity and the demonstrated enterprise of its inhabitants. New businesses opened—a sewing machine agent set up shop in Greenville, and the number of peddlers nearly doubled—and a healthy economy was evident as the number of drugstores swelled from one to four. Moreover, Greenville now offered new and augmented amusements to the bored countryman or traveler. An opera house opened its doors, four circuses visited the town, the number of soda fountains doubled, and there were now more than twice as many establishments offering liquor by the gallon.[88] Greenville and Washington County were growing quickly after 1878, and most citizens credited the indigenous railroad's activity with brightening the area's future.[89]

Greenville and Washington County continued to expand and diversify their commerce in the 1880s. Some articles, like bricks and ice, were now manufactured in town, but most finished products still came from outside the region. In the ten years following the GC&B's construction, Greenville's population more than doubled in number, and inhabitants demanded an increasingly specialized array of goods.[90] In 1887 a large number of general stores (thirty-nine) still served patrons, as did seven "Chinese notion shops," but there were also four milliners and two men's tailors. The nineteenth-century version of southern junk food had also made its appearance on Greenville's streets: one might snack at any of its four catfish stands or wander through six stores devoted to confectionery, fruit, and oysters. Greenville's 1887 population was estimated at 5,000 souls, many no doubt convinced that moving to the city brought them "out of the sylvan wilds into the great stream of progressive civilization."[91]

The physical manifestations of a progressive civilization did not all arrive on the first train. Civic improvements varied widely; settlers who gazed too long at the latest imported goods might find themselves sinking into the sidewalkless Delta mud. Although Greenville installed boardwalks in its business district and wealthier neighborhoods in the 1870s and 1880s, these structures frequently rotted underfoot or were damaged by use and abuse. A contract for a citywide network of concrete walks was not let until 1905. Nor were visitors advised to walk in the streets. Although loose dogs were banned in 1875, and unpenned hogs subjected to impoundment after 1877, other perils awaited the unwary walker. There were no paved, bricked, or graveled thoroughfares in town before an 1894 experiment using slag on two blocks of Washington Avenue in the central business district. The footsore could, however, avail themselves of the mule- and horse-drawn streetcars that plodded through the town as early as 1887, and a two-street electric streetcar network began service in 1900.[92] Still, municipal improvements did not keep pace with the town's growth.[93]

Residents were understandably impressed by the inaugural run of the electric streetcars, but the Delta town class proved itself eager to celebrate any step toward that elusive goal, progress.[94] Consider the hyperbolic newspaper coverage in September 1886 of Greenville's first steam-powered cotton compress: "Previous to the ceremonies Colonel Percy delivered an eloquent and feeling address. He sketched the foundation of our young city, and reviewed the many difficulties and trials of its course—the scourge of fire, the ravages and demoralization of overflow, the desolation of pestilence, and the caving bank which engulfed the fruits of many years of labor and the entire mercantile population. But with an indomitable resolution and pluck Greenville has risen superior to calamity and has overcome all obstacles."[95] After Percy's oration, "Miss Robertshaw pulled the lever, the powerful mechanism of the 90-inch Morse Compress was set in motion, and with a puff like a cannon-shot the first bale was compressed. Messrs. McBath, Carter, Hallet, and Musgrove of the cotton buying fraternity, assisted by the Honorable Peter Mitchell, county member of the Legislature, tied the hoops, and the ceremony of christening by breaking a bottle of champagne over the bale by Miss Percy followed."[96] Introduction of this cotton compress was a significant event, for its tightly pressed bales could be shipped from Greenville to purchasers anywhere in the world. Portentously, the *Times* declared the event marked Greenville's "advance to station as a commercial centre, instead of a mere shipping point."[97]

In 1886 Greenville stood on the banks of a well-traveled river and at the end of two growing railroad systems. Steam and animal power carried thousands of immigrants to the Delta each year; steam, water, animal, and man power cleared the forests; and animal and man power cultivated the crops. But while a state representative and members of the "cotton buying fraternity" tied the pressed cotton fibers tightly in place, the prospects of small farmers were also being restrained. Over the coming decade agricultural credit became an instrument for separating farmers from their property, and politics was shaped into a tool guarding the privileges of wealthy planters, businessmen, and professionals. None of this was evident when the banker's daughter set the compress in motion, and the lawyer-planter's daughter cracked open the champagne, but within ten years no one could deny that opportunity was narrowing in the Delta. By 1896 concerns for regional development no longer led planters and merchants to extend generous opportunities to freed people. Instead, whites bought, swindled, and crop-liened black farmers loose from the land. The region was shifting from the New South's promised land to "Mississippi's Mississippi." Predictions of wealth and influence rang out in 1886, however, as the Delta's rising white elite moved off to celebrate their bright future amid the champagne mud of the dusty compress building.

6

Closing the New South Frontier

The Delta's black farmers experienced a thorough deterioration of their economic and political prospects in the last dozen years of the nineteenth century. While the region's interior assumed a settled air as its vast wilderness surrendered to cultivation, the African Americans whose labors were responsible for many of these changes found themselves the victims, not the beneficiaries, of development. The frontier's hardships had been largely overcome, but some opportunities—like a dependably lucrative market for small farmers' timber—were lost in the process. Worse, the agricultural depression that enveloped the cotton South after the mid-1880s encouraged Delta conservatives in their political chicanery and financial transgressions. Ballot boxes were transformed from receptacles of democracy into targets for fraud, and black customers' patronage and credit needs became invitations for the avarice of white merchants and planters. The very character of the region, its offer of a modicum of economic and political independence for hardworking black farmers, was lost in the 1890s. By 1900 few black farmers, even the most ambitious, held realistic expectations of buying good Delta land. Instead, they struggled to escape peonage.

Whites realized by the early 1870s that in a region where African Americans comprised at least 80 percent of the potential electorate, politicians dedicated to resurrecting white supremacy could not hope for victory in uncompromised elections. There were too many black voters to defraud, intimidate, or block them all from the polls. White politicians thus sought temporary accords with the majority electorate before each election. Influential whites and blacks came together early each summer, divided offices between the races and parties, and resolved to promote a common ticket; newspapers frequently carried the names of both black and white power brokers at these joint "nominating conventions."[1] Whites usually gained nomination for the most lucrative and powerful positions, but blacks—even ardent Republicans—usually favored fusing with white conservatives over engaging in a bitter campaign. Blacks clearly resented taking second place in the division of political spoils (and hesitated to "fuse" if a viable Republican ticket seemed likely), but the fusion arrangements that dominated Delta politics could not have existed without black support.[2]

It was Delta conservatives' eagerness to overthrow Republican Reconstruction that introduced this approach to the region. In forming the Taxpayers' League in 1874, prominent white conservatives appealed to successful blacks— some of whom had learned a client's role as privileged slaves in the region before 1865—to join the crusade for fiscally responsible government. The incorporation of deferential freedmen lent a biracial cast to the movement and partly absolved white conservatives from the charge of racist politics. Recall how former slave driver Bohlen Lucas was invited to the Washington County Taxpayers' League meeting and, when he proved supportive, was named one of the group's spokesmen. His speeches to black audiences proved so effective that Lucas was invited to help negotiate the 1875 ticket that "redeemed" Washington County from Republican administration; indeed, Lucas won nomination and election to the office of county treasurer in that election.[3]

Redemption's success in 1875 was not based solely on patronage and other ties between freedmen and their former masters: many prominent black supporters of the Taxpayers' League were lapsed (or forcibly converted) former Republican officeholders. One such, former Washington County sheriff J. Allen Ross, not only joined the effort to overthrow the Republican Party he had earlier directed, he made public "confessions" of his earlier transgressions. Ross drew a compelling insider's picture of Republicans' misrule in stories serialized by the *Greenville Times* throughout the summer of 1875. The conservative convert Ross detailed judicial corruption, bribery of the local board of registration, and fraudulent tax collections with confessions conveniently timed for use by anti-Republicans on the political hustings in the 1875 campaign. To no one's surprise, Ross and other ex-Republican supporters of the Redeemers' ticket were complimented for their efforts by the "property-owning citizens of Washington County" after "the great and triumphant redemption." Ross was singled out for his "eloquence and ability" in detailing Republican misdeeds, and "a position of prominence in the future" was predicted. The *Greenville Times* reported that Ross intended to canvass for the Democratic nominee for president in the next year's campaign.[4]

Conservatives also welcomed white Republicans, long vilified as carpetbaggers or scalawags, to the conservative banquet table. Those who crossed over to join the Redeemers were urged, like Ross, to make a clean breast of their past partisanship and expose the devilment of their former allies in the Republican Party. Joshua Skinner, a white man who sought the sheriff's office previously held by the fusionist Ross, also took his new faith to the *Greenville Times* in the weeks before the 1875 local elections. Skinner publicly renounced pursuit of the Republican nomination and apologized for his earlier behavior on the hustings. He was particularly rueful regarding the "phrenzy of an unstudied and impromptu speech" he had recently delivered to a crowd of black citizens at Silver Lake. Fearing his remarks in support of the Republican ticket had been "misconstrued and exaggerated," Skinner prayed the community would recall "his record as a confederate soldier and his past conduct as a citizen" and "judge him in charity."[5] White conservatives exacted a high price from their would-be allies, for former Republican officeholders of both races were expected to recant their prior words, deeds, and alliances publicly.

Their success in mobilizing black voters and candidates in the "redemption" of local offices in 1875 encouraged white conservatives to employ fusion tactics in subsequent elections. The next year the *Greenville Times* carried an editorial openly solicitous of Washington County's black electorate. "The white people of the county do not wish to deprive you of any rights or privileges," the editorial assured black voters. "They do not wish as did the carpet bag horde, to monopolize all the offices. At the last election a division was agreed upon, and it has worked satisfactorily to all," the writer proclaimed. "There has been more peace and a better state of feeling in the county."[6] Fused tickets of white conservatives and black moderates, this editorial made clear, were the political path preferred by the plantation district's white power structure. Having dislodged the Republican Party the previous year, the Delta's white conservatives were loath to risk hotly contested elections with independent parties and candidates — even if continued office holding required bargains with former slaves.

Fusion's strength and viability, like the dominance of plantation agriculture, were defined by the region's emerging settlement patterns. Whites found it easiest to bring patronage to bear along the Mississippi River and in other accessible precincts. Black voters in the riverside plantation district were treated to barbecues and heard conservatives speak to their special concerns, such as the danger of nearby convict farms. The dwindling number of black Republicans who, like congressional candidate John R. Lynch, continued to campaign for the party of Lincoln in the plantation districts were careful to temper their rhetoric in the fusionist stronghold. Of one Lynch appearance in 1876, the conservative *Greenville Times* commented approvingly that "the speech was free from rabid appeals . . . to race prejudices; it was affable and considerate in its references to the Democratic element. Quite a contrast with the invariable Radical speeches of the past."[7] On the other hand, white conservatives judged the swelling number of freedmen renting and buying backcountry farms too distant, too individualistic, or too partisan to concede to fusionist appeals. Although the wink and nod of "future considerations" might appeal to sharecroppers struggling among the expanding plantations, it was less effective in bringing black voters of the backcountry into the fusionist fold.

Many conservatives were not satisfied to share government with black officials; their sense of racial pride demanded a larger role. Consider the perspective of Bolivar County white supremacists in the 1880s. The county's white population was increasingly outnumbered as the decade wore on. Their minority status — only 14.4 percent of the county in 1880 — grew more pronounced each year. By 1890 whites accounted for less than 11 percent of the Bolivar population, most of them huddled in the plantation district along the Mississippi River.[8]

Although fusion kept some prominent whites in political office despite their minority status, the presence of powerful blacks in the county's government and as its representatives in Jackson galled many former slaveholders. The offices held by black politicians were not mere tokens dispensed to distract the black majority. African Americans represented the county in the Mississippi Senate from 1872 through 1876 and from 1880 through 1888. With the exceptions of 1876–79 and 1883, there was always at least one black Bolivar countian in the state's House of Representatives. The sheriff's office, whose occupant was responsible for collecting taxes as well as preserving the peace, remained in the hands of Republicans for most of the 1870s, and blacks filled the county treasurer's post for most of the 1870s and 1880s. Finally, a black Republican held the office of clerk of the probate and circuit courts — which administered the criminal dockets and the disposition of estates — from 1880 through 1895. Thus, black officeholders were responsible for keeping the peace, collecting taxes, formulating the county's budget, regulating criminal proceedings, and ensuring fair conveyance of inheritances. Moreover, white Bolivar countians were regularly represented in the Mississippi Senate and House of Representatives by black men.[9] Instead of regarding this outcome as appropriate to the county's African-American majority, many white supremacists began to chafe against the fusion system they blamed for black prominence.

By the 1880s some Bolivar whites searched for ways to diminish the impact of black voters in the backcountry. W. B. Roberts later recalled how the county's "older men called me into conference with them and in deep earnestness explained to me that to retain even a show of white supremacy, which they regarded as necessary, it was my duty as a young lawyer and citizen to use my brains and skill to devise ways of preventing negro control by any means in my power." Roberts was a natural choice to aid the conservatives, for in addition to his ambition and legal training, he lived in a precinct with twenty black voters for each white citizen. "One can imagine the difficulty of making that box show a Democratic majority," he remarked.[10]

If the predominantly black frontier precincts could not be convinced to join the fusion ticket, Roberts's confederates reasoned, the impact of their votes must be lessened. The distance between backcountry voting precincts and the Bolivar County Courthouse along the Mississippi at Rosedale presented them with a number of opportunities. Roberts admitted that a "favorite scheme was to mix bills of lading at the river and ship by mistake a ballot box to St. Louis while a coil of rope or bale of cotton was sent to the county site to be counted." After the backcountry received train service in the mid-1880s, a new way to lose black votes was discovered: "the ballot box might, accidentally, be dropped out of the window of a train." Even when distance and technology did not cooperate so readily, Roberts and his henchmen found ways to dilute the black vote. "Any trick might be employed," he confessed, "that seemed to promise a chance of success."[11]

When Republican and independent candidates repeatedly garnered fewer votes than the county's preponderant black majority suggested they might expect, Bolivar County blacks grew suspicious. Soon freedmen insisted on appointing dependable observers to witness both the casting and counting of votes. Again, W. B. Roberts detailed how white conservatives distorted the tally. A box with an overwhelming Democratic majority had been secretly prepared, and the Bolivar whites planned to substitute its contents for the actual votes in a largely black precinct. The only obstacle to the plan was the diligent presence of two African-American election officials. The "two negro inspectors positively refused to leave the room even for supper," and Roberts feared the honest ballots might survive his scheme. "Under this stress, one of the white managers, who was a doctor, told them this was one time when the colored and white folks would eat together: and he went out and returned presently with a number of boxes of sardines and crackers." Unbeknownst to his allies or rivals, the doctor had employed a hypodermic needle to inject "croton oil, or some other violent drug, into the two boxes handed the Negroes. In a very few minutes the

Negroes were sick and had to leave hurriedly, and the box showed at the count a big majority for the Democrats."[12]

Roberts, who represented Bolivar County in the Mississippi Senate from 1920 to 1940, was not unashamed of his role in subverting elections. He later described his exploits during the 1880s as "ludicrous occurrences." Nor was Roberts an unremitting white supremacist. He praised a number of black leaders of Bolivar County, singling out town founder Isaiah T. Montgomery, state representatives J. H. Bufford and George Gayles, Sheriff and Clerk of the Probate and Circuit Courts J. E. Ousley, and United States senator Blanche K. Bruce as exemplary individuals. Yet the young white lawyer was willing to invalidate his county's elections and deny full suffrage to men he claimed to respect. As if to explain his actions, he recalled occasions when he had "appeared in court as a lawyer with all the court officials, the twelve men on the jury, and the lawyers on the other side, as well as all witnesses, being black." Despite his professed respect for notable black individuals, Roberts would not countenance democratic rule if it was exercised by the area's African-American majority. The social and economic mobility that made the Delta a promised land to many southern blacks in the 1870s and 1880s repelled Roberts, and he used "this condition" as justification for his fraud.[13]

The political chicanery of Roberts and his ilk was paralleled in the late 1880s and 1890s by increasing mercantile mendacity. The credit terms imposed by lenders hardened, black farmers were required to pay more for agricultural loans, and the passage from sharecropper to tenant to landowner was impeded. Much as in politics, changed financial conditions eroded the independence of black Delta farmers.

The declining price of cotton had concerned southern farmers of both races for decades. High postwar prices (inflated by four years of unpredictable supply) encouraged many farmers and investors from outside the region to try their hands at cotton farming in the just-failed Confederacy. But cotton prices fell abruptly from 1865 to 1867, squashing the agricultural ambitions of most outlanders before the new decade commenced. Although the pace of price declines slowed thereafter, the direction of cotton prices remained downward. Between 1874 and 1877 the average price for southern cotton stood at just over 11 cents per pound of lint. Twenty years later, in the midst of the agricultural depression that played havoc with the nation's farming between 1888 and 1899, the average cotton price was less than 6 cents per pound. In responding to falling prices, a cotton farmer faced three options: grow more cotton to make up the loss in price, find another cash crop, or suffer a decline in his standard of living. Most farmers actively pursued the first option, and some were able to exercise the second choice, but few escaped the latter fate.[14]

By the late 1880s even farmers in the fertile Delta were hard-pressed to remain out of debt. Many of their costs were obvious. Rent (or land-purchase installments) had to be paid, laborers compensated for plowing, chopping, and picking the cotton, and implements purchased and repaired. Farmers faced less apparent costs, as well. The lint had to be ginned free of impurities, pressed and bound into commercial bales, and delivered to commodity agents for sale—all at the farmer's expense. These combined cultivation and processing expenses cost a farmer over $21 for every acre planted in cotton, about 4.57 cents for each pound of lint. The farmer must then feed, clothe, and shelter himself and his family for a year, retire debts, pay his taxes, and meet incidental expenses with the return in excess of 4.57 cents per pound. That was a difficult feat near the end of the century, for the selling price of cotton hovered between 6 and 8.5 cents per pound throughout the latter 1880s and 1890s. By the mid-1890s, when Delta cotton prices averaged 7.14 cents per pound, farmers had to produce 297 pounds of cotton per acre just to meet the costs of cultivation.[15]

This combination of substantial costs and cotton's low price proved disastrous for many landowners and tenants after 1888. In 1893 Sharkey County planter Dr. A. J. Phelps testified before a Senate committee investigating the plight of southern cotton growers. Phelps estimated that two-thirds of his neighbors were in danger of losing their land or becoming trapped in inescapable tenancy. The planter disclosed that the average cotton yields in the region for the 1890–92 crop years stood at about 300 pounds per acre, just at the break-even point. "They are universally in debt," he reported; "many are insolvent." He drew a stark contrast with the Delta's earlier economic climate, stating that "the present condition of cotton growers in this district is worse than three years ago, worse than ten years ago, or twenty years ago."[16]

Farmers searched for ways to reduce their costs. The most dramatic change came in the amount of grain raised for human and livestock consumption. Unwilling to reduce the number of acres devoted to cotton, many Delta farmers had previously purchased much of their grain from outside the region. Phelps estimated that many farmers, goaded into home production of foodstuffs by the poor cotton prices of 1891 and 1892, were approaching self-sufficiency in 1893. Leflore County planter W. H. Morgan concurred and testified to his own experience. Morgan had escaped debilitating debt by "raising my corn and roughness for my stock. I raise at home everything to eat I can, and all the forage I can." In 1892 Morgan divided his fields equally between cotton and corn, even though most farmers grew cotton on at least 75 percent of their cultivable land. Farmers raising their own corn and forage, Phelps agreed, fared better in the agricultural depression than those who continued to incur debts for Iowa corn.[17]

Landlords with tenants on their property began experimenting with other tactics. In response to their diminished incomes from cotton sales, these land-lords and subleasing renters sought to squeeze greater returns from their tenants. Planter Morgan described his own methods. He did not use wage laborers or renters on his property: the former required frequent payment (an additional credit cost for the planter), and the latter demanded lower fees for use of the land than did share workers. Morgan used only sharecroppers to grow his cotton and corn. The planter's calculations did not stop at considering what system of tenancy or labor was most lucrative: he actively sought to lure his sharecroppers into frequent trade and trap them in his debt. Morgan candidly reported that "it only pays to raise cotton in order to have a market at home." This "market," Morgan's sharecroppers, were expected to trade with him and were the primary purchasers of his large stock of grain. Every manufactured item or bushel of corn purchased by sharecroppers diminished Morgan's dependence on the slumping cotton market, and if a worker became mired in debt through these transactions, Morgan could invoke his lien against the farmer's personal property or compel his labor for the following year. "Your tenants or farm laborers are your patrons," the planter explained, "and just so far as you can make them so, you are successful." Morgan did not detail how far this strategy required him to go in trapping sharecroppers into debt peonage.[18]

Planters were not alone in squeezing extra income from their business transactions. Merchants, especially those lending money and extending retail credit to farmers, also sought new sources of cash in the declining cotton market after 1888. During the 1870s and most of the 1880s, agricultural credit was predictably simple. In the first quarter of each year, farm owners and tenants contracted with merchants, cotton factors, or planters for cash advances and retail credit for the coming crop year. Cotton growers generally pledged the year's crops against the nascent debt, and those who already owed sums to their lender usually promised their livestock, implements, and other personal property as proof of their ability to repay the loan. Landowners were generally required to lien all or part of their real estate to the lender to further safeguard the transaction. Should the borrower fail to repay the full loan amount, the creditor could renegotiate the loan for another year in hopes of full compensation, or he could immediately activate the lien. If he chose the latter course, the debtor's property (land, crops, farm implements, and personal items) was auctioned to the highest bidder in public sale, with the proceeds going to pay arrears. Any sum exceeding the debt and cost of auction was apportioned to the debtor.[19]

Significantly, the creditor did not hold a mortgage or automatic claim to the debtor's property upon the latter's default. The debt had to be satisfied by public sale. As a result, creditors could not simply swindle a farmer into great debt and then claim to own the debtor's holdings. In fact, public auctions for debt in the late 1880s and 1890s commonly failed to return the full amount owed to the creditor. Many merchants received less from auctions than they had loaned to failed farmers. Hence, merchants and other lenders had incentive to find ways to profit within the lending arrangement and reason to avoid public auction in the depressed market of the 1890s.[20]

Agricultural loans to wealthy whites differed little from those negotiated with black tenants in the first postbellum decades. In return for advances of up to $4,543, New Orleans cotton factors Richardson and May charged white planter S. M. Spencer 10 percent interest on his debt, required that he pay an additional 2.5 percent fee for all goods purchased on credit, took a lien on the crops, implements, and livestock at his Alps plantation in Issaquena and Washington Counties, and made him promise to ship his entire cotton crop to their Louisiana warehouse. Local lenders offered similarly restrictive terms to white elites.[21]

From the late 1880s creditors searching for additional profit augmented loan agreements with a host of costly conditions, fees, and requirements. Lenders had long charged high interest rates for agricultural loans (usually 10 percent), merchant lenders customarily charged higher prices for goods purchased on credit than for items sold for cash, and cotton factors and some landlords demanded that the entire cotton crop be delivered to them for marketing. But as the price of cotton slipped down near the break-even point, deeds of trust began to demand that borrowers deliver a specified number of bales to the lender, with charges—usually $1 to $1.50 per bale—levied for each bale missing from the expected total. The figure of $1.50 was more than cotton traders were then charging in sales commissions. A 450-pound bale of cotton that sold for 7.5 cents per pound brought cotton traders charging the customary 2.5 percent commission only 84 cents. Some lenders further demanded that borrowers pay a flat storage fee for each bale of cotton delivered to the merchant's storehouse, a levy which more than compensated lenders for the time between receiving cotton and selling it on the cotton market. Lenders increasingly speculated on the international cotton market—a practice encouraged by Greenville's steam-powered cotton press, which allowed Delta cotton to be shipped directly to buyers in any part of the world—and expected debtors to pay them to do so. Thus, in addition to repaying his loan with high interest, a borrower was asked to underwrite the lender's cotton trading.[22] While planters like W. H. Morgan were finding new ways to draw their "patron" sharecroppers into purchases and debt, the Delta's urban merchants and lenders experimented in new methods for compounding debt and prolonging costly credit obligations.

Acquisitive landlords and creditors were not above the temptations of fraud. Numeracy, like literacy, was not common in the early generations of freedmen. Whereas 97 percent of white planters were literate in 1900, only 57 percent of black male farm owners (and barely 50 percent of black male farm tenants) evinced similar education.[23] Storekeepers might overcharge, double charge, and miscalculate with near impunity in the first decades after emancipation. The worsening economy seems to have inspired many merchants to overcharge for goods. Indeed, the mendacity of white Delta merchants became legend by the turn of the century, motivating criticism even from fellow whites. White merchants' fraud became so galling to Washington County planter and attorney LeRoy Percy that he publicly denounced their greed and called for greater expenditures on black education to help combat the merchants' advantage in transactions. Addressing a meeting of the Mississippi Bar in Greenville, Percy reminded his listeners that "there is no greater temptation known to man than the hourly, daily, yearly dealing with an ignorant, trusting people. There has been no race known to history that could long withstand this deadly, insidious attack." Blacks must be better educated, or white merchants would continue to yield to the allures of unjustified acquisition. Percy predicted that the effects of white merchants' fraud would be felt by both races. "The money improperly taken because of his helplessness from the negro, it is true, leaves him little poorer, but it definitely degrades him who takes it. There are no two brands of honesty. You cannot be dishonest in dealing with the negro, and remain honest in your dealings with other men."[24] But there is no evidence that Percy's appeal substantially decreased the habits of fraud that were refined in the 1890s.[25]

Not all black borrowers simply submitted to the tightening screws of credit. Deeds of trust negotiated in this period reveal a great diversity of obligations and requirements. Farmers succeeded in bargaining down the number of bales they were required to deliver, the cost assessed for each missing bale, and the storage fees charged for cotton delivered to their creditors. They were generally unable to eliminate or reduce the 10 percent interest rate, however, and the provision charging higher prices for goods received on credit than for items bought with cash was nearly universal. Some desperate debtors, usually renters and sharecroppers, fled their creditors, even abandoning crops standing in the field to escape seizure and auction of their other property. Consequently, deeds of trust became increasingly specific regarding liens against the borrowers' personal property. Wagons were described in detail; plows, hoes, and axes were counted and categorized; the physical characteristics and names of horses and mules were entered into deeds of trust.[26] Lenders clearly hoped these provisions would dissuade debtors from surreptitious relocation or would aid in recovering the property of fleeing defaulters.

Borrowers found few alternatives to local lenders. National and international mortgage lenders were largely absent from the region's credit market during the agricultural depression. I have located only one black farmer who fully escaped the tightening local credit market. Nelson Bliss, a particularly adept Sunflower County farmer, negotiated a deed of trust in 1893 with the Investment Guarantee Trust Company of Hull, England. The loan was a small one ($700 repayable in five years with 10 percent interest), and Bliss was probably regarded as a good credit risk, for he had owned his eighty acres for over ten years. Still, the Britons were cautious and required that Bliss insure his personal property, home, and other farm buildings as a condition of the loan; the lenders wanted assurances that Bliss's holdings would be auctionable should he fail to retire the deed of trust. But Bliss was uncommon. Creditors feared that the prospects of dependable repayment evaporated with the declining price of cotton, and the prevalence of the deed of trust dissuaded most outside lenders who might otherwise have risked lending in hope of repossessing fertile property.[27] Thus, black and white Delta farmers of all levels of wealth operated within a credit market strongly influenced by worsening economic conditions.

That local credit market could seem diverse, for Polish Jews and Chinese merchants were lending money and extending credit to Delta farmers in the 1890s. Yet European or Asian origins did not render a creditor more generous than his native-born, Caucasian counterparts. Consider the efforts of Wong Chung, a Chinese immigrant who was moderately active in Greenville commerce during the 1890s. In 1895 Wong negotiated a deed of trust agreement with Henry and Rosa Jones, black farmers owning forty acres in Washington County. The Joneses had fallen $75 into the merchant's debt in 1894, and Wong demanded a lien on their farm, crops, and personal property to safeguard his investment. Like other area merchants, Wong demanded the debt (and any increase) be repaid with 10 percent interest, included a bale obligation in the Joneses' deed of trust, charged them $1 for each bale under the requirement, and assessed a 2.5 percent commission for selling the cotton they produced. He agreed to furnish supplies for the 1895 crop year but insisted on charging higher prices for any goods extended on credit.[28] The terms of this agreement were common by 1895, and the Joneses would have encountered the same restrictions and fees from most of the native-born merchants lending money in the area during the depression.

One year later Henry and Rosa Jones had not retired their debt to Wong Chung; indeed, the sum had grown to $91.55. Wong was willing to renew the deed of trust, however, and imposed the same conditions on the new agreement. Cotton prices remained inert that year, but the Joneses' debts to Wong did not; by January 1897 the black farmers owed the Chinese merchant $216. Henry and Rosa Jones must have been discouraged by their situation. Cotton prices had been down near the break-even point for cotton growers for almost a decade by 1897, and no end was in sight. Moreover, the couple's debt had swollen to more than twice the previous year's amount. Other farmers were losing their land, and the Joneses must have feared a similar fate. Still, with no better options among the merchants and lenders of Washington County, the farming couple renewed their deed of trust with Wong Chung in early 1897.[29]

Details of Henry and Rosa Jones's 1897 finances do not survive, yet we can assume they were again disappointed in the prices received for their cotton. The staple's price did not increase dramatically, and their debts probably swelled as a result. But this is certain: Wong Chung activated his deed of trust. The Joneses received word of the action, a trustee advertised the sale in the *Greenville Times,* and a public auction was held on the steps of the Washington County Courthouse. Wong may have hoped for a high and competitive bidding for the property, but he was disappointed. Even though the agricultural depression would soon lift, few buyers were able to purchase land, even public auction land, in the spring of 1898. Desultory bidding kept the price low, and fearing a sale that would not repay the Joneses' obligations, Wong stepped in to purchase the land himself. He won the bidding at $160 for the forty acres—a sum he need not pay because it was owed to himself—and took possession of the property. Henry and Rosa Jones lost the farm they had struggled to hold through the worst agricultural depression in American history, and merchant Wong Chung now held a plot of land that would not even bring the price of his loans to the Joneses. The debt was finally settled, but no one was pleased by the results of the auction.[30] Wong Chung was a small-time lender, vulnerable to the smallest economic downturn and without the capital reserves or extensive credit necessary to make many loans to struggling farmers like Henry and Rosa Jones. More experienced lenders, even some of the region's most established merchants and cotton factors, were also left holding the bag of empty liens at Delta land auctions.

It was hardly the life Herman and Nathan Wilczinski expected when they left their home in Posen (now Poznan, Poland) 135 miles east of Berlin to travel to America in the 1870s. Their brother Leopold and other family members had settled into trade in Greenville and reported a bustling region with growing trade. The Wilczinskis sold goods, bought and sold land, and made loans to farmers; by 1874 Herman was operating a store containing $8,000 worth of merchandise. Nathan was voted Man of the Year by the local Knights of Pythias organization in 1875, and all of the Wilczinski brothers were active in civic affairs.[31]

Although the 1870s and early 1880s were generally prosperous for the Wilczinskis, no merchant on this New South frontier escaped conflict. Consider the Wilczinski brothers' dealings with white yeoman farmer Dock Early. Early initiated purchase of a particular sixty-six-acre parcel of land in 1879. But the property was sold at auction in 1880 — and purchased by Herman and Nathan Wilczinski — after the farmer defaulted on a deed of trust they held. As high bidders, the Wilczinskis took over the property, but Early was determined to buy back the land. The Wilczinskis resold him the acreage, known as "Early's Deadening" in recognition of the farmer's efforts to clear the forest. But Dock Early defaulted again, and the land was once more auctioned and again purchased by the Wilczinskis in 1883. The Wilczinskis resolved to break the pattern of sale, default, and repurchase and sought other buyers. Two black farmers stepped forward to purchase the land in 1884, and the Wilczinskis conveyed conditional title to the property to Ajax and Thomas McPherson in return for promissory notes totaling $665. But the McPhersons found that paying for the land was the least of their troubles, for Dock Early refused to leave the property and would not let them cultivate the land he had cleared. The black farmers apparently abandoned their attempt, and the Wilczinskis — unable to locate renters or buyers willing to confront Early — went to court for an ejectment order against the white farmer. Although the Wilczinskis won their ejection suit, Early continued to occupy the farm, and the merchants could not locate anyone who dared rent or purchase the property. At this impasse, the Wilczinskis negotiated another sale to Early, stipulating that he must abandon the property by the end of the year if no money was paid for the land's use or purchase. He failed to pay and finally quit the premises. In the six years of their involvement with Dock Early and the disputed land parcel, the merchants made loans to Early of up to $962.82, but they do not appear to have ever collected any repayment of the principal or interest, rental fee, or purchase installment.[32]

By the 1890s the Wilczinskis had more to contend with than one stubborn debtor. Like many Delta merchants, they found their cash reserves strapped by the faltering economy. Worse, their own lines of credit, both within and outside the region, were fraying. In 1892 the Wilczinskis were reduced to dubious financing. After borrowing $2,500 from the Merchants and Planters Bank of Greenville (and giving the bank a deed of trust for 479 acres, including the still-unsold Early tract), the Wilczinskis looked about for other funding. They did not pursue creditors nearby, lenders who would know of the Merchants and Planters Bank's prior lien on their holdings. Instead they negotiated a second deed of trust on the property with Mrs. M. Pollock of Baltimore, Maryland, in return for $3,150.[33]

Should the Wilczinskis find themselves unable to repay these loans, their liened land — like the farms of Henry and Rosa Jones, Dock Early, or any other failed Delta land purchaser — would be sold at public auction. As the first lien-holder, the Merchants and Planters Bank of Greenville would receive its full recompense from the sale before Mrs. Pollock was paid any money. There is no evidence that she fully understood the loan's level of risk. Indeed, it was likely that Mrs. Pollock would not reap any repayment if the property fell to auction, for the loans against the land amounted to an average of $11.80 per acre, a high price for mixed land during the depression. Wong Chung, after all, only had to bid $4 per acre to gain the Joneses' cleared land, and the Early field portion of the Wilczinskis' property had proved itself virtually unsalable. Fortunately for the Wilczinskis and their various creditors, the merchants managed to stave off bankruptcy through the remainder of the decade.[34] The Wilczinskis' experience demonstrates, however, that respected and well-established Delta merchants found themselves making shady deals to stay afloat during the 1890s.

Caught between falling cotton prices and the increasingly avaricious tactics of lenders, relatively few black farmers bought farms during the agricultural depression. The rate of land purchase plummeted from the early 1880s' brisk pace to a dearth of activity during the late 1880s and 1890s. Between 1889 and 1897, the worst years of the depression, the average yearly number of black land buyers fell to one-quarter of its 1880–89 average (graph 6).[35] In some counties years passed without one black farmer registering a land purchase.[36] Delta blacks' climb up the agricultural ladder was effectively halted in the 1890s.

Graph 6. Black land purchasers, Washington County, 1880–97

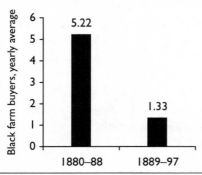

Source: Washington County Deed Records.

Not all Delta farmers surrendered to worsening conditions. Some, embold-ened by the cooperative vision of the Farmers' Alliance and the Colored Farm-ers' Alliance, set out to find joint solutions to their common credit and supply problems.[37] Thus did a curious establishment styled the Tchula Cooperative Store rise up in Holmes County at the Delta's eastern edge. By 1890 the Tchula Cooperative was attracting business from farm owners (but not tenants) throughout the Delta's eastern reaches. The store sold goods, made loans, and helped market the cotton crop at its railside location approximately halfway be-tween Yazoo City and Greenwood. The Tchula store loaned money and ex-tended credit to black landowners in nearby counties and generally required a deed of trust on land as surety for the credit.[38] Significantly, the cooperative charged no interest on debts or advances, although it did charge higher prices for goods purchased on credit than for items bought with cash.

Black farmers William P. and Rosina G. Cross of Sunflower County negoti-ated a typical loan with the Tchula Cooperative Store in March 1890. They of-fered a deed of trust on their eighty-acre farm in return for assumption of a $165 debt and credit for the crop year. The lender's lien included the Crosses' land, their four cows, two oxen, one mule, crops, and tools. The couple's personal and real property was liable for auction if they did not repay the debt and pay for goods and advances by 1 November 1890.[39]

William and Rosina Cross may have paid off the Tchula store for their debt and purchases in 1890, but by 1893 they were again in need of credit. The live-stock holdings of the Cross family had declined in the three years since their last negotiation. Now they had only one (instead of four) milk cows and were without any oxen. Although three beef cattle had been added, the loss of the oxen left the family only one mule with which to cultivate their fields. In May 1893 they signed a deed of trust encompassing their land and personal property to the Tchula Cooperative Store in order to carry over their $283.18 debt and gain further credit during the 1893 crop year. Again, the Crosses agreed to pay credit prices for their purchases but were not charged interest on their debt or advances.[40]

Despite the absence of interest on their debts, the Cross family was becoming immersed in the same cycle of debt that bedeviled borrowers across the South. By 1895 the Cross debt at the Tchula store had grown 16 percent, and the family again gave a deed of trust on their land to gain continued access to credit. The next year, the farmers may have found reason for hope; their debt declined slightly (from $328.41 to $301.98), and they were not compelled to eat or sell any more of their field animals. In fact, the family was able to buy another mule in 1897 without increasing their debt by more than 10 percent.[41]

The Tchula Cooperative Store was less fortunate, however, for it made no loans after 1897 and vanished from the public records. Although the cooperative experiment in interest-free lending did not survive the end of the decade, its humane lending policy had a salutary effect on black farm owners in the eastern Delta: none of the farmers borrowing money from the Tchula Cooperative Store lost their land during the relationship.[42] True, some (like the Cross family) liquidated other property and took on a larger debt during the period, but the store's refusal to add interest charges to their burden no doubt helped many keep their heads above the sea of arrears that drowned the hopes of other black landholders. Although the Crosses' 1897 debt was several times its 1890 figure, they still owned their land at the end of the century, and four years passed before they next needed to negotiate a deed of trust to gain credit.[43] Had credit mechanisms such as the Farmers' Alliance–inspired Tchula Cooperative Store been more common in the Delta, more of the region's black farmers might have held onto (or purchased) farmland in the 1890s and beyond.

The paucity of interest-free lending establishments in the Delta during the 1890s was no accident. Both planters and merchants opposed Farmers' Alliance operations as threats to their influence in Delta agriculture, trade, and politics. These concerns had some basis in reality, for the efforts of an alliance chapter in Leflore County—and the responses of militant whites—brought the region to the verge of race war in 1889.

Oliver Cromwell arrived in Leflore County in the summer of 1889. Cromwell, it soon emerged, pursued two overlapping but potentially contradictory goals. He was both a Colored Farmers' Alliance organizer and the commission agent for a cooperative store, the Durant Commercial Company, located outside the Delta. Whether Cromwell was more dedicated to publicizing the alliance's agrarian mission or to selling supplies and equipment to the region's black farmers is difficult to discern; indeed, there was much debate among his potential followers and customers regarding his primary allegiance. Cromwell's incentives aside, it is clear that his activities disturbed powerful whites in the nearby plantation district.[44]

This black missionary of cooperative buying and selling did not believe in surreptitious conversions. Cromwell traveled from plantation to plantation, farm to farm, meeting the black tenants and landowners of Leflore County and delivering the good news of an escape from crop liens and high prices. Join the Colored Farmers' Alliance, he seems to have implored, and discover how the united purchasing power of black agrarians can reduce your debts and end your reliance on white creditors. In individual conversations and bold speeches throughout Leflore, Cromwell advocated the alliance's philosophy and made special mention of the bargains available from the Durant cooperative store. His message was well received in the eastern Delta, and Cromwell's new adherents soon ordered shipments of goods from the alliance outlet.[45]

By mid-August, Cromwell's efforts had attracted the suspicions of local whites, who doubtless disliked his condemnation of the area's economic relations. Planters, especially those with sharecroppers on their lands, may have been uneasy with the allianceman's growing popularity among their workers, for his influence implicitly undermined landlords' control. Merchants had even greater cause for concern. Cromwell disparaged their business methods, drew away customers' dollars to the Durant store, and poisoned minds against white traders. It was rumored that he had instigated a boycott of white-owned stores.[46] This disruption and competition coincided with landlords' and merchants' desperate search for ways to increase their business and offset the effects of the slumping cotton economy. For local whites Cromwell's mission (and success) could not have come at a worse time.

Consequently, Leflore whites moved to undercut the allianceman's authority. Rumors began to circulate throughout the county, probably spread by white merchants. According to one tale, Cromwell was not the upright advocate of agrarian ideals he professed to be but an ex-convict who once led a gang of horse thieves. Another rumor claimed Cromwell's advocacy of the Colored Farmers' Alliance was just a pretense, a calculated scheme intended to separate poor farmers from their alliance dues. Cromwell was probably not even affiliated with alliance, it followed, but simply pocketed the membership payments of duped agrarians.[47] Cromwell cared much more about his income than the welfare of Leflore County blacks, these allegations suggested, and the true friend of the poor farmer was his accustomed patron, the white planter or merchant.

Some of the county's black farmers believed these rumors, and Cromwell was called before the new chapter of the Colored Farmers' Alliance to defend his actions and motives. Perhaps local blacks wondered why newcomer Cromwell so loudly proclaimed to be their friend and advocate, what made him so eager to risk the enmity of powerful whites, and whether his support would vanish if they were unable to buy his goods (or if whites retaliated against the embryonic alliance cell). Having endured years of frontier hardship only to watch the price of cotton fall so low that it mocked their efforts, Leflore's black farmers may have begun to doubt the wisdom of Cromwell's plan. The organizer was clearly ambitious, for who else would ride alone into the Delta backcountry preaching economic salvation and wealth through cooperation? Perhaps, the newfound converts speculated nervously, Cromwell was simply playing on their frustrations and fears of poverty to sell an empty promise. Maybe the only one to benefit from their alliance membership was the man who collected the dues.[48]

It was a tense meeting. The charges were examined, Cromwell's efforts came under scrutiny, and he defended his actions. Eventually the matter was brought to a vote. Even among the members of the local alliance, some black farmers remained skeptical of Cromwell's intentions and urged that a better-known farmer from the area be elected as their leader. A majority, however, supported Cromwell. The chapter drafted a resolution expressing confidence in the organizer's character and activities and decided to share their verdict with the broader community.[49]

Then the alliance cell made a critical miscalculation: rather than highlight their support for Cromwell and release their majority resolution as the informed opinion of the local organization, the members chose instead to exaggerate their numbers and militancy. Perhaps Cromwell's oratory swept them away, perhaps the group's collective patience snapped at having to defend their advocate against persistent falsehoods. Whatever the explanation, the resolution that should have been a simple document supporting the work of one activist was transformed into a threatening manifesto when the group of black farmers signed themselves "Three Thousand Armed Men." Seventy-five armed members of the local alliance then marched in "regular military style" to deliver the declaration to whites in the nearby hamlet of Shell Mound.[50]

Delta whites were liable to overreact when confronted with displays of this sort. The disparity in numbers played a large role in magnifying white perceptions of imminent danger: Leflore County contained more than five black inhabitants for every white resident at this time. The county's 2,597 white settlers were aware of the numerical advantage that 3,000 armed black men would enjoy if the races fell to conflict. Older Delta whites recalled their antebellum dread of slave uprisings, and the bloody specter of Nat Turner haunted the region in the wake of the Shell Mound demonstration. Leflore whites buzzed over rumors that Cromwell had already organized the black alliancemen for armed resistance against any attempt to molest him.[51]

Delta whites' morbid imaginations were sustained by relatively recent experience. Large bands of armed blacks and whites had clashed in the region since the Civil War. Leflore County whites and blacks may have recalled similar events transpiring at the Mississippi River town of Austin just fifteen years earlier.

Austin, in Tunica County, was a rough-and-tumble river town, but even its crime-hardened citizens were shocked by the developments of August 1874. A white resident, one Dr. Smith, fell into argument with a black man about an unknown dispute. Smith, who may have been losing the debate, drew his sidearm and began pistol-whipping his adversary. The gun discharged in their struggle, but neither man was struck. Instead, one bullet flew off into the crowd gathered to view their combat, and a young black girl was killed. Smith was promptly arrested and charged with the girl's murder, but the magistrate allowed the white man to go free on bail.[52]

Tunica County blacks were outraged that the innocent girl's killer might be suffered to walk the streets, and several hundred freedmen formed a posse to recapture the physician. He was easily apprehended, and the group returned him to the Austin jail, after which they left the scene. Smith was then freed again, however, for the jailer could not reincarcerate a man whom the magistrate had just released. After Smith left the cell, word quickly spread that the killer was again loosed upon society, and hundreds of blacks congregated near the town. Sheriff Vannoy Manning, who had twice given Smith his freedom, judged the gathering's mood to be ugly and promptly fled the town. Other Austin whites, similarly fearful of the damage an aggrieved, armed black majority might do, followed the sheriff's lead. Some of the assembled blacks, seizing a unique opportunity for unsupervised acquisition, looted the town's stores. Whites in Tunica County and much of the northern Delta were appalled that a misunderstanding of due process could bring about armed uprising and theft on a massive scale. Their expectations of order were not restored to Austin until 300 armed white men, many of them Civil War veterans, arrived under the command of former Confederate general James R. Chalmers via steamboat from Memphis. Chalmers's irregulars captured eight black men whom they believed were intent on inflaming local blacks to mob action, and local whites soon returned to the riverside town. Sheriff Manning returned after the troops' arrival and with a sixty-man posse spent weeks scouring the county for other leaders of the late disturbance, eventually capturing and incarcerating twenty-five blacks. [53]

The Austin insurrection convinced many Delta whites that the region's freedmen were too fond of their newfound rights and might require the pacifying influence of a steady application of armed force.[54] Alarmed by the prospect of a large number of armed blacks devoted to Cromwell, Leflore County whites sent their women and children out of the rural districts to the county seat, Greenwood, and larger cities beyond the region's borders. The county's white men had learned from the Austin disturbance that completely abandoning the territory would encourage some blacks to theft, and many stayed behind to guard their farms. The outnumbered whites were "convinced that serious trouble would soon follow" and appealed to others of their race in neighboring counties to send men and aid before an armed black uprising erupted.[55]

The confrontation between Cromwell's armed alliancemen and fearful Leflore whites escalated quickly. First, the black alliancemen had overreacted to criticisms of Cromwell and advertised themselves as armed and dangerous. Then, recalling the actions of earlier whites fearing black violence, the county's white residents adopted a siege mentality and sent for reinforcements. Within a context of frontier violence and economic desperation, Leflore whites and blacks acted and reacted with a series of increasingly bombastic miscalculations. A rough backcountry setting alone was not enough to trigger this deadly impasse, nor was the collapsing cotton economy. Even the provocative Cromwell, alone, was hardly enough to justify race war. Yet this combination of irritants and each group's eagerness to construe the actions of the other in the worst possible light led, by the end of August, to an explosive showdown.

In nearby counties whites heard (and spread) rumors that Leflore County blacks had gathered a huge stockpile of arms and were massing for violence. Perhaps these rumors were cousins of the tales previously circulated about Cromwell. Irrespective of veracity, these tales galvanized the white citizens of the Delta. By 31 August armed whites were streaming into Greenwood to halt an imagined black uprising against the remaining white settlers. Armed blacks, meanwhile, gathered around Minter City, roughly twenty-five miles northwest of Greenwood along the Tallahatchie River.[56]

According to one Delta newspaper, "The whites were irritated and indignant that they should have so unwarrantedly been drawn into collision." Whites at a distance from Leflore County believed the alliancemen and their supporters had been seduced into an armed confrontation by the prospect of numerical advantage over area whites. Blacks in Leflore County, one editor speculated, were "inflated with the feeling of having flaunted their array [of men and arms] unchecked." They did not realize that, as in Austin fifteen years before, Leflore County whites could quickly call in sympathetic forces from outside the Delta. Black insurgents, the newspaperman concluded, "were blinded to their deadly and certain danger." On 31 August armed Leflore blacks held another parade, this time at their camp along the Tallahatchie.[57]

Leflore County's white sheriff, L. T. Baskett, rode north from Greenwood to treat with the black insurgents. He found them resting in their riverside encampment after the parade and urged the assemblage to disband. Some were nearly persuaded by his speech. But when one of their number moved off to abandon the camp, he was challenged by a leader of the group, shot, and killed. Sheriff Baskett, convinced that the insurgents were "beyond his power," quickly left the camp. Unable to contain or control the violence, the sheriff telegraphed Mississippi governor Robert Lowry to send troops to quash the uprising.[58]

Lowry sent three companies of the Mississippi National Guard and personally accompanied the rail-borne troops to Greenwood, all arriving by the afternoon of the next day, 1 September. Lowry and the troops found they were not the first detachments to answer Sheriff Baskett's call; white vigilantes had thronged to Greenwood from other parts of the Delta and from the neighboring hill counties. Afraid the undisciplined whites might degenerate into a blood-crazed lynch mob, Governor Lowry spoke to them at length regarding the state troops' abilities and reminded his listeners of the shame that would burden the area's reputation should vigilantism ensue. Lowry was cheered by the irregulars, many of whom then left the area. Suspicious of the remaining white mob, Governor Lowry took an additional precaution and forbade any volunteers to join the state troops.[59]

Late that night the troops boarded a steamboat and proceeded up the Tallahatchie in search of the armed band of blacks. Sheriff Baskett met the steamboat at Minter City and led the troops (with some local whites) in a protracted search for the insurgents. About forty blacks were arrested on 2 September and in the days that followed, and 220 "improved Winchester and Spencer rifles" were confiscated from individual black agrarians, but the guardsmen never captured the main body of armed blacks or maneuvered them into a pitched battle. As in the Austin insurgency, a force from outside the region arrived to disband the angry freedmen, successfully captured a few ringleaders, and then left the field to local whites.[60]

The number of casualties suffered in the Leflore County upheaval is uncertain. Northern Republican newspapers were eager for high estimates of southern bloodshed in those weeks before their state and local elections and ran a bewildering array of body counts. Most of the stories did not identify the sources of their intelligence, which seem to have been based on hearsay and speculation. Although no whites were reported killed in the wide-ranging and violent search, a welter of reports placing the number of black dead between 30 and 100 souls circulated among the newspapers of the urban North.[61]

Oliver Cromwell escaped, lending some credence to merchants' earlier charges that he was motivated more by self-interest than by unswerving commitment to Leflore County's black farmers. Indeed, Cromwell left the county before the guardsmen arrived. He may have taken the train south to Jackson before Governor Lowry and the troops headed north; a number of people reported seeing Cromwell on the streets of Jackson on 1 September, the day the guardsmen arrived in Greenwood.[62] But Cromwell's assistant, George Allen, did not escape the scene. Someone, probably Sheriff Baskett, identified Allen as the gunman who shot the potential defector to prevent reluctant insurgents from quitting their Minter City camp after Baskett's speech on 31 August. On the night of 3 September, with armed whites searching the county for the insurgents, Allen led a group of armed blacks to an isolated store in search of more ammunition. Refused entry by the merchant, Allen set fire to the building. He was captured later that week, charged with "incendiarism," and executed on 9 September. Four other prominent members of the uprising were captured and either shot or hanged for their roles in the affair. A sixth man, Lewis Mortimer, was accused of murder and lynched at Shell Mound three days later; his death was probably attributable to the white vigilantes who roamed the area for days after the state troops departed.[63]

Even if only six black men were killed in the disturbance—and it is probable that many more perished—its message was unequivocal: white supremacy, in commerce and politics, now demanded that the white minority employ disproportionate force in response to any challenge to the status quo. The events in Leflore County energized whites' racism and provoked actions that severely limited black opportunity in the Delta.[64]

Planters from the eastern Delta met on 20 September to discuss what they believed to be the root cause of their recent troubles: the Durant Commercial Company's operations. Whites were particularly disturbed by the hundreds of modern rifles that Leflore County blacks apparently had procured via Cromwell from the alliance store. The planters argued that their "own lives as well as those of our families, and the existence of our best interests depend upon the discontinuance of dealings of this character." The assembled whites demanded that the Durant store cease sales and shipments to the Leflore County black alliancemen and informed the editor of the Colored Farmers' Alliance newspaper, the *Vaiden Advocate,* that the journal should not be sent to Leflore subscribers. The planters did not specifically outlaw the local branch of the alliance but resolved that "the colored farmer's alliance is being diverted from its original and supposed purpose and is being used by designing and corrupt negroes to further their intentions and selfish motives."[65] The Colored Farmers' Alliance was thus served notice in 1889 that any further attempts to organize Leflore blacks against their deteriorating economic position would be met with white outrage and possible violence.

The Leflore County disturbance placed the question of white supremacy in sharp relief. By the late 1880s Bolivar's W. B. Roberts and other Delta Democrats had grown weary of their complicated treachery. Plantation district sharecroppers might be lured, threatened, or bribed into complicity with the fusion system, but the black-dominated interior was more difficult to subdue and control. Moreover, a growing number of whites were disaffected with the chicanery and fraud endemic to the fusion system and appalled at the intimidation employed to silence defiant black citizens. In Leflore (and perhaps elsewhere), blacks were listening to "outside agitators," abjuring long-established bonds of patronage, and threatening whites with financial ruin. Worse still, backcountry blacks had taken up arms to defend their leaders and property and were overcome only by troops and untold bloodshed. The prospect of a revitalized Republican Party (or fusion-resistant independent movements) loomed large: would Delta whites wait until armed black voters asserted their vast numerical majority and installed officials unsympathetic to planter interests?

In the wake of Leflore, and believing themselves in the twilight of fusion politics, Delta whites joined Democrats from across the state in calling for a constitutional convention to reconsider suffrage. Ironically, white Deltans had long opposed this course and were instrumental in defeating calls for a new constitution only two years earlier. Now the prospect of armed black insurgency and black political control pushed conservatives to abandon their strategy of fusion and fraud.[66] As B. F. Jones wrote to the *Jackson Clarion-Ledger,* "The old men of the present generation can't afford to die and leave their children with shot guns in their hands, a lie in their mouths, and perjury on their souls, in order to defeat the negroes. The constitution can be made so this will not be necessary."[67]

Isaiah T. Montgomery, founder of Bolivar County's all-black community at Mound Bayou, was the sole African American and the only self-described Republican elected to Mississippi's 1890 constitutional convention.[68] The gathering's central purpose was unadvertised but broadly understood: the convention's principal objective was to disfranchise as many black voters as possible. By 1890 many Democrats had become bitterly opposed to relinquishing any offices to ex-slaves under the fusion plan. Other whites expressed horror at the violence that attended truly competitive elections. And a growing number of conservatives were openly perturbed by the accelerating militancy of the state's blacks: Jackson had hosted "the largest colored convention" in Mississippi history one month before the Leflore County upheaval. There, black delegates urged federal intervention in the state's political process to "break up lawlessness and ballot-box stuffing" and "bring about respect for the rights of citizens."[69] The degradation of Mississippi politics vexed members of both races, but the constitutional convention stood as white conservatives' preemptive strike against those who might bring national forces to bear on the franchise and state governance. Mississippi whites were guided partly by their perceptions of a shifting national political climate. In 1889 Republicans gained control of both houses of Congress and held the presidency. White anxieties focused on Henry Cabot Lodge's bill to require federal inspectors at congressional elections (dubbed the "Lodge Force Bill"), legislation that threatened to end the ballot-box tampering described by W. B. Roberts.[70] Before leaving Mound Bayou for the August convention, Montgomery told black supporters that he had little hope that the meeting would improve the state's worsening political climate.[71]

As he journeyed to Jackson, Montgomery must have realized that his fellow delegates would offer little support for his views. Among the 134 delegates at the convention, 130 were Democrats. The Republican Montgomery was set apart with one "National Republican," a self-designated "Conservative," and one supporter of the Greenback movement. Montgomery's potential allies against disfranchisement left much to be desired: all three opposed an equal franchise for blacks.[72]

The constitutional convention posed a sharp dilemma for Montgomery. He might single-handedly condemn the racist foundation of the convention's main mission, hope that his lonesome opposition drew federal attention, and pray that some combination of local shame and outside interference could prevent Mississippi conservatives' from enacting their disfranchising design. Or, he might avoid controversy and attempt to shape the way the disfranchising statutes were conceived and implemented. Without allies, there was no chance his lone voice would drown out the disfranchising chorus. In some fashion the will of white conservatives would surely be enacted into the state's fundamental code. Montgomery had to choose between continuing to fight a battle that was already lost or influencing the peace.[73] Mound Bayou's founder chose the latter course.

Although Montgomery conceded to the disfranchising legislation, he did so with a challenge to white delegates: apply the new constitution's voting requirements equally to both races, he demanded. This son of Joseph Davis's plantation manager publicly agreed with conservative delegates that race relations had generally worsened since emancipation. But he disputed the inevitability of political hostility and denied that blacks were solely responsible for the widening rift. Whites must acknowledge their debt to the once-enslaved blacks, men and women whose toil had created Mississippi's plantations, places where "every acre represents a grave and every furrow a tear." Freedmen, he conceded, did not always act wisely in politics, but whites must share much of the blame, for "you have suffered your prejudice to set bounds and limits to our progress." Although he supported the convention's professed goals of ending the "bloodshed, bribery, ballot-box stuffing, corruption, and perjury" that stained Mississippi politics, Montgomery wondered if white lawmakers were capable of fair administration. The state's black citizens, he counseled, "lack confidence in your professions of good will." Yet he would cast his vote in favor of the document despite these criticisms.

Montgomery saw his qualified support for the disfranchising constitution as a last-ditch effort to rescue the state's race relations. He voted to strip the franchise from many of his race in order to "bridge a chasm that has been widening and deepening for a generation—to divert a maelstrom that threatens destruction to you and yours, while it promises no enduring prosperity to me and mine," he told whites at the convention. Acknowledging estimates that two-thirds of black voters might be disfranchised by the provisions under consideration, Montgomery termed this loss a "fearful sacrifice laid upon the burning altar of liberty." It was a sacrifice offered to "restore confidence, the great missing link between the races; to restore honesty and purity to the ballot box and to confer the boon of political liberty upon the Commonwealth of Mississippi." The value of blacks' sacrifice, however, depended on whites' implementation of the new constitution. Unless whites resolved to approach racial disputes "upon the enduring basis of Truth, Justice and Equality," Montgomery feared that the concession of black suffrage would be for naught.[74]

For most Mississippi whites, Montgomery's complicit vote spoke louder than his critical words. They pointed to his approval of the disfranchising clauses as proof of blacks' willingness to be rendered politically mute but ignored his plea for "Truth, Justice and Equality." Conservatives enacted a host of provisions sure to restrict black citizens' ability to register to vote, carefully avoiding specific mention of race as a qualification for suffrage. Like the convention that designed it, the 1890 constitution was a hypocritical exercise proclaiming itself color-blind and nonpartisan while enacting laws that increased the political advantages of white Democrats. Although the document did not specifically forbid blacks to vote, the suffrage requirements crafted by conservative delegates smoothed whites' path to the ballot box while confronting the prospective black voter with obstruction and misdirection.

Conservatives expected the constitution's literacy test and understanding clause to do the yeoman's work of disfranchisement. In a state where educating black slaves had been illegal just twenty-five years before, delegates knew that many black adults still could not read or write, and they consequently demanded literacy as a requirement for suffrage. Many Mississippi whites were similarly uneducated, though, and disfranchising poor whites and freedmen might give impetus to a political uprising based on class grievances. Independent political movements might thus become the beneficiary, not the victim, of the conservatives' work. So a loophole was devised for white registrants: if they could not read, candidates for the franchise could gain suffrage by proving they understood a section of the state constitution when it was read to them. White registrars, the delegates expected, would do their part to uphold white supremacy by favoring white candidates and excluding blacks. A correspondent to the *Jackson Clarion-Ledger* revealed conservatives' thinking when he wrote, "If every negro in Mississippi was a graduate of Harvard, and had been elected class orator . . . he would not be as well fitted to exercise the right of suffrage as the Anglo-Saxon farm laborer . . . whose cross 'X' mark, like the broad arrow of Locksley, means force and intellect, and manhood—*virtus*."[75] Although the literacy test and understanding clause did not openly discriminate against blacks, drafters expected that blacks' unique disadvantages—slavery's legacy of illiteracy and the racism of white registrars—would combine to end the problem of black voting.

Delta blacks were rapidly gaining literacy despite slim funding for their segregated schools; threats of disfranchisement intensified educational efforts for adults and older adolescents. Before the constitutional convention concluded its session, the *Jackson Clarion-Ledger* warned the disfranchisers that "night schools for negro men have already been established in the Delta." After the convention Isaiah T. Montgomery returned to Bolivar County to aid the adult education effort, determined to limit blacks' "sacrifice" of voters to the fewest possible number. Black candidates for registration in the Mound Bayou area could find help in the town's established schools, but Montgomery feared that other areas of the county, especially near the towns where most whites lived, would be less amenable to furthering black literacy. He was especially eager to establish a black school at Cleveland, a booming railroad town and future seat of the county's government. When Cleveland whites balked at the idea, Montgomery secured white support from outside the county. Among those advocating Montgomery's plan for black schools were the white editors of Greenville and Greenwood newspapers. James K. Vardaman, editor of the *Greenwood Enterprise,* reprinted a *Greenville Times* editorial supporting Montgomery's efforts, reminding readers that "the stand which this man has taken for the improvement and elevation of the negro . . . entitle[s] him to the hearty encouragement and material support of the white citizens and property owners of the Delta."[76] Some Delta whites seemed moved to magnanimity by Montgomery's sacrifice of black voters' equal suffrage.

Like white conservatives, many of Montgomery's black contemporaries (and subsequent scholars) listened to his vote, not his voice. Despite a professed hope that voting in favor of the 1890 constitution would bring "Truth, Justice and Equality," Montgomery's actions at the convention have not been judged favorably. For black politician John R. Lynch, any vote in favor of the disfranchising provisions was incompatible with Montgomery's "reputation of being honest and honorable" and would remain "an inexplicable mystery." J. Saunders Redding was less charitable, accusing Montgomery of selling his vote to prevent "the white man's intrusion upon his private domain" at Mound Bayou. Still, Montgomery's willingness to challenge Cleveland whites over black education suggests that his interests extended beyond his "private domain."[77]

No fairly administered literacy test would give whites an electoral majority in the Delta. Indeed, an honestly construed voter registration plan granting suffrage to literate males of at least twenty-one years of age probably would have resulted in a large majority of black voters. In 1900, the first year for which dependable literacy figures are available, more than half of the region's black males over twenty-one could read and write. An estimated 13,455 voting-age black males could prove literacy while the Delta housed only 3,474 literate white males over twenty years of age. In the Delta, where blacks comprised over 87 percent of the population by the turn of the century, more than a literacy test was required to return politics to white control.[78]

Mayre Dabney, who had served as a delegate to the 1890 constitutional convention, toured the Delta's courthouses in 1896 to determine whether the literacy test had rendered its expected service in disfranchising black voters. He was surprised, however, to find the clause seldom employed. One registrar told the inquisitive conservative that he had refused suffrage to only one man on account of the literacy provision, and others claimed to have never denied the franchise to an applicant on those grounds.[79] It seems Delta Democrats were able to regain political control without resorting to the literacy test.

There was no shortage of clauses restricting the franchise, however, and other restrictions trapped black applicants who easily navigated the literacy test. The poll-tax requirement proved especially detrimental to potential black voters in the Delta. The annual $2 poll tax was not a significant sum, but the stipulation that the amount be paid in cash well in advance of elections and the receipts be shown registrars eliminated unwary voters. Prospective voters who could not prove they had paid all of their taxes (poll, land, levee, etc.) were denied ballots as a provision of the 1890 constitution. In the frontier Delta, where the focus of black settlement lay many miles inland from the riverside courthouses, this seemingly inconsequential provision erected formidable barriers to black voting. Mayre Dabney found only 338 registered black voters in Washington County in 1896; an additional 8,834 blacks were delinquent in their poll-tax payments and thus ineligible to vote. In that same year 1,280 white citizens of Washington County held the franchise. The new constitution's requirement that a voter be able to prove residence in the state for the two previous years and in his current election precinct for at least one year was another standard that proved difficult for some black Deltans to meet. Farmers new to the area might spend years moving from field to field, searching for the best acreage, landlord, and farm purchase arrangement. Moreover, the backcountry's lack of well-defined governmental boundaries made it easy for unscrupulous registrars to claim that a candidate for suffrage had lived outside his election precinct the previous year and deny him the franchise. The constitution's authors added insult to injury in their designation of voting registrars. Local court officials were no longer empowered to register county voters; under the 1890 constitution all of the registrars were to be appointed from the state capital. The white Democrats who controlled the constitutional convention and state government were determined that their handpicked surrogates would shape the electorate, and the black justices of the peace of the Delta backcountry could no longer safeguard the voting lists.[80] Although all of these provisions were aimed broadly at Mississippi's black populace, their cumulative effect proved especially troublesome to the majority of would-be Delta voters.

Even after finding a sympathetic registrar and proving literacy, payment of taxes, and term of residence, a prospective black voter might still be denied suffrage under the multilayered provisions of the 1890 constitution. In searching for ways to disfranchise the maximum number of blacks, the constitution's drafters focused on a variety of petty offenses that the freedmen might have once committed; conviction on any of these counts forever disqualified a citizen from voting. Anyone ever convicted of bigamy, for example, could never register under the 1890 constitution. Few whites would be affected by this clause, but many blacks—who, as slaves, were forbidden to marry and were subject to transfer from plantation to plantation—had spent the latter 1860s sorting out their tangled conjugal affiliations, and some had been convicted of bigamy.[81] One could also be disqualified from voting if convicted of petty theft, an offense many hungry ex-slaves were driven to commit in the lean years after emancipation. By contrast, grand larceny was forgiven of prospective voters. Thus, a black man who once filched a pig or chicken could never vote, while whites discovered embezzling thousands of dollars continued unmolested in their franchise. Without ever mentioning race or color, the conservative disfranchisers concocted a document strongly detrimental to black rights. While some delegates hid behind the constitution's supposedly neutral language, claiming that there was "not a word in the constitution of 1890 which discriminates against the colored people," other framers were more blunt. "In Mississippi we have in our constitution legislated against the racial peculiarities of the Negro," one Democrat admitted. "When that device fails, we will resort to something else."[82] Such were the props of white supremacy by the 1890s.

Not surprisingly, whites dominated the Delta electorate by 1892. Although more than 80 percent of the region's inhabitants were black, in that year over two-thirds of the eligible voters were white. Only 1,358 blacks were registered to vote in that year, less than 6 percent of the Delta's estimated 23,478 literate black males over age twenty. By contrast, the 3,075 whites registered to vote in the Delta represented 85 percent of literate white males age twenty-one and older.[83] The disfranchising clauses of the 1890 constitution had been employed with great success by Delta Democrats.

Despite the thoroughness of the laws, the purge of blacks from the voting rolls proceeded unevenly. In Quitman County, for example, blacks still comprised a majority of the voters, outnumbering registered whites 142 to 124 (graph 7). And figures for Bolivar County suggest that Montgomery's public "sacrifice" of the black franchise won his neighbors some respite. Although Bolivar whites held the majority, their margin was only 13 out of 759 voters: they had to continue to pursue fusion tickets, scare black voters from the polls, or risk challenges to Democratic candidates. In fact, the fusion system continued in Bolivar and Sharkey Counties well into the 1890s, with black representatives elected to the state legislature in 1892 and 1894. In Leflore County, where black agrarians had purchased Winchester rifles from Oliver Cromwell just three years earlier, Democrats were much more thorough in guaranteeing white control. The franchise was limited to only 28 black men there, while 462 whites registered to vote. Washington County, where so many black farmers bought land along Deer Creek, was similarly repressive of black suffrage. Slightly more than 13 percent of Washington's 985 voters were black, too few to threaten the local Democratic machine.[84]

Graph 7. Delta voters, 1892

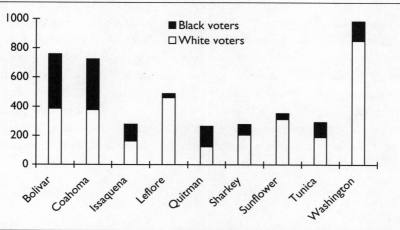

Source: James H. Stone, "A Note on Voter Registration under the Mississippi Understanding Clause, 1892," *Journal of Southern History* 38 (1972): 293–96.

White Democrats were clearly in control of Delta politics at the decade's end, despite local discrepancies in disfranchising zeal. Even the determined black voters of Bolivar were quelled by 1899, when the county's white Democrats no longer pursued fusion agreements with Montgomery and other local black leaders.[85] The days of compromise and biracial coalitions were over; the Democrats had finally grasped control, and they were jealous of their long-delayed ascendancy. By the turn of the century, the black vote was merely a curiosity in the Delta, the relic of a vanished age.

During the agricultural depression of the late 1880s and 1890s, the Delta's black farmers saw their prospects for political and financial independence melt away. Whether they believed their right to vote had been "sacrificed" on the altar of public virtue as Isaiah Montgomery claimed or stolen by scheming Democrats, black Deltans' franchise was lost for decades. Black economic opportunity was similarly imperiled as white merchants and planters, their profits sagging along with cotton's slump, resorted to increasingly acquisitive business practices. The sale of merchandise became a way to trap patrons in debt, loans and credit were shaped into tools for separating struggling farmers from their meager possessions, and sharecropping and tenancy came to look more like dread sentences than starting points toward land ownership.

In some ways, the 1889 events in Leflore County were prophetic: black farmers threatening the supremacy of the Democratic Party or the incomes of white merchants and lenders henceforth did so at their own peril. Delta storekeepers and other creditors, made frantic by the falling price of cotton and prospects of bankruptcy, now grasped for profits with fresh avarice. Planters no longer perceived a dire shortage of labor. Landowners came to prefer timber leases with lumber companies, not free-use contracts with renters, as a means to clear backcountry land. Delta whites lost interest in attracting ambitious black migrants to their fields and forests. Instead, they grew anxious for economic and political control. In their panic they squandered the region's reputation as a promised land of the New South. The lesson of Leflore was unmistakable by the end of the century: black opposition to the region's growing imbalance of power would bring swift white reaction. As the price of their independence, blacks might be forced to sacrifice their political voice, their property, or their lives.

7

The Plantation Empire

Holt Collier never doubted the practical purposes of violence. He had come to the Delta as a slave and quickly appreciated the wildness of the land and its inhabitants. He remained there long after emancipation, and though he saw cotton bloom and mules trod where oak and panther once reigned supreme, Collier understood that civilization was as slow to grace the wilderness as equality was slow to replace slavery. Call it "Southern honor," "frontier excess," or any other name that connotes prickly, well-armed assertiveness, the Delta accepted a strikingly high level of violence in the last third of the nineteenth century.[1] It was no haven for a man who could not, or would not, defend his reputation against slurs or encroachments, and it was a dangerous place for slander.

An ill-advised defamation made Holt Collier a legend in the region. Shortly after the Civil War, an officer in the Union army publicly disparaged Collier's former owner, Colonel Thomas Hinds. The colonel replied by knocking the slanderer flat to the ground. The Yankee arose with a knife clutched in his hand, but bystanders restrained him. Later told of the northerner's behavior, Collier declared, "If I had been here I would have killed him." When the outlander was found shot to death, suspicion focused on Collier, for his malevolent remark had been widely circulated. Collier was tried, defended by planter W. A. Percy, and exonerated of the crime, even though most contemporaries believed the ex-slave killed the Union officer to revenge the slight against his former master.[2]

Acts of violence did not cease with the departure of Federal troops or the end of Reconstruction. Weapons, not courts, remained the preferred means for settling disputes, redeeming soiled honor, and achieving economic and political advantage. Delta whites and blacks shot, stabbed, hanged, gouged, and beat each other throughout the late nineteenth and early twentieth centuries. Along with Holt Collier, they lived and died by a rough creed.[3]

In the first postbellum decades, violence often arose among whites in response to perceived insults to their sense of honor and other inflated grievances. Such was the case in the dispute of E. T. Bradshaw and Eugene Gordon. One Sunday night in 1874, while the two white men were talking in Floreyville (a Bolivar County settlement along the Mississippi), they fell into disagreement. A witness reported that "they had some words," and "Bradshaw, who is of a bold and unsuspicious disposition, supposing the affair terminated, paid no further heed to the matter." He had no chance to leave the scene, however, for "Gordon up and stabbed him, the knife entering the left side about four inches from the heart, creating a very dangerous and . . . fatal wound." Although the victim Bradshaw was a "gentleman well and most favorably known in the county," his murderer evaded capture for the crime. Indeed, violent resolution of personal disagreements was so widely accepted in the area that a local magistrate, the town constable, and a prominent doctor all abetted Gordon's escape from prosecution.[4] Gordon's mortal reaction to "some words" was deemed, if not routine, at least acceptable.

Bolivar County was not the only home to white Deltans determined to defend their honor at any cost. William Stone and T. L. Brown had competed for a city lot in Greenville, which the latter successfully purchased for an addition to his hardware store. But the friction did not end with Brown's purchase. Stone was sensitive after not gaining the valuable property and provoked an argument with Brown at his store. Although Brown had won the property, he was unwilling to endure Stone's abuse of his business practices and soon returned insult with insult. Now doubly aggrieved, "Stone said to Mr. Brown that he was acting in an ungentlemanly manner toward him; upon which Mr. Brown, taking up a small iron bar, advanced upon him." Stone then drew his pistol and shot the merchant.[5]

Violence was widespread, not a tactic limited to the Delta's "young gentlemen" and merchants. Consider the confrontation of two white tenant farmers near Lake Washington in the plantation district. According to the local newspaper, "Two white men farming on the place, named Morrow and White, near neighbors, had a trivial difficulty on Monday evening. The next morning as White was passing Morrow's house on his way to the field, he was shot and instantly killed by Morrow, who fired from the window of his house."[6]

Nor were the upper and lower ranks alone in seeking violent resolution of grievances: the region's white yeomen farmers also fell to bloody conflict over insults and bad manners. W. H. Beller and D. N. Cress both farmed near the Issaquena-Washington County line but could not coexist peacefully. As the *Greenville Times* reported, they "had some difficulty and threats passed, but no actual violence had occurred." Then Cress's long-festering grievances moved him to action: he hid in the woods near a trail oft-traveled by his rival, and as Beller rode near, Cress fired on him from the forest. Beller was killed, and Cress made his escape.[7]

Thus, honor and a postwar culture accepting harsh reprisals frequently spurred white Deltans into violent acts. Planters, merchants, small farmers, and tenants were all eager to revenge insult with force, and the region was bloodier for their efforts. Whether resolved in face-to-face combat or from ambush, the disagreements of white Delta residents too frequently devolved into mortal confrontations. Yet, in the late nineteenth century, the standards of law and the exertions of lawmen were beginning to intrude on individuals' pursuit of personal justice. Although the mortal code of honor still guided many settlers in their actions (and reactions), it was becoming more difficult to escape prosecution by pleading affronted honor. A magistrate, constable, and prominent Bolivar County doctor might aid an honor-bound killer in escaping jail, but they would be held accountable for sanctioning the murderer's flight. Similarly, the ambusher Cress felt required to flee Washington County after his deadly deed, and William Stone was prosecuted for shooting hardware merchant T. L. Brown.[8] The shift from personal, honor-driven settlements to reliance on courts was slow in the Delta, but even in this frontier of the New South, whites resorted less to vengeance as the century came to a close.[9]

Hence, the 1897 Avon shootout was deemed remarkable by local observers and newspaper readers. Will Able and Paul James were both "well known and highly esteemed in Avon" and were identified by the *Greenville Times* as descendants of the region's early settlers. Although they were also first cousins, kinship and respectability did not prevent rivalry.[10] The friction between the two cousins centered on a third relative, Paul James's sixteen-year-old niece Jimmie Blanche Wright, who lived with James and his mother. The forty-year-old Will Able had prevailed upon the young woman to elope with him, and the two were married without notifying their kin. Paul James took great umbrage at these developments: the girl had been taken from his home without warning by a man many years her senior. Kinship did not excuse the slight, James maintained, nor did the fact that most Delta wives were much younger than their husbands.[11] To explain his pique, the *Greenville Times* noted that the young niece was living with "a young unmarried man" and his mother. James's widely proclaimed embarrassment at the elopement, some believed, was a poor attempt to disguise his sexual jealousy and anger at the man who had won the girl's hand in marriage. He confronted his newly wedded cousin the next day in Avon's compact commercial district.

The encounter began without visible rancor. Bystanders reported that after discussing the matter, the cousins "apparently came to an amicable understanding." They parted, and James walked away. But James's display of amity seems to have been contrived to lull his rival into lowering his guard, for the jealous younger cousin suddenly turned, drew his pistol, and began shooting at Able. "Able immediately returned the fire and the two men deliberately stood and continued the fusillade, although both were mortally wounded, until they each fell dying on the ground." The "dispute was settled," and James's jealousy or dishonor revenged, but both combatants were killed in the process, and the object of their rivalry was left a widow. Such frays, once common in the region's frontier days, had grown rarer by the end of the century; in fact, this eruption was so unusual that a local newspaper dubbed the occurrence "the most remarkable exhibition of courage and nerve ever before witnessed." Humiliation and sexual jealousy had not vanished from the Delta, but whites rarely exorcised these demons with pistols by 1897.

Delta freedmen had also shown themselves prone to violence in disputes over women. In early August 1875 wage laborer Bill Cargil employed a shotgun loaded with buckshot to slay Sam Grass, another laborer. Both coveted the same woman, and Cargil was willing to kill to keep her. The same summer a tenant disappeared from the Robb plantation in southwest Washington County. The man's remains were discovered in November of that year, and his murderer confessed to the crime. Sexual jealousy had prompted this violence as well. In the frontier Delta, as throughout the South, black men were loath to bow to any slight to their sense of honor, especially when it involved the loss of their companion's affections. Rather than seek redress in the law, they used violence to prevent or avenge wrongs. As historian Edward L. Ayers has determined, "Just as the antebellum Southern aristocracy believed itself to be above the law and thus adjudicated conflicts by using the means of honor, so did postwar black Southerners know themselves to be *outside* the law."[12]

Black males' sense of their honor and household prerogatives sometimes led to the abuse of family members.[13] The *Greenville Times* detailed one such case of abuse in mid-1875. A black tenant farmer returned home after dark and discovered his female companion missing; he eventually found her in a neighbor's cabin. Before witnesses, he demanded she go home and cook his supper. When she refused, he threatened to whip her, as he had done the night before. The threat failed to move her, however, and the man stalked back to his house alone. He soon returned armed with a pistol. Placing the gun against her head, he declared, "So you won't go home and cook my supper." She did not move, and he shot her in the head while she held their infant child in her arms. His neighbors did not challenge the man's right to order, whip, or verbally abuse his woman, nor did anyone move to prevent her murder. After the act, the armed murderer escaped from the plantation.[14]

In the Delta, as in much of the vanquished Confederacy, most black violence was aimed at other blacks, and whites usually attacked those of their own race. Ayers has found that "violence in the postbellum South, as in the antebellum South, usually developed among social equals," and this was largely true of northwest Mississippi.[15] When Delta whites and blacks did clash, factors other than honor were usually to blame.

Most white-black confrontations emanated from economic disputes. In many cases during the 1860s and 1870s, former slaveholders acted as if freedmen were still their property to use and abuse. If freedmen complained or opposed this treatment, some whites relented, but others—especially planters along the Mississippi River—redoubled their assault. Thus, when Coahoma County planter and former slave trader Nathan Bedford Forrest had a "personal difficulty" with a laborer on his Green Grove plantation in 1866, the ex-Confederate general killed the disputant. The incident enraged nearby blacks, who surrounded the Forrest home and built huge bonfires to guarantee that the murderer did not slip away at night. Forrest was arrested by the county sheriff and required to post $10,000 bail to regain his freedom. Forrest, who later helped found the Ku Klux Klan, was acquitted of the murder charge; the sympathetic white judge framed the jury's charge so narrowly that they had little option but to credit the ex-general's plea of self-defense.[16]

Over time, riverside planters were dissuaded from much of their accustomed brutality. Freedmen's Bureau inquiries and the negative reputation that followed, prosecution by freedmen, and blacks' unwillingness to work for planters with confirmed records of abuse all encouraged more circumspect behavior from white landowners. Some ex-slaves explored harsher measures. In at least one instance, freedmen conspired to murder a riverside employer they deemed cruel.[17] Even in the backcountry, where planters struggled to attract settlers to their half-wild acreage, whites abused and sometimes killed freedmen.

John Penrice loaned a horse to a black backcountry farmer named Sam. The animal later died while in the freedman's possession. Penrice demanded compensation, but Sam could not or would not pay for the dead horse. Their disagreement erupted one afternoon when both happened into a Deer Creek general store at the same time. They fell to quarreling — the local paper described their debate as "abusive" — and the black farmer picked up his gun and left the store. Penrice then grabbed another man's gun and fired at Sam from behind, killing the freedman. Penrice was arrested and tried for the murder. Penrice's trial was remarkable, for at least five of Greenville's most prominent lawyers from three legal firms cooperated in his defense. Their efforts were worth the cost to their client, however, for the judge freed Penrice. The magistrate was "satisfied by the testimony that the killing was accidental."[18] Thus, even during the years of blacks' greatest economic opportunity — when white landowners were most concerned for the region's reputation among freedmen — violence could go unpunished, and the collaboration of white elites might contribute to the miscarriage of justice.

White planters were not alone in the use of violence against economic subordinates, however. Six months after the Penrice decision, another example of planter extremism was evinced in nearby Issaquena County: this time the planter was a black man. Jerry Myers, an African American, apparently used sharecroppers on his riverside property in northern Issaquena County. One of these sharecroppers was Brutus Johnson, and in July the two men began arguing over Johnson's crop. The precise point of their dispute is unclear, but Myers seems to have judged Johnson derelict in hoeing the weeds from between his cotton plants. Much like Nathan Bedford Forrest, the black planter would not tolerate contradiction. Jerry Myers grew enraged, drew a gun, and shot Brutus Johnson dead.[19] In this case the two African Americans' class differences proved more important than their common race.

Backcountry blacks sometimes took advantage of their numerical majority and the distance from white lawmen, carrying out attacks against isolated whites. Such was the case along Washington County's Deer Creek in 1878. The white clerk at Spingarn's store was aroused by a loud knocking at the establishment's door one Saturday about midnight. As he opened the door, "a gang of negroes rushed in, seized the clerk, and while some of the crowd held him and choked him, others loaded a wagon at the door with flour, meat, sugar, coffee, etc. And the party drove off with the spoil, after coolly informing the terrified clerk that they would pay him another visit as soon as he replenished his stock."[20] Spingarn's store was not the first backcountry store plundered by black gangs. Leflore County merchant B. Lowenstein was murdered when several blacks robbed his establishment in 1873. That same year several whites living in a Sharkey County store were killed when the building was looted and set afire by a band of blacks.[21]

Despite the rash of robberies and murders in the 1870s, backcountry whites lived in greater dread of fires set by disgruntled employees or former tenants. Planters blamed numerous blazes on black arsonists in the first decades after emancipation. After the building that housed his steam-powered cotton gin and sawmill burned to the ground (destroying machinery and seventeen bales of cotton), a Bolivar County planter loudly proclaimed the conflagration the work of arsonists. A Washington County planter reached the same conclusion after his cotton ginhouse and a building used to store unginned lint both burned down on two separate occasions.[22]

In addition to honor-based violence and economically motivated abuse, political contests contributed to the high level of personal violence in the region after the Civil War. This was the case in the beating of Bohlen Lucas. The former slave driver joined with white conservatives to put forth a fusion ticket to "redeem" county offices from the Republican Party in 1875. Lucas was an enthusiastic supporter, even joining the ticket to run for the office of Washington County treasurer. Returning from the polls, whence he had escorted his tenants to guarantee they voted properly, Lucas was set upon by unknown assailants, probably freedmen who would not tolerate his working against the party of Lincoln and helping to return secessionists to control of local government.[23]

A similar case of politically motivated violence erupted the next year. Greenville whites were tense in the weeks approaching the 1876 presidential election. Rumors that carpetbaggers and their local black allies had tried to burn down the town contributed to the jitters of its conservative inhabitants. A white Democrat, C. A. Platt, had already survived one attempted assassination by political foes when a second attack occurred. The town's Democratic paper reported that a female boarder in Platt's home was standing near her window "when a [gunpowder] cap popped and some one ran off. The miscreant evidently mistook her for Mr. Platt." Platt and a friend were just returning to the house and saw a man running through the backyard. "The gentlemen emptied their revolvers at the flying villain, but did not succeed in arresting him."[24] Politics was serious business provoking intense passions and, not infrequently, bloodshed.

Although Delta violence found blacks more sinned against than sinning, both races indulged in injurious acts between the end of the Civil War and the late 1880s. The region's attractiveness to southerners of both races assured the continuing acceptance of their notions of honorable behavior and the resulting possibility of bloodshed. The frontier character of the place—specifically, its paucity of peace officers and lack of institutions to discourage and punish wrongful behavior—also invited tempestuous acts. The late war and emancipation, moreover, encouraged bad feelings between blacks and whites and gave justification to brigands who would prey upon those of another race. All of these factors combined to foster an atmosphere of violent impermanence in the first decades after 1865, particularly near the waterways of the region.

In an unusual example of self-criticism, an 1874 issue of the *Greenville Times* reflected that "all the worst vices of society in the South and the Far West seemed combined and concentrated in the society of the Mississippi cotton ports." The crux of the problem lay in the fact that "besides the few merchants, the white population of such a town is largely made up of gamblers, river roughs, and desperadoes of various kinds, fellows who go about bristling with pistols and bowie knives which they are never slow to use." The situation in the towns and riverboat landings was exacerbated, the *Times* editor declared, by the fact that most of the freedmen who gravitated to the urban spots did so because they disdained agricultural work: "The colored population contains the very scum of the plantations, poor darkies who earn a little money now and then on the river steamers and spend it for drinks." The journalist concluded that "of course there are decent whites and decent blacks, but in every one of these towns there is a preponderating element of rowdyism that is easily stirred up to violence."[25]

The character of "rowdyism" changed as the century progressed, but the problem did not abate. Although the level of individual violence—motivated by honor, economic advantage, or political chicanery—declined steadily through the late 1870s and 1880s, mob violence grew in incidence and severity. By the 1890s Delta mob activity was synonymous with lynching. But it was only after the turn of the century that lynching invariably asserted white supremacy.

Lynching was frowned upon in the region well into the 1870s. Whites, the usual instigators of this community-sanctioned murder in the South, had a variety of reasons to oppose lynching in the Delta. Some paternalists no doubt felt they could accomplish more by suasion and veiled threats than by outright intimidation. Labor-hungry landlords, moreover, were reluctant to frighten off potential workers or tenants with vigilantism. Finally, there was the issue of who would lynch whom: in a society where "desperadoes" went about "bristling with pistols and bowie knives which they are never slow to use," who would bother knotting a rope? Pistol shots cracked in the streets, and rivals were gunned down in their fields; although the community gave mute acquiescence to this bloodshed, lynch mobs were seldom convened.

Greenville seemed a likely spot for a lynching in October 1875. One month before the local elections in which conservatives hoped to overthrow Reconstruction, two white men, both well-respected planters whose families boasted long residence in the region, were found "foully murdered" between Greenville and Deer Creek. A black man was arrested and charged with the slayings, and two prominent Republicans were appointed to his defense. One of the leaders of Mississippi's festering Redemption, W. A. Percy, then volunteered his services to the prosecution. The lines of racial and political conflict intersected at the prisoner's jail cell, and the town braced itself for upheaval.[26]

Indeed, a company of armed horsemen soon appeared in the streets of Greenville. They were the friends and neighbors of the slain planters and included members of both races. After the accused was remanded to jail to await trial, "the armed crowd began to fall in, silently, steadily, but with an air of determination which told the lookers-on that the prisoner's life hung upon a word." The Delta had seldom indulged in lynching, but this occasion seemed as liable as any to warrant a summary execution. Then three prominent conservatives, including prosecutor Percy, stepped forward into the throng. Imploring the mob to desist and disband, the trio of Confederate veterans insisted that the accused be left to the law, not slain for a crime he might not have committed. Perhaps the three conservatives stressed the stain that a lynching would bring to the county's reputation among immigrants, perhaps Percy shared the strength of the prosecution's case against the accused and predicted certain conviction, or perhaps they emphasized a much-needed commitment to justice in the rough-and-tumble river town. Their arguments against the lynching have been lost, but their efforts were successful. The mob, "shocked and outraged as they were by the brutal murder of their friends, with magnanimity almost unparalleled, gave the trembling wretch they had come to slay the benefit of the doubt of his guilt and left him in the hands of the law."[27]

Not all such incidents were as judiciously resolved, even in the 1870s. In Johnsonville, then the seat of nearby Sunflower County, a mob met little resistance to its vigilantism. A black man had been murdered "under circumstances of unusual brutality," shocking even the violence-hardened settlers of the backcountry. Worse, the murderer—a white man—"openly boasted of the deed." Such behavior could not be countenanced. A lynch mob coalesced, took the murderer from his cell, and hanged him. "Public sentiment," a Delta newspaper emphasized, "excuses the lynching."[28]

The lynching of white men was not uncommon in the Delta's frontier era. Indeed, Delta whites were at greater risk from lynching than were blacks through 1901. Although whites comprised only 12.3 percent of the region's population in this period, they accounted for 16.6 percent of the area's lynching victims. Whites were thus lynched at a rate 35.5 percent above their proportion of the Delta's inhabitants. Blacks, on the other hand, were lynched at a rate below their share of the population.[29] This was extremely unusual in the postbellum South, where blacks were lynched by a ratio of more than 8:1 when compared to whites.[30] Most of the black victims in Delta lynchings were blamed for crimes against persons (table 2). Murder and attempted murder were cited in more than half the lynchings, and rape was held to justify another 15 percent of the executions. Delta whites, by contrast, were most often accused of crimes against property; 42 percent, it was claimed, had committed theft. The next-largest group of white lynching victims, comprising 29 percent, were accused of murder.[31]

Lynching followed a clear seasonal pattern in the Delta, for the colder months were also the deadliest. Blacks faced particular risk from early autumn until spring: 70 percent of the black lynchings fell in the seven months (58 percent of the year) from September through March. This suggests that lynching activity corresponded to rhythms in the crop cycle (table 3). From September through December, the cotton was picked, debts were revealed, and profits (or losses) realized. The following period, from January through March, saw tenants without field work and frequently relocating to negotiate better farming

Table 2. Alleged crimes of Delta lynching victims, 1889–1918 (in %)

	Murder and attempted murder	Race roit and race prejudice	Rape	Assualt	Arson	Theft	Unknown and others
Whites (*N*=7)	29					42	29
Blacks (*N*=88)	58	8	15	3	6	4	6

Source: NAACP, *Thirty Years of Lynching in the United States, 1889–1918* (New York, 1919).

contracts. These months were tense, for as the price of cotton fell throughout the 1880s and 1890s, landlords and tenants placed extra stress on the contracts they negotiated. Whether concluding old contracts or discussing new arrangements, they frequently came into conflict in these months and sometimes fell to blows.[32] These were also the months in which murder was most frequently cited as the cause for a lynching (graph 8).

The introduction of thousands of blacks from outside the Delta heightened stress between January and March. Black woodsmen flocked to the region from the Midwest during the winter when cold temperatures kept termites and other wood-boring insects dormant and the best timber could be gathered.[33] These transient sawyers lived in tented camps and roamed the backcountry and remaining forests near the plantation districts. At the same time the riverside attracted hundreds and sometimes thousands of levee laborers. Each winter the

Table 3. Seasonal pattern of black lynchings, 1889–1918

	Murder and attempted murder	Race roit and race prejudice	Rape	Assualt	Arson	Theft	Unknown and others
September	7				2		1
October	6		3	1		3	
November	2						
December	6		1				
January	5		2	1	2		1
February	8					1	
March	6	3	1				
April	2						1
May			2				
June	2	3	3	1			
July	6		1				1
August	1	1			1		1

Source: NAACP, *Thirty Years of Lynching in the United States, 1889–1918* (New York, 1919).

Graph 8. Blacks lynched for murder, 1889–1918

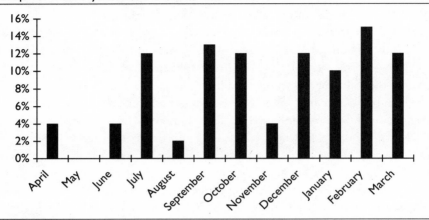

Source: NAACP, *Thirty Years of Lynching in the United States, 1889–1918* (New York, 1919).

region braced itself for the spring floods, and levee contractors arrived with great camps of workers. In March and April these laborers would be occupied around the clock firming up the levees and adding sandbags against rising water, but in January and February the men had opportunity to come and go from the camps. Like the sawyers, most of the these workers were black males in their late twenties; unlike the woodsmen, however, the levee workers were true outlanders. Nearly two-thirds of those laboring on the levees were from outside Mississippi (table 4). This concentrated influx of newcomers was reflected in the victims of lynching, for nearly one-quarter of the men lynched between 1889 and 1918 could not be identified by name, and the great majority

Table 4. Levee and sawmill workers, Coahoma County, 1900 (in %)

	Black	White	Male	Female	Literate	Mississippi-born	Average Age
Sawmill laborers (N=51)	82	18	96	4	66	63	27
Levee laborers (N=265)	97	3	98	2	44	37	28

Source: Twelfth Census, Population MS for Coahoma County, Miss.

of these victims were killed in the winter months. Of the Delta's unidentified black lynching victims, 85 percent died between October and March.[34]

There is no single explanation for the Delta's late nineteenth-century lynching patterns.[35] Indeed, a variety of factors—some broadly shared among the cotton-producing sections of the South, others peculiar to the Delta—influenced violent mob reprisals. One may, however, isolate a few leading themes. Strained landlord-tenant relationships, disputes between creditors and debtors, and the arrival of thousands of unknown sawyers and levee workers combined to make the months between the gathering of the cotton crop and the spring floods the most likely time for mob violence. Individual conflicts within these tension-filled contexts summoned up bloody passions and brought forth lamentable results. It would, for example, be simplistic and incorrect to regard the lynchings of the late nineteenth century either as clear manifestations of white supremacy or as explosions of mindless racism, for whites then faced a greater risk of lynching than did blacks. Although always deplorable, lynchings were neither so numerous nor so hegemonic that they impeded the region's late nineteenth-century reputation as a land of opportunity for black farmers.

But the tenor and implications of Delta lynchings began to shift. Lynching became a more ominous threat, for its frequency increased markedly at the turn of the century.[36] Between 1889 and 1899 the Delta witnessed an average of 2.27 lynchings each year. From 1901 (when eleven men were lynched in the region) through 1908, the average more than doubled.[37] But not everyone was at equal risk after the turn of the century. Although whites had been lynched at a disproportionately higher rate from 1889 through 1901, not one white was lynched after the latter year. Befitting the end of the Delta's frontier era, the last whites lynched were accused of cattle rustling.[38] After 1901, lynch mobs made blacks their sole targets. In the twentieth century Delta vigilantism finally became predictably joined to white supremacy.[39]

Just as lynching was becoming a method of white control over the Delta, opportunities for blacks to purchase farms declined precipitously. The wholesale value of cotton jumped sharply upward in 1900, with lint demanding a price 31 percent higher than in the previous year. Planters, speculators, and merchants sensed a coming cotton boom and focused their attentions on control of land. Less fertile fields were pressed into cultivation, and farmers hurried to clear wooded tracts. The proprietors of one plantation in northeastern Washington County, for example, increased their cultivable acreage by 29 percent between the 1900 and 1901 plantings. The price of land rose dramatically amid this search for extra fields. As late as 1897, large tracts were offered for as little as

$7 per acre; one settler later recounted "seeing one forty acres traded for a cow and another forty acres traded for a Winchester rifle" during the agricultural depression. By 1900, however, a land-rush mentality gripped the Delta: the average price of land had already climbed to $25 per acre. Large numbers of plantation district speculators began investing in interior land for the first time since the 1850s.[40]

Most of the bidders for Delta land after 1900 were white and enjoyed at least moderate wealth. Few poorer farmers of either race were able to buy land. Most had taken on heavy debts in the 1890s; cotton's low price and the rising cost of credit left them so burdened with arrears that many were untouched by the twentieth-century cotton boom. Those who did own land struggled to pay off past debts and prevent seizure, while tenants (who were similarly debt-ridden) could seldom convince sellers that they were a good credit risk. Although a few black farmers managed to purchase property in these early years of the new century—usually buying poorly drained or inaccessible acreage disdained by planters—most of the region's agrarians remained trapped in tenantry or desperate to avoid it.[41]

The Delta land market in this period encouraged the extension of planter-dominated agriculture into the former backcountry. Wealthy whites exercised their credit advantages in negotiating loans for land purchase: planters' extensive holdings furnished attractive collateral, and their business connections put them in touch with individuals and companies willing to lend large sums for lower rates than were common in the region. Thus, George Faison and his Sunflower County clan paid only 8 percent annual interest on their debts to the Scottish-American Mortgage Company, although poorer farmers in the region routinely faced interest charges of 10 percent. Cheap loans helped the Faisons expand their operations as cotton prices climbed upward, and in 1907 George Faison, Sr., owned 3,500 cultivated and 2,000 uncleared acres in Sunflower County alone. He and his sons also held large tracts in Bolivar and Sharkey Counties. International credit resources assisted planters and merchants like the Faisons as they escaped the hard times of the 1890s and rushed for expansion in the first decade of the new century.[42]

The types of land on the market in the early 1900s further encouraged plantation expansion. By the turn of the century, lumber companies had been denuding Delta forests for over a decade, clear-cutting valuable hardwoods and hauling the felled lumber away on railcars. Timber companies preferred arrangements that allowed them to lease rights to the wood without buying the land. Many proprietors of wild lands also favored the timber lease because they continued to own the land while someone else quickly cleared the property and paid for the lumber. But timber companies also bought extensive acreage outright. The Yazoo and Mississippi Valley Railroad, a large owner of wooded backcountry land, was eager to sell off these holdings in the 1890s and early 1900s, partly to escape paying taxes on the property.[43] Great sections of wilderness passed from the railroad to lumber company ownership in this period. After clearing, however, the price of the "improved" land was often beyond the means of poorer farmers. The absence of wood also dissuaded farmers who hoped to sell lumber for cash in the off-season from buying these acres. Thus, black farmers who might have earlier purchased these remote tracts for mixed farming and off-season lumbering now found the property too dear and too bare.[44] Yet plantation owners were increasingly eager for cleared land on which they could place sharecroppers.

The fate of Washington County's northeast corner illustrates the diminished allure of lands "improved" by lumber companies. In 1892 the land tax rolls of Washington County listed the Louisville, New Orleans and Texas Railroad as owner of 8,342 wooded acres lying northeast of Leland. The railroad's name was changed to the Yazoo and Mississippi Valley Railroad later that year, after the company's purchase by the Illinois Central Railroad, and the land—valued at $2 per acre—passed to the new owners. The acreage was then sold to the George T. Houston Company, a Chicago-based lumber company buying and clearing tens of thousands of acres of Delta hardwoods. After deforesting the acreage, the Houston Company attempted to sell the land. Land agents were contracted and huge maps distributed to tout the property. But few Delta farmers were able to buy extra acreage during the agricultural depression. Transactions picked up as the cotton economy revived after the turn of the century, but none of the purchasers were black. The prices asked by the agents of the Houston Company were too steep, the prospect of farming fully cleared land was unappealing, and many black farmers lacked the cash or credit to buy property. The tract—comprising almost fifty-five square miles—was sold to white planters over the next few years.[45]

In the first years of the new century, many planters feared that the supply of tenants would not meet their accelerating demand. Landlords of new and expanded plantations, unable to attract farmers to all their fields, perceived a labor shortage. By late 1901 Delta planter Alfred Holt Stone declared that "there is scarcely a planter in all this territory who would not gladly make substantial concessions for an assured tenantry."[46] Landlords became convinced they had outgrown their supply of workers. Some experimented with novel solutions.

Stone resolved to attract good tenants with favorable terms and comfortable living conditions. "There was nothing philanthropic about it," he later insisted. "It was a business proposition, pure and simple." Stone thought prospering tenants would remain on the plantation of their good fortune: "The problem before us was to place in the hands of these people the means of acquiring something for themselves." Good terms would solve "the labor problem, having attracted to the plantation by ties of self-interest a sufficient number" of well-compensated tenants. Stone therefore set out to "select a number of negro families, offer them the best terms and most advantageous tenant relation, and so handle them and their affairs as to . . . [promote economic] independence." Stone and the tenants agreed that renting would return the largest profit to the workers, and his entire Dunleith plantation was reserved for fixed-fee rental.[47]

Stone's "business proposition" resembled the means by which freedmen ascended the backcountry's agricultural ladder in the 1870s and 1880s. But the landlord made no provision for his renters to become landowners. Indeed, he seems to have forgotten that the hardworking and ambitious renters of earlier times had been working hard in pursuit of their own ambitions — not a landlord's. Stone and his tenants held contradictory expectations: the planter desired an "assured tenantry" while his renters regarded tenancy as a means to acquire their own land.

Although many enjoyed a profit, Dunleith renters did not develop loyalty to the plantation. In the first year nearly 45 percent of the renters left after the crop was gathered. Stone replaced the departed renters with others of the same tenure and continued the experiment. But the following year, after profits more than twice those received for the first crop, another 22 percent of the tenants abandoned the plantation. Good treatment and prosperity, Stone was learning, did not guarantee dependable renters. Indeed, the planter determined that offering contracts which allowed renters to accumulate money and property only exacerbated his labor woes. "We demonstrated our ability to make independent, property-owning families out of poverty-stricken material," Stone insisted. "These families in turn demonstrated the fact of their independence by severing relations with us almost as promptly as we put them on their feet."[48]

No doubt, Stone's former renters would have disputed whether it was the landlord's efforts alone that imbued them with initiative and "put them on their feet." Yet his focus on their independence is appropriate, for what successful farmer would want to work under another man's general supervision? The Delta's demand for tenants was at a new high; it is no surprise that Stone's prosperous renters left his fields behind to parlay their success into better, more profitable arrangements with other landlords. Some may have still cherished hopes of saving enough money for a down payment on a small farm.

Stone described the efforts of one renting family in detail. "In December, 1900, we moved in a crew of 7 people. They all represented themselves as working hands, though one of the men was over sixty-five, with a wife past sixty. Their entire outfit consisted of a horse, worth at a liberal valuation $50, and $58 worth of miscellaneous and indescribable household effects." The family was poor even by the standards of tenantry, and Stone expected that assuaging their destitution would win him dependable loyalty. This group of renters prospered and remained at Dunleith beyond their first crop. Still, it was Stone's plantation, not theirs, and they felt no compelling reason to ignore other prospects. "In December, 1903, while riding over the place one day, my attention was arrested by a procession slowly approaching me. It consisted partly of two wagons, one buggy, two mules, one horse, three cows, two calves, and five dogs—the property of this same crew of seven. In addition, they had with them outside wagons enough to assist them in hauling away 285 bushels of corn, $190 worth of household effects (including a sewing-machine for each woman and a gun for each man), and a half-dozen crates of hogs and several of poultry." By Stone's estimate "they carried away $1,100 worth of personal property" in addition to their farming equipment and livestock. The family subsequently leased land from a nonresident landlord and negotiated advances from a nearby merchant. They had not achieved complete independence, but they had found a farm to till without daily interference. Stone, although bitter at their departure, understood the renters' main motivation: "They left to get rid of the supervision incident to plantation management."[49]

Although he made money renting his lands, Stone spurned the arrangement in the third year of the experiment and henceforth sought only sharecroppers for Dunleith. He increased supervision, gave sharecroppers smaller plots, and scrutinized their expenses more carefully. A sharecropper might buy his own livestock for use in the fields, but Stone refused to "sell him these things on long time, nor do we otherwise personally encourage their purchase." By 1905 Stone had all but abandoned his experiment to inculcate tenant loyalty, and he no longer sought ways to assist renters in "acquiring something for themselves." Although Stone still resolved to treat the workers well, his inability to secure a dependable supply of ambitious renters through good treatment had left him bitter. "In short," he declared, "we are no longer engaged in the altruistic enterprise of converting shiftless and empty-handed negroes into desirable and well-equipped tenants for the temporary benefit of other planters."[50]

Few other planters attempted anything approaching an "altruistic enterprise" during the post-1900 labor shortage. Most landlords imposed more, not less, control over their tenants from the start of the cotton boom. Whereas Stone first offered profitable rental contracts and amenable conditions, many Delta planters insisted instead on wage labor or closely supervised sharecropping arrangements. Some planters went even further to control their labor supply: after 1900, rumors of peonage began drifting out of the Delta. Peonage—where debts to an employer were used to hold a tenant or laborer in his position—had a long history in labor-scarce areas throughout the world, and Delta planters were not the only southerners to employ the tactic in the early twentieth century. Turpentine manufacturers in Florida, cotton growers all over the Deep South, and railroad construction companies in various parts of the region all justified involuntary servitude (and, sometimes, physical abuse) by pointing to employees' real or padded debts to the boss or company. Delta entrepreneurs operating an Arkansas plantation were accused of holding Italian farmers in peonage in 1907, and in 1908 a wealthy Tunica County planter was convicted of the crime.[51] Compared to the avarice and inhumanity of the peon masters, Alfred Holt Stone's disgruntled racism seems mild.

Although the Tunica planter's 1908 conviction may have dissuaded many planters from entrapping their laborers in a quagmire of debt, another factor provided relief from fears of a crippling labor shortage. Louisiana and southern Mississippi, where the boll weevil wreaked far worse damage than in the Delta, began to hemorrhage impoverished farmers eager for fairer fields. Delta planters soon dispatched labor agents to woo these distressed cotton farmers north to the alluvial region. Sometimes the agents' words alone were sufficient to bring about relocation. On many occasions, however, creditors (especially landlords) would not allow a tenant to depart their area in arrears. Thus, Delta planters and their agents often paid a prospective laborer's debts in order to gain a new field hand.[52] Despite cultivating more fertile acres in their new locations, these workers had little chance of achieving landownership in the Delta.

The rapidly changing structure of Delta agriculture played a prominent role in frustrating newcomers' hopes. The plantations these new arrivals encountered after 1908 were not amenable to black farmers' ambitions. The backcountry–plantation district dichotomy that characterized the Delta in the frontier era was fast disappearing. In the Delta's interior plantations were still smaller, less capital intensive, and more amenable to cash renters than along the riverside. But these factors increasingly marked distinctions of degree rather than differences of kind. Throughout the region planters now expressed a preference for wage laborers or sharecroppers over renters. Even on the decreasing number of plantations that still allowed fixed-fee tenancy, overseers made frequent examinations of a renter's crop and sometimes demanded extensive changes in cultivation. "All tenants," these planters believed, need "very careful supervision" lest the land yield up an inferior or diminished crop. Visitors to the Delta, especially those who had previously encountered the region in its frontier era or who were familiar with southern cotton farming, often remarked upon the "growing desire of the planter to control absolutely the labor, crops and stock on his land."[53]

And these planters, it seemed, were everywhere. Although many had abandoned isolated plantation houses years earlier in pursuit of the more active social life that accompanied town residency, they had not forgotten the agricultural foundations of their wealth. Indeed, the cotton boom and land rush experienced in the first two decades of the twentieth century only increased their attentions. The arrival of automobiles greatly simplified planters' desire to live in town and make periodic inspections of their dispersed properties. By 1909 Greenville already boasted competing dealers of Ford, Overland, and Buick cars, and Delta counties were undertaking expensive road repairs "to render autoing a pleasure" to planters.[54] Mondays through Saturdays, a planter's greatest pleasure came in seeing his fields grow heavy with cotton.

Large, closely supervised plantations were already emerging in the Delta in the early 1900s, but the boll weevil's arrival in 1908 intensified this trend. Entering Mississippi in 1907, the insect chewed its way into the Delta's southern reaches in the following year. By 1915 the scourge had spread throughout the region, and crops were annually threatened by the weevil's appetite. Midway through the invasion, agricultural agent Alexander E. Cance surveyed the Delta and reported the tightening grip of planters and other landlords on the region's farming population.[55]

Landlords reexamined their tenant relationships and land-use patterns when faced with the prospect of a cotton-devouring insect loosed upon the region. Planters most eager to control the way their fields were cultivated—especially concerning whether to diversify crops and how to poison the weevil—were increasingly drawn to using wage laborers and sharecroppers in their fields. But the tendency toward closer supervision of plantations reflected more than a simple desire to exercise maximum hegemony over labor. By the late 1890s Delta planters like J. B. Wilson of Yazoo County were experimenting with plowing techniques that enhanced crop yields on long-used lands. The arrival of the boll weevil made increased cotton production even more important, and fertilizers came into widespread use in the region after the turn of the century. Owners of large tracts were at the forefront of these efforts and also led experiments with a variety of poisons aimed at killing immature boll weevils. Although any farmer might attempt these innovations, wealthier farmers had better resources, large plantations offered a more efficient environment for testing pesticides, and planters could obtain chemicals and fertilizers at a lower price because they bought in larger quantities.[56]

Innovative planters reconsidered long-established trends in Delta tenancy. An emphasis on maximizing efficiency made them increasingly reluctant to rent their property to small operators. By the second decade of the twentieth century, more profitable means could be found to cultivate the land. Wage hands were subject to the instructions of their employer as a matter of course and would carry out orders or risk discharge. Sharecroppers on large plantations were not much more autonomous. By virtue of the pseudopartnership that granted these tenants access to the landlord's property, sharecroppers usually agreed to follow the "advice" or "management" of the landowner and his agents. The approach of the boll weevil and the attendant plantation reorganizations thus made sharecroppers and wage laborers more attractive to planters.[57]

But what of the fixed-fee renter? Like Alfred Holt Stone, many Delta landlords were decreasing their reliance on renters by the close of the twentieth century's first decade. Despite a resurgence in cotton prices, the proportion of Delta farms worked by renters fell from 44 percent of the total in 1900 to 41 percent in 1910. In that same period sharecroppers increased their cultivation from 46 to 50 percent of all Delta farms. The shift from renting to sharecropping and wage labor quickened after 1910. By 1920, 74 percent of the Delta's farms were cultivated by sharecroppers, while a mere 19 percent housed renters.[58]

In some cases former renters now requested to work for shares of the crop. According to agricultural agent Alexander Cance, "following a bad year or dire prophecies" of boll weevil activity, black renters actually preferred sharecropping to the potential burden of a fixed cash rent. The boll weevil introduced "fear of the future" into renters' considerations and "influenced the negro to submit more willingly to control. Many are asking help and advice of the white overseers. While the last years have been profitable to the renter for cash[,] he feels more safe when following the orders of his planter." For these farmers renting was no longer a step up toward landowning; it was a ledge from which a bad crop might knock them into inescapable poverty. Better, many calculated, to farm on shares for the landlord and be assured a percentage of something than to risk a weevil-shorn crop with a large rental bill. Even when they contracted to rent land, many fixed-fee tenants now encountered supervision indistinguishable from that imposed upon a plantation's sharecroppers. By 1911 the plantation manager "dictated to renter and share hand alike the kind of crop to grow, the place to grow it, the seed to plant, the methods of cultivation and tools to employ, the time of picking, the place to gin and market his crop."[59]

Despite the costs of change, many planters proved eager to undertake new techniques after 1910. Landlords came to prefer using sharecroppers on their land, even if overseers must be hired to supervise their work, than cede a modicum of control to renters. Interviewing Delta whites, Alexander Cance found the belief that "no large plantation can preserve its fertility, keep up its permanent improvements and return a profit to its owner for a term of years under a non-supervised tenant system" was "practically unanimous" in the second decade of the twentieth century.[60] The era of widespread farm renting—and the opportunities it afforded to black farmers—was passing quickly in the 1910s.

The boll weevil was the most obvious factor in the planters' decision to phase out renting, but other considerations also intruded. The rental arrangement had benefited both landowner and tenant when ambitious tenants cleared backcountry land and improved its value. This attraction, however, was made obsolete by the rail-borne sawyers with their steam-powered saws and log-retrieval systems. Planters judged themselves better served by short-term timber leases than several years of haggling over rental contracts. Especially when purchasing land cleared by a lumber company, planters saw little incentive to allow renters on the property.[61]

With diminished need for renters' improvements, landlords focused on the fees paid by these tenants. Significantly, the return from renting land after 1900 was usually inferior to the sums gained when using sharecroppers. Delta landlords in the early twentieth century could depend on a return of 6 to 7 percent of the land's value from renting the property. By contrast, the return from sharecropping seldom fell below 6 percent and sometimes brought landlords 18 percent of the property's worth. A study of the 1913 crop found that cash renters returned an average of 6.6 percent of the farm's value to landlords. The income from plots worked by sharecroppers, however, stood at 13.6 percent of the land's worth. The larger profits promised by sharecropping and landlords' ability to clear acreage without using renters induced many planters to abandon fixed-rate tenancy on their property.[62]

Planters also came to prefer sharecropping because tighter supervision enhanced a landlord's hegemony over his tenants. The disgruntled Alfred Holt Stone summed up many plantation owners' views of black autonomy just after the turn of the century. White Deltans' "greatest objection" to renting land to blacks, he insisted, was that it "allows the Negro privileges which he too often abuses."[63] The black Delta farm renter, Stone emphasized, did "not take kindly to suggestion or direction as to what he shall plant." Worse still, "he thinks he should be left free to work his crop when and as he pleases."[64] Renters' control of mules, either leased or owned outright, further irritated the intrusive Stone: "He thinks he should enjoy the privileges of riding them about the country, when both he and they should be at work, and of neglecting them and poorly feeding them, if he so elect."[65] After his plantation experiment with fixed-fee tenants, Stone believed that "the Negro as a renter is generally undesirable, often troublesome, and that his cultivation of land causes deterioration." Landlords who could not find sufficient sharecroppers or wage laborers and signed on renters to ensure full tillage of their fields may have heeded Stone's advice: use a "contract specifying in detail what was undertaken by each party, and reserving to the plantation management absolute control over all plantation affairs."[66]

Alexander Cance's analysis of the Delta one decade later suggests that many planters were close to achieving this degree of control. In 1911, as in 1861, a typical day on a Delta plantation began with the ringing of the plantation bell and the gathering of workers to receive their day's assignments.[67] Following the overseer's instructions, the renters, sharecroppers, and wage laborers dispersed to the fields. Eventually, the planter's car arrived in a cloud of fine, pale dust.[68] The landlord verified the progress since his last visit and sometimes added tasks, such as fencing, ditching, or road repair, to the manager's list of projects. The planter then departed to inspect his other properties and attend to business or pleasure, as the mood struck him.[69] Next, the overseer toured the premises. "Even if the tenants are reliable hands," Cance reported, the plantation boss "visits them during the day to see that some work is going forward, and to advise and direct that work." To the planter his overseer's efforts were vital in the effort to reserve "full control of the crop[,] from plowing to ginning[,] in the plantation management." Any alternative, it was believed, would "dissipate energy and demoralize cropping systems by giving this control over into the hands of more or less irresponsible tenants."[70]

After the cotton was gathered, few tenants were allowed to sell the crop at their discretion. Most planters coordinated the marketing of all lint raised on their place, regardless of the grower's tenure status. Indeed, a producer was seldom compensated according to the merits of cotton actually grown on his assigned plot. Twentieth-century planters preferred to pool the proceeds from selling lint of divergent quality, then divide the aggregate sum according to the weight of each tenant's yield. This technique punished tenants' initiative, but planters defended the practice (which some probably used to defraud workers) on the grounds that "price discriminations or differences breed trouble among the tenants and discourage rather than stimulate the growing of a better grade" of cotton. In selling cotton, as in growing the crop, "supervision close and exacting was the rule throughout the district" by 1911. Ominously, Cance reported that many Delta planters were "in favor of more exacting supervision."[71]

The economic prospects and living conditions of black farmers were quickly deteriorating. Only "exceptional negroes" now purchased land in the Delta. The best land they could afford was usually isolated from transportation and markets and "frequently rather difficult to cultivate for some reason or another." The number of black land purchasers was not liable to increase any time soon, either, for tenants' savings rates were very low. Although the number of tenants with bank accounts increased, few saved enough money to buy land in the inflationary Delta market. To make matters worse, most of the bank accounts opened by black Delta tenants did not pay interest. Even those rare tenants who purchased livestock in this period usually did so on credit, and a farm was now far more expensive than a cow.[72] Although black farmers had dominated the ranks of landowners in the late nineteenth century, a 1911 observer might understandably conclude that the "great mass have no genius or desire for land ownership."[73]

If not toward livestock, land, or savings, where was the money earned by Delta tenants and sharecroppers going? One need look no further than the plantation store. As late as the 1890s, most of these outlets were limited to dealing in clothing, farming implements, tools, and a few trinkets and taste treats. By the 1910s, though, the store was an emporium of much more exotic goods. Cance was surprised to find that the Delta stores had "as complete a stock of merchandise as a well-furnished country store anywhere in the Middle West." Tenants' consumption patterns followed suit. In the rising cotton market of the early 1900s, the black farmer's "wants [were] increasing with his increasing returns."[74] Whether access to this broadened selection of goods increased a farmer's standard of living is debatable, but it surely reduced the amount of money he might save for investment in land or livestock.

Despite the lure of Delta stores' augmented selection of consumer goods, black farmers grew increasingly restive with their deepening tenancy and searched for means of resisting dependence. As on Alfred Holt Stone's Dunleith plantation earlier in the century, many tenants refused to work for any planter for longer than one year. Some sought better contracts or conditions with new landlords; others moved to assert what was left of their dwindling economic independence. Whatever their motivations, many tenants took to the roads in late December and early January in search of a new Delta home. Turnover was highest where "supervision" was the most rigorous. "On some of the very carefully managed plantations, 60 percent of the tenants moved" in 1910, "the great majority to become tenants elsewhere" in the region, according to Cance. At plantations where landlords seldom interfered with a farmer's work, "one is likely to find less than 10 percent of the tenants changing yearly." Planters with a "reputation for fair, generous and mild treatment had no problem of labor migration to contend with." Cance's estimates were confirmed by another agricultural agent, M. A. Crosby, in 1914: "Some of the plantations have plenty of labor on them, while others are very short." In Crosby's ambiguous phrase a plantation's supply of labor depended "largely on the personality of the managers."[75]

Some planters continued to respond to labor shortages by importing laborers, now seeking workers from areas worse affected by the boll weevil than the Delta. These "purchased" laborers also chafed under the new Delta methods, however. "They fret somewhat under the yoke," Cance confirmed, "which is heavier than in their former homes." After paying the planter for their transportation and debts, these farmers were particularly "inclined to be migratory."[76] They had good reason to move, for black farmers—both longtime residents and recent arrivals from distant parts—were being ground into irredeemable poverty in the Delta during the early years of the twentieth century.

The boll weevil's arrival not only encouraged tighter supervision of plantations and diminished the availability of renting positions, its depredations also bankrupted some black farmers.[77] Black farm owner Henry Johnson, Jr., was among the weevil's victims. Johnson's father bought his first Delta land in 1887. He paid cash for 60 acres, and although the agricultural depression necessitated several loans and deeds of trust in the following years, Johnson held onto the land and added another 66 acres to his holdings. His son and namesake inherited the property in 1898 and added another 100 acres to the farm in the early 1900s. By 1909 Henry Johnson, Jr., owned 226 acres of good Washington County land and was one of the largest black property owners in the region. He had to borrow money and give deeds of trust on his farm to finance operations in many years, but credit was a constant factor of Delta life, and the rising price of cotton belied the potential risks.

Then the boll weevil reached his farm. Johnson's poor 1911 crop left him with an impossible debt (he owed over $5,000 to one lender), and his creditors closed in. Lacking any bargaining power, Henry Johnson, Jr., sold—for only $10 cash and forgiveness of his substantial arrears—the 226-acre farm his father had started more than two decades earlier. Other creditors seized the family's personal property—seven mules, three horses, one wagon, and their cotton and corn crops—for sale at auction. By February 1912 a man considered among the most successful black farmers in the region a year earlier was without farm, livestock, or implements.[78]

Henry Johnson, Jr., was not alone in suffering the weevil's appetite. Wealthier landowners were also exposed to the pest, and yields on large plantations fell markedly. On Alfred Holt Stone's Dunleith plantation, cotton production declined by more than one-third in a single year. In 1910 Dunleith fields averaged 315 pounds of lint per acre; one year later, after the boll weevil's entrance, the average yield had fallen to only 207 pounds per acre.[79]

The next year Stone and every other farmer in the Delta faced another natural disaster: the region's perennial threat, flood. In one of the worst overflows to date, floodwaters covered much of the Delta, delaying, and in many cases preventing, cotton planting. Over half of the lower Delta lay under crevasse flooding (through Mississippi River levee breaks) or backwater (as tributary rivers of the interior swelled over their banks). The upper Delta fared little better; another 400,000 acres were submerged in the northern counties. Altogether, 2,763 square miles of the Yazoo-Mississippi Delta suffered inundation in 1912. Extensive flooding swept the Delta again in 1913, leaving approximately 10,000 inhabitants of the lower Delta homeless after water poured through two separate crevasses in the main line of Mississippi River levees.[80]

Cotton growers who had struggled against boll weevils and spring floods probably expected to redeem their fortunes in 1914. The international cotton market interfered with those high expectations, however. With European declarations of war in August 1914, the international commodity markets were thrown into disarray. As a result, American cotton buyers—interstate cotton factors and small-town merchants, alike—hesitated to buy lint for fear they would not be able to ship the bales to European markets. Without international demand, cotton speculators expected the staple's price would fall considerably. Thus, while merchants awaited indication of the market's direction, many farmers searched in vain for buyers for their crop. Those few speculators who bought cotton from farmers at this juncture paid prices well below the current market value. Historian Manning Marable estimates that southern farmers lost $500 million in the two months that followed cotton-picking time. "Black farmers who borrowed money to purchase their land suddenly had no way to pay annual mortgage payments. Sharecroppers who owned no property were not as threatened with sudden economic ruin as were small black owner-operators." Mississippi farmers did not see cotton prices return to their 1913 level, when lint was purchased for just over 12.5 cents per pound, until 1916.[81]

Delta farmer Bazil Brown was one of these endangered landowners. Brown had always tried to avoid debt. When he bought his land in 1881, the black farmer purchased an isolated tract. In fact, the eighty-acre farm was so distant and difficult to work that its previous owner had allowed the property to be seized for back taxes of only $24.64. Brown, by contrast, was careful to pay his taxes and avoided giving anyone a deed of trust to his land. Despite the hard times that descended upon the region in the 1890s, Bazil Brown remained debt-free for twenty-nine years. But in 1910 Brown had grown old and may have been competing with the boll weevil for the cotton grown on his farm. In that year he gave his first deed of trust to a merchant in order to have cash for farm operations. Although he switched his debt to another lender in 1911, Brown was unable to leave behind his new debtor status. The same was true in 1912, although that year's crop gave Brown just enough money to retire his arrears and farm without credit in 1913. But by 1914 the farmer had again accumulated a debt, necessitating a deed of trust to a third lender, one C. S. Rowe. Teetering on the edge of solvency, Brown was one of the farm owners whose independence did not survive the 1914 "cotton crisis." The property was sold at auction in 1915.[82]

If the Brown family had been able to hold onto their land beyond 1915, they might have soon rejoiced in cotton's rebounding price. Between 1915 and 1916 the average price paid for Mississippi lint increased 58 percent. The next year, prices jumped again, rising 52 percent. Although the gain for 1918 was smaller, with cotton prices gaining less than 2 percent, the price stood at a profitable twenty-eight cents per pound. Cotton farmers were even more fortunate in 1919, when the staple's value escalated to just over thirty-six cents per pound. But many black Delta farmers, men and women who began the decade tilling land they owned, had already lost their property. Between 1910 and 1920 the number of black farm owners in the Delta declined for the first time since emancipation.[83]

While owners of small- and medium-sized farms struggled to preserve their property, larger plantations experienced breakneck expansion. Planters remained eager to add cultivable acreage to their holdings, especially as the wartime demand for cotton pushed its price substantially upward. Albert Luandrew was a young boy living with his father, a Coahoma County tenant farmer, when "this new white man, he started puttin' up fences." The new planter's enclosure efforts were aimed at maximizing his cotton acreage. According to Luandrew, the plantation owner "fenced all the niggers into their land so they couldn't come out, [and then he] plowed up the road comin' into town." Faced with virtual imprisonment to supply a neophyte landlord's avarice, the Luandrew family left the plantation and contracted to work another planter's property.[84]

Many Delta blacks did more than substitute one master for another. Desperate to escape penury on the business plantations of the Delta, these men and women looked beyond the region for better prospects. As a Greenville man wrote, "I want to get my famely out of this cursed south land[:] down here a negro man is not good as a white man's dog."[85] War and the labor needs of northern manufacturers presented new opportunities to discouraged Delta farmers.

The outbreak of hostilities had not only interfered with the cotton market, it also blocked European migration to the factory towns and cities of the United States. Faced with a costly decline in available labor, some manufacturers dispatched labor agents to the South and instructed these representatives to spread the news of abundant work and better lives in the North. Ignoring their own solicitation of workers from Louisiana and southern Mississippi just one decade earlier, prominent white Deltans decried northern labor agents as "outside agitators" and warned tenants that life in the cities of the North would be far worse than cotton farming. But conditions had grown so harsh in the Delta that few formal overtures from northern industrialists were needed; the farm tenants and laborers of the region were already searching for better prospects. As Charles S. Johnson wrote in the National Urban League's journal, *Opportunity*, a desire to escape persecution played a large role in inducing departure from the South. In the Delta hundreds of blacks subscribed to the militant *Chicago Defender* and in its pages found reason to hope for dignified lives outside the region. The *Defender* carried advertisements of work in Chicago business and invited "all to come north" and take advantage of the ready opportunities. The Delta's easy access to the manufacturing centers of the upper Middle West facilitated relocation. From the alluvial basin migrants could ride north to Chicago on the Illinois Central Railroad and its subsidiary, the Yazoo and Mississippi Valley Railroad. Rumors of labor agents seeking workers willing to relocate to Chicago or Detroit helped fuel interest in migration, but the increased danger of lynching, weariness with sharecropping, encouragement from the *Defender,* and news of friends and relatives who had successfully emigrated to northern climes were just as important in persuading potential migrants to abandon the Delta.[86]

Many black Deltans left the region for better chances in the urban North, generally riding the railroads to Illinois.[87] By autumn 1917, 600 blacks had already departed Greenwood for the North, and Greenville migrants abandoned 200 houses. Pouring out of the Delta, this hopeful crowd swelled the poorer neighborhoods of Chicago and lesser cities downstate, like Decatur, along the Illinois Central's main line. Within a few years the agglomeration of ex-Deltans was reshaping the population of urban Illinois. Although less than 5 percent of the nonwhite population of Illinois hailed from Mississippi in 1910, the proportion of Mississippi-born persons topped 20 percent only one decade later.[88]

Plantation owners did not stand idly by while their fields were abandoned. Although a representative of the Mississippi Chamber of Commerce urged landlords to treat workers better and cease cheating their tenants, many planters ignored this advice. Rather than give their black employees incentives to remain in the Delta, these landlords continued to bully, defraud, and abuse sharecroppers and laborers. When workers attempted to leave, some found their way blocked by the planters' surrogates: Greenville police were frequently employed dragging northward-bound blacks from trains. Determined migrants, however, found ways to avoid being trapped in the Delta. Many Washington County blacks caught trains in Leland, and those leaving Greenville sometimes walked the twelve miles between the two towns to avoid having their departure discovered and aborted.[89]

Desperate for laborers, the Delta's planters again looked outside the region for replacements. Agents were dispatched beyond the bluffs and rivers that ringed the region, searching for farmers who might still be willing to give cotton, and the Delta, another chance. The region's nineteenth-century reputation as a good place for ambitious black agrarians remained strong enough to attract a substantial flow into the Delta even as many disillusioned veterans of the place fled north. A special United States Department of Agriculture study of farmers' movements found that although almost all of the Delta migrants went to the northern cities, relocating farmers from other areas of the state remained within Mississippi. In fact, "those migrating from other sections of the state went for the most part up into the Delta—to some extent taking the places of those who left."[90] Some black farmers still believed the Delta was the promised land of the New South. Those who had lived and worked there knew better, however, and they made the region the jumping-off place for the Great Migration.

By 1920 the Delta's days of frontier opportunity were long passed. It stood, instead, as a plantation empire. White planters and merchants lorded over the region, and cotton was their tribute. As in slave times, most black farmers were relegated to retainer status and inescapable poverty. Children and grandchildren of the region's first emancipated black migrants could no longer expect to climb the agricultural ladder to landowning: farm prices had skyrocketed beyond their reach, and landless labor was now a life sentence. At the close of the twentieth century's second decade, black farmers faced lives hemmed in by the demands of plantation owners and creditors, the prospect of peonage, and the threat of lynching. Save for a narrow band of privileged white elites, the Delta was a promised land no more.

Conclusion

But of others there is no memory;
they have perished as though they had never existed;
they have become as though they had never been born,
they and their children after them.

Ecclesiasticus 44:9

Bohlen Lucas, Lewis Spearman, and William Toler—these were not famous men. Yet their stories are rich in the postbellum Delta's ways of life and patterns of hope. In his own way, each pursued and attained the region's central promise, landowning. In circumstances all too common, each also labored to hold onto his land and economic independence as cotton prices fell, credit terms grew harder, and onetime benefactors became competitors. They rode the swell of prosperity as the Delta frontier was opened after the Civil War, and they and the rest of the region's inhabitants foundered as that swell crashed into agricultural depression before the century's end. Well-known, prominent, emulated, and admired in their own day, Lucas, Spearman, and Toler have since been disregarded and forgotten.

Bohlen Lucas was the most celebrated (and scorned) of the three. From his days as a slave driver along Deer Creek through his election as Washington County treasurer in 1875, Lucas occupied a prominent place among Delta blacks. Yet, despite his ambition and attainments, he was regarded with ambivalence by members of both races. The several hundred acres Lucas owned or leased in the 1870s came with strings attached—ligaments of obligation held and occasionally manipulated by white planters, some of whom had been using Lucas as their puppet since his days as a privileged slave. As a bondsman, slave driver Lucas had enjoyed the authority and perquisites of a position based on forcing his fellow African Americans to do the agricultural bidding of their master and his overseer. Lucas remained the beneficiary and captive of obligation even as a freedman. Indeed, he may have sought out patrons, for he was now well formed to a client's posture.

In 1875 Lucas redeemed his many obligations by marching black tenants to the polls to overthrow local Republicans, secure his election as treasurer, and end political Reconstruction in Washington County. But Lucas's moment of electoral triumph was also the point at which he became expendable. His candidacy had imparted a biracial hue to the conservative ticket, and his election deprived Republicans of an important office, but what use was an illiterate county treasurer once the votes were counted? Similarly, Lucas's financial success in the late 1860s and early 1870s might have made him a figure of local black pride and something of a demipatron among the freedmen, but who among them would willingly countenance a man who so avidly worked against the party of Lincoln? Small wonder that Lucas was attacked on his way home from the polls on that election night; no surprise that the range of potential assailants—both black and white—was so broad that no suspects were ever identified or pursued. Physically crippled at the height of his political and financial success, Bohlen Lucas sank toward obscurity. By 1880 this former slave driver, entrepreneurial farm renter, landowner, political boss, and county treasurer was reduced to cultivating a rented twenty-acre plot.[1] Such were the wages of patronage in the postbellum Delta.

Lewis Spearman more accurately represented the strivings and difficulties of backcountry African Americans in the Delta's frontier stage. Lacking well-established patrons, he moved gradually through tenancy toward his goal of landownership and amassed 249 backcountry acres near the Yazoo River in the 1870s and 1880s. His family's labor, not the fickle patronage of white gentry, accounted for his success: sons, daughters, and grandchildren lived with or near Spearman and contributed to the family enterprise. In all of this, Lewis Spearman was illustrative of the Delta's ambitious African-American farmers. Although his move from tenancy to landownership was quicker than most, and his acreage one-third larger than the plots owned by the average black landholder, his path to success was well trod. Like Spearman, most of the freedman buying Delta land in this period located in the backcountry where prices were lower, hardwoods offered a supplement to farming income, and white planters were few. And, again like Spearman, they prospered most when relying on the household economy to provide labor and reduce external costs. Their children might not spend much time in the inferior schools available to Mississippi blacks, and their long-term options might be narrowed as a result, but the family's pool of labor and prospects of short-term production were maximized. Like the patriarchs of old, Spearman and his peers presided over broad acres and an expanding lineage.

But neither a patriarchal establishment nor the cheap labor and productions of their household could fully protect these farmers from the decay of the market economy they supplied. As cotton prices fell across the late 1880s, even thrifty agrarians like Lewis Spearman were forced to borrow money. Cotton prices continued to fall, and Spearman's debts grew. He tried other lenders, but to no avail; in March 1895 the last of his land was sold at auction to satisfy debts he could not repay as a cotton farmer. By this time Lewis Spearman was an old man, and he lacked the strength or energy to start over in the adversarial conditions of the 1890s' agricultural depression. He died before the decade's close; his eldest son and namesake—who had been Lewis Spearman's mainstay in the two decades of property holding—never acquired land of his own.

Unlike Spearman or Lucas or most of the Delta's postbellum black farm owners, William Toler managed to preserve his accomplishment and transfer a landed legacy to the next generation. He carefully navigated the credit channels in which so many of his peers capsized. Although he farmed in the Delta's remote backcountry, he proved himself adept at negotiating with the region's urban merchants and lenders. Indeed, the ex-slave's ability to endure hard times while maintaining a modicum of financial independence suggests that he often bested the boomtown commercialists.

Toler's story paralleled the experiences of Spearman, Lucas, and their fellow farm purchasers in many ways. His success also became clear in the 1870s; he bought an eighty-acre farm in the backcountry of Washington County in 1875 and added an additional eighty acres soon after. Much of the land was wooded when he arrived; hence much of his energy was devoted to clearing, fencing, and maintaining the farm. Although this improved the value of his land, it also cost time and money, and William Toler's debts grew throughout the decade. By 1878 he owed local merchants $800; five years later his debt had more than doubled—all this in the relatively strong cotton market of the late 1870s and early 1880s. It seems that Toler was less cautious about debt than his fellow landowner to the east, Lewis Spearman. By 1890 Toler's creditors presented him with a complex and restrictive agreement he was compelled to sign or take the less appealing option of surrendering his land. Toler's finances suffered in the early 1890s, and he was unable to reduce his debt. Like Spearman's, his farm was sold at auction in the mid-1890s.

But the parallels end there. Lewis Spearman lost his land and never recovered from the sheriff's sale; William Toler revealed his true abilities in this new adversity. He convinced the farm's purchaser to sell the property back to him for $285 more than the auction price. Although he dependably paid the 10 percent interest on his account in following years, he never retired his debt. When pressured to settle his account or again face auction, Toler persuaded another merchant to loan him money to pay off his note. Six years later, when that merchant grew eager for his money, Toler found yet another lender willing to provide the cash. Toler essentially kept his farm, paid only the interest on his debt each year, and found new creditors when presented with an ultimatum to pay off the note or get off the land.

Some might suspect that William Toler was as much ensnared in patronage as Bohlen Lucas had been. After all, he always managed to find whites willing to lend him money, and he was never forced to fully repay his debts. Was he bought off by white creditors as Lucas had been bought off by white politicians?

Apparently not. If one knew the man only through his financial records, it would be tempting to characterize his life as a study in serial clientage. But the full story was more complicated, and the man was more impressive. Unlike Lucas, Spearman, and most other black farm owners, William Toler purchased his land from real estate brokers, not nearby planters. This removed some of the leverage for local pressure. To further minimize the possibility of a patron-client relationship, he borrowed money from cotton factors, distant town merchants, and bankers—not from former owners or overseers (as Lucas had). In short, he kept his finances separate from other aspects of his life, dealing only with individuals who had no prior hold on or interest in his affairs. He also differed from Bohlen Lucas in his political beliefs and actions. Unlike the Redeemers' toady, William Toler never strayed from the party of emancipation. Even when Mississippi's new state constitution made disfranchisement of African Americans a predictable feature of the political landscape, Toler remained an active Republican. He was so prominent in the party, in fact, that he was appointed to one of its few spoils positions, serving as local census enumerator for a section of Washington County in 1900. Toler could not have filled that role—and certainly would not have left behind census manuscripts written in a fine, clear hand—had he been illiterate, like Lewis Spearman, Bohlen Lucas, and most of the other African Americans who bought farmland in the Delta's postbellum era of opportunity. Like them, William Toler was unlettered at emancipation; by contrast, he learned to read and write before 1880. Finally, Toler was distinctive even in his response to chronic indebtedness. Although we may be tempted to equate debt with dependence, one doubts that the lenders who knew how hard he worked to clear and cultivate 160 acres, educate himself, raise a vigorous family, promote the rights of black Republicans in the heart of the solidifying white supremacist South, and retain ownership and control of his hard-won property would have regarded him as a mere appendage.[2]

It is tempting to ask, how did these other qualities and abilities bear on Toler's unusual success in passing on the land he pioneered to the next generation? If every African-American farming family in the Delta had emphasized literacy for old and young, if they had sacrificed some of their children's immediate labor so they could attend school more frequently, if parents had used their own education to supplement the miserly educational facilities Mississippi offered its black citizens, if they had employed the skills acquired to more closely examine their contracts and more thoroughly seek out distant creditors—would this have kept them afloat through the difficult depression years of the 1890s? Or, if every eligible black voter in the region had remained devoted to the Republican Party in the 1870s and beyond, if they had vigorously exercised their right to vote, and if they had resisted apathy, fraud, and discouragement with dedicated intensity—would this have been enough to retain their political viability and guarantee them self-government despite the Democratic Party's push for dominance across the South? Might William Toler's methods, assiduously employed by other black farmers, have prevented the fearful erosion of economic and political power suffered by the Delta's African Americans in the 1890s and thereafter?

It seems unlikely. Despite William Toler's example, a more active focus on education and unremitting dedication to political principle probably were not enough to help most Delta blacks by the 1890s. Consider the numerous forces arrayed against small farmers by the turn of the century: disfranchisement, race-based lynching, the end of the backcountry's isolation, and, undergirding these tensions, the heightened competition for acreage after the economy's post-1898 rebound. The last of these bears special consideration, for as the price of cotton increased, the interior land of black farm owners became the target of any white planter or merchant eager to grow the pale lint. This greed, this acquisitive fever, was difficult to escape—especially for aging black farmers who had not been able to escape the agricultural depression debt-free. Most could not pass on their land to the next generation, and those who did leave property often passed along crushing debts as well. Soon these farms would fall under the auctioneer's gavel, and the descendants of Lewis Spearman and so many others lost the tangible proof of their family's too-brief success.

Recall what the children of the pioneers inherited: debt-saddled acres, the avaricious gaze of their creditors and local planters, and soil that no longer possessed the full vitality of earlier years or offered the valuable hardwoods that had supplemented many early farmers' incomes. William Toler's heirs held on to their land in keeping with the family tradition. Like their progenitor, subsequent Tolers proved adept at negotiations. But by 1912 even this family was compelled to look beyond the Delta for fair creditors. The local people were too land crazy. In that year the next generation of Tolers secured a loan from a Memphis woman; a few years later they took their business even farther afield, gaining a loan at only 8 percent interest from a Chicago source. But just as few of William Toler's peers were his equal in evading the pitfalls of debt, so too were few of their contemporaries as resourceful as Toler's heirs in the 1910s and 1920s.

Evidently, the fullness of the Delta's promise differed for each generation. Freedmen emancipated in the region or traveling to it after 1865 found a unique set of possibilities. White landowners, clinging to their riverside plantations, offered rental or sale of backcountry acres on unusually generous terms in those days. The first generation of freed African Americans thus enjoyed rare opportunities to purchase their own farms in the 1870s and 1880s, and they built communities where black men and women were the focus of authority and emulation in the pioneered interior. Their children were less fortunate. The second generation contributed their labor to the family's success but were less likely to emerge with their own property. The agricultural depression of the 1890s, the debts generally incurred in that uniquely hard time, and the sharpened competition for land at the turn of the century made it unlikely that the second generation would be able to duplicate the successes of their parents and difficult for them even to safeguard their inheritance. Some of this second generation did buy land, but it was mostly marginal acreage offered by the railroads—land white planters deemed unappealing for one reason or another. Still, it was not the children but the grandchildren of the pioneers who suffered most. For them, the Delta's promise was long since broken. What their forebears had seen there, and maybe even grasped for a while, faded before this generation came of age. Instead of offers for lucrative rental or land purchase, they found only sharecropping or wage labor. Neither of these options now seemed steps on the road to landholding; their likeliest destination was inescapable debt. Little but inertia and the proximity of relatives remained to hold the third generation in the Delta, not while lynch mobs swelled, creditors penciled down a poor man's profit, polling places were closed to the black majority, and their forebears' dreams of independence twisted into nightmares. No wonder the Delta became the jumping-off place for the Great Migration north during and after World War I. For the third generation of free African Americans, the Delta was more a place to be escaped than a promised land of agrarian opportunity. It was their native land, true, but few felt welcome there.

Each generation of whites also experienced a different Delta. In 1865 white adults faced a world much changed by the preceding four years. A war had been fought and lost, the bonds of chattel slavery had been tested and broken, and the destruction and neglect of the region's agricultural infrastructure had reduced the plantation district to a thin strip of broken-down establishments caught between the unrestrained Mississippi and the untamed wilderness. It is understandable that planters—amid physical devastation, social change, and military defeat—would attempt to retain as much of their prewar world as possible. Most planters sought some continuity in their labor relations, hoping to preserve a degree of paternal, if not physical, control over their workforce. But the freedmen proved eager for freedom, not a slightly improved bondage, and it was difficult to attract and keep workers on plantations marked by slavish conditions.

The Delta's marked disjunctures—holders of rich land fearing its loss or inactivity, a black population that outnumbered whites by a ratio of four to one, and the large majority thus amenable to Republican appeals—brought forth extreme responses from threatened whites. Many soon favored compromise, but others fell back on coercion. Some of the latter group, like convict lessee Edmund Richardson, brought a bondage worse than slavery to their riverside holdings. But these convict masters were relatively few in number and largely scorned by their peers. A far greater proportion of Delta landlords were soon compelled to surrender the perquisites of their antebellum mastery. Like Henry T. Ireys and Frederick Metcalfe, most planters gradually moved away from gang labor, through the squad system of organization, and eventually to family units working separate plots. Ever concerned about a shortage of labor in their fields, these men tried a variety of land tenure and employment options (Metcalfe and a few others even went so far as to engage Chinese laborers). By 1870 many landlords accepted sharecropping as their most profitable option in the plantation district. But the rising taxes that accompanied Reconstruction brought another crisis: unable to pay their obligations, many landowners feared losing their less developed property. Again, they sought the path of least change. Planters offered fair rental and sale terms for distant backcountry acres as a way of generating funds to help them retain their home plantations in the more settled districts. This opportunity brought tens of thousands of freedmen to the Delta in the 1870s and 1880s and generated the remarkable growth in black landholding.

These crises passed for landed whites, and the range of economic possibilities broadened perceptibly for their children at the turn of the century. Cotton prices rose, taller and stronger levees offered more dependable protection for low-lying acreage, and large timber companies arrived offering to pay landholders to clear their remote tracts. All of this made the extension of existing plantations into the interior economically attractive, even as it rendered traditional arrangements with backcountry renters obsolete. The Delta's de facto bifurcation, with wage labor or sharecropping plantations along the major rivers in contrast to more modest establishments owned or leased by black farmers in the interior, was blurred by the turn of the century and had largely vanished by 1920.

Planters' expanding horizons were accompanied by changing attitudes toward African Americans. Frederick Metcalfe muddled his way from paternalistic slaveholder to paternalistic (and largely unprofitable) landlord; his son, Clive Metcalfe, proved much more vigorous in bending freed blacks and their offspring to his economic will. The former slave master tried to motivate his workers with incentives and abstained from physical measures; his son gloried in violence.[3] When Frederick Metcalfe's grandchildren came of age in the twentieth-century Delta, whites were firmly ensconced at the top of a hierarchy predicated upon control of resources and capital, race-targeted lynchings, and the disfranchisement of most black citizens. As it had before 1861, white skin again betokened unassailable privilege by 1920. History had not simply repeated itself—the business plantations of the twentieth century were difficult to confuse with Old South establishments, either in their specific technologies or in paternalism's repudiation by the new age—but it was difficult to ignore the twentieth century's parallels with the antebellum years.

By the end of World War I, capital-intensive agriculture was well established throughout the Delta, and racial oppression was one of its chief tools. In these sad facts the Delta was hardly unique. The expansion of capitalist assumptions and methods has been a main theme of postbellum southern (and American) history; racism has, in one way or another, been a key factor in southern lives since the arrival of the first African slaves in 1619. These interlocking themes—

the persistence of racism and the inescapable advance of capitalism — have justifiably occupied center stage as scholars re-create the drama of the southern past for the present age. No one even dimly familiar with the historical literature on the postbellum South now doubts that many whites employed class and race appeals to enhance their power and influence over African Americans, sometimes cloaking their self-interest as fealty to an organic society imagined from the past and sometimes advertising it as the path to future prosperity.

So, what shall we make of the generation of black pioneers who sought unique opportunities for independence in the Delta interior, and of the white elites whose compromises encouraged them in this pursuit? Were they mere blips on the screen of time? Ambered figures in a transitory moment? Archaic modes and expectations crushed beneath the inexorable development of capitalist agriculture? In the long view of southern life, where race prejudice seems endemic and capitalism appears unstoppable, what insight do they offer?

Rather than impose our contemporary perspectives on the men and women of the frontier Delta — stressing the long-term futility of resisting white supremacy before the Civil Rights movement, for example — we should approach their world as they encountered it. It is crucial that we remember that their prospects were at least as unpredictable as ours, that their paths toward safety and prosperity were even less clearly marked. Indeed, historians of the postbellum South are unusually unified in emphasizing the chaotic nature of life in the immediate postwar era. The chaos permeating 1865 and the years beyond was more than mere context, however, for it could shape actions and justifications in those crucial years. C. Vann Woodward refined the notion decades ago, emphasizing the disjunctures created by Confederate defeat and slavery's abolition. "After the curtain fell on the Old South in 1865, the same cast of characters had to be taught strange roles and learn new lines." For Harold Woodman, this was essentially a revolutionary drama, yet without the beginning, middle, and end of traditional theater. The "Civil War and Reconstruction achieved only half a revolution; they destroyed an old economic system but created nothing to replace it. Moreover, this destructive half of the revolution . . . did not result from an internal upheaval by a class armed with the experience, the ideology, and the vision of a new society. It was imposed from the outside." Consider yet another metaphor reinforcing the notion of postbellum confusion, this drawn from Barbara Jeanne Fields: "Amid the apparently kaleidoscopic movement of the fragments of prewar southern society, a clearly definable process was underway, to which the unwitting and unwilling contributed as surely as the witting and the willing." Evidently, those were tangled times, as individuals searched for ways to bring their present and the future into harmony with the better parts of their past, as institutions flirted with obsolescence, and as the region that failed to become a nation retreated into itself. Woodman describes it well: "What appears to be confusion often approaching anarchy becomes comprehensible when we recognize that people held varying views shaped by a past experience that had become irrelevant. They were looking backward as they stumbled uncertainly into the future."[4]

Part of the confusion arose from the fundamentally reshaped structures of life after years of destructive war. But the quandary of white and black southerners was exacerbated by the absence of any clear guidelines, model, or historic example. Theirs was a world without parallel, either foreign or domestic. Steven Hahn recaptures the unprecedented disruption southern planters faced:

> Nowhere else were so many servile laborers liberated in one stroke or soon after provided equivalent civil and political rights. Indeed, for some time, it seemed that a major program of land reform might be initiated. Even with the failure of land reform, black enfranchisement and the active organizing of the Republican party presented a serious political challenge to planters who had already suffered military defeat and heavy economic losses. The freedmen pressed their claims, came to sit in southern state legislatures, and—in numerous plantation belt counties—took command of the local government.[5]

But Hahn's insight need not be limited to white elites; African Americans faced a related tumult. Their goals might be divergent, even antagonistic—for in every planter's dread there was a freedman's hope, in every dependable tradition there was a legacy of oppression to escape or eradicate—but all endured a context without precedent. Even as they viewed the present through different pasts, whites and blacks shared a changeful world lacking certainty and clarity.

This flux persisted longest on the margins of the South: in the mountains, as timber, rail, and mining companies introduced large-scale extractive operations where market-focused agriculture had thin roots; on the prairies, where stockmen hoping to supply the meat protein needs of America's urban population battled farmers and each other for use of the Southwest's arid topsoil; in coastal plains, where the sparsely settled (if sandy) acreage drew multitudes eager to leave the plantation districts; and in those swampy bottomlands the antebellum generation had found too difficult to cultivate but which now offered a fresh start to migrants eager to escape the old plantation or the Old World.[6] These

rough-and-tumble societies in marginal settings — despite their obvious difficulties — were home to hope as well as disruption, for the South supported poor
farmers' landholding ambitions best upon its margins. Edward L. Ayers's history of the New South exposes the geographic pattern encountered by the
poorest of the poor, the freedmen: "About 45 percent of blacks owned land
along the coasts and in the mountains, but only 8 percent in the Black Belt
managed to attain that status."7 Although firmly within the borders of the
plantation swath, the Delta's tumultuous opportunity placed it for decades
among the marginal places on that edge of the South where hope and disappointment were so delicately balanced. It beckoned to anyone who would not
endure the thwarted prospects all too common in the settled South.

Some learned of the Delta's rich promise from labor agents dispatched across
the South by riverside planters, others from travelers who had passed through
the alluvial region, a few from newspaper or magazine articles, an unknown
number by word of mouth. More important than the source of information
was their response to the news: tens of thousands journeyed to the region during the post–Civil War era. To tell their story another way, tens of thousands
abandoned established homes, leaving behind friends, relatives, and accustomed work to try life in the wilderness of northwest Mississippi. For these
men and women — be they freed blacks, immigrants from eastern Europe, or
investors from northern states — the risk and labor demanded in the new region
held out greater promise than the familiar lives they abandoned.8 Indeed, the
Delta's promise had burned so bright after 1865 that even when it was extin-
guished by the wave of twentieth-century business plantations, migrants drawn
by the afterglow continued to arrive in the region, eager to take the places of
those who left for points north during World War I. For those who heard of the
Delta's promise and especially for those who sought new lives in the region, its
essential meaning derived from its unusual opportunity. Decades passed before
its reputation was recast as a Siren's song.

The Yazoo-Mississippi Delta is no longer a New South frontier. Indeed, the
curious dichotomy of riverside plantation district and backcountry disappeared
decades ago. Huge tractors now prowl lands cleared more than a century ago by
Lewis Spearman, Bohlen Lucas, William Toler, and the other black frontiersmen; chemical-laden aircraft swoop low over acres once guarded by towering
oaks. Mound Bayou remains, but its mission of black uplift has been surrendered to the stubborn realities of endemic rural poverty. Present-day travelers to
the Delta are seldom impressed by the features that once made the region re-

markable—the rich soil, the great forests, the tall cotton. Instead, they are struck by the shocking disparities wrought with mechanized agriculture, for in today's Delta, some of the nation's richest white farmers live surrounded by the country's poorest unemployed blacks. Several counties in the region are regularly listed among America's most impoverished, and their infant mortality rates would embarrass many Third World countries. Yet hefty agricultural subsidies still inflate the incomes of white planters and their cotton-based corporations, and a new extractive industry, casino gambling, distracts visitors from the prevailing hopelessness of the rural poor.[9] Big plantations and white success, cramped shacks and black poverty—these are the vivid juxtapositions that now emanate from the region. This is the modern Delta, successor to the small farmers' postbellum promised land.

Many of the region's current citizens are surprised to learn that the Delta was once known for much more equitable prospects. Present-day residents are so accustomed to a society where race determines place that they cannot imagine black farmers flocking to the Delta, much less prospering there. Few realize that the region pivoted from a frontier full of opportunity for small farmers to the home of "business plantations" within the span of three hectic decades. Instead, they assume that African Americans have always endured hard times in "Mississippi's Mississippi." Delta native and bluesman B. B. King summarized this perspective in a Public Broadcasting Service program about the region's contributions to American music. At the beginning of the twentieth century, King narrated, the region's blacks still "lived much as they had in slave times. . . . The Delta has not changed."[10]

But much has changed, and much has been lost. In the first decades after emancipation, a generation of ex-slaves sought and partially achieved economic independence in the Delta, and their white contemporaries allowed and sometimes aided that progress. The next two generations encountered far different prospects. With the onslaught of full-blown white supremacy between 1890 and 1920, blacks' political rights were stolen, their fragile economic independence was eroded, and lynching became their unique nightmare. The Yazoo-Mississippi Delta from 1865 to 1920: one tumultuous region, two distinct—almost contrary—eras, and countless men and women for whom change was the clearest certainty. Affirming the intensity of their hopes, we comprehend the depths of their disappointments and recall these lives from forgotten time.

Notes

Abbreviations

BRFAL	Records of the Bureau of Refugees, Freedmen, and Abandoned Lands, National Archives
ICN	Newberry Library, Chicago
Ms-Ar	Mississippi Department of Archives and History, Jackson
NA	National Archives
RG	Record Group
SHC, NcU	Southern Historical Collection, University of North Carolina–Chapel Hill
Sunflower Co. Deed Records	Sunflower County Deed Records, Sunflower County Courthouse, Indianola, Miss.
ViBlbV	Virginia Polytechnic Institute and State University, Blacksburg
Washington Co. Deed Records	Washington County Deed Records, Washington County Courthouse, Greenville, Miss.
Washington Co. Land Tax Roll, 1870	Washington County Land Tax Roll, 1870, County Courthouse, Greenville, Miss.
Washington Co. Land Tax Roll, 1892, 1904	Washington Co. Land Tax Roll, 1892, 1904, MSS, Mississippi Department of Archives and History, Jackson
Washington Co. Probate Records	Washington County Probate Records, County Courthouse, Greenville, Miss.
Washington Co. Will Book 2	Washington County Will Book 2, Washington County Courthouse, Greenville, Miss.

Introduction

1. The Yazoo-Mississippi Delta is not a delta at all; it does not spread out from the mouth of a river. The region is instead an alluvial basin carved out over eons by the meandering Mississippi River and its tributaries.

2. Robert L. Brandfon, *Cotton Kingdom of the New South: A History of the Yazoo-Mississippi Delta from Reconstruction to the Twentieth Century* (Cambridge, Mass., 1967), 40. Although a dependable introduction to what many elite whites regarded as the region's political economy, Brandfon's work too often neglects the less celebrated majority of Deltans and the history they made out of sight (and out of mind) beyond the planter's "big house."

3. Department of the Interior, Census Office, *Twelfth Census of the United States*, "Agriculture," vol. 5, pt. 1 (Washington, D.C., 1902), 96–97. Blacks owned between 71 and 81 percent of the farms in three counties in the South Carolina–Georgia low country, but unlike the cash-crop farmers of the Delta, these landowners were a subsistence economy "peasantry." Loren Schweninger, *Black Property Owners in the South, 1790–1915* (Urbana, Ill., 1990), 163.

4. For examples, see Brandfon's *Cotton Kingdom,* James C. Cobb's *The Most Southern Place on Earth: The Mississippi Delta and the Roots of Regional Identity* (New York, 1992), or Leon F. Litwack's *Trouble in Mind: Black Southerners in the Age of Jim Crow* (New York, 1998). Figures derived from Department of Commerce and Labor, Bureau of the Census, *Thirteenth Census of the United States,* "Agriculture," 6 (Washington, D.C., 1913), 872–79; Department of Commerce, Bureau of the Census, *Fourteenth Census of the United States,* "Agriculture," vol. 6, pt. 2 (Washington, D.C., 1922), 522–29.

5. Some of the more influential works on the region's mid-twentieth-century history include Neil R. McMillen, *The Citizens' Councils: Organized Resistance to the Second Reconstruction* (Urbana, Ill., 1971); Stephen J. Whitfield, *A Death in the Delta: The Story of Emmitt Till* (New York, 1988); and Nicholas Lemann, *The Promised Land: The Great Black Migration and How It Changed America* (New York, 1991).

6. Blacks constituted a majority of farm owners in seven of the Delta's nine counties by 1900. In these areas the proportion of black farm owners ranged from 55 to 80 percent. Overall, blacks comprised 66 percent of all Delta farm owners at the turn of the century. *Twelfth Census,* "Agriculture," vol. 5, pt. 1, 96–97.

7. The proportion of owners to sharecroppers was reversed between 1880 and 1920. Owners worked 63 percent of the Delta's farms in the earlier year, compared to sharecroppers' 16 percent. But in 1920 farm owners accounted for only 7 percent of farm operators, and sharecroppers fully 74 percent. Department of the Interior, Census Office, *Tenth Census of the United States,* "Productions of Agriculture," 3 (Washington, D.C., 1883), 66–67; *Fourteenth Census,* "Agriculture," vol. 6, pt. 2, 522–29.

1. Homecomings

1. William D. McCain and Charlotte Capers, eds., *Memoirs of Henry Tillinghast Ireys,* Papers of the Washington County Historical Society (Jackson, Miss., 1954), 2, 9–17, 24–28.

2. One wonders how the Ireys brothers were received by the Delta's former rebels. Their wartime neutrality would have been a profound social liability had Henry initially disclosed that "my brother John and I wished to take part in the battle for the Union, but were prevented by the earnest appeal of our mother." Ibid., 18, 29–31. Lawrence N. Powell's work on first-time planters in the 1860s places the Ireyses' secret in regional perspective. See his *New Masters: Northern Planters During the Civil War and Reconstruction* (New Haven, 1980).

3. Steven Hahn, "Class and State in Postemancipation Societies: Southern Planters in Comparative Perspective," *American Historical Review* 95:1 (Feb. 1990): 84; Harold D. Woodman, "The Reconstruction of the Cotton Plantation in the New South," in *Essays on the Postbellum Southern Economy,* ed. Thavolia Glymph and John J. Kushma (College Station, Tex., 1985), 100. These social and economic dilemmas would also attain a political dimension in time. Thavolia Glymph's analysis is helpful in understanding the connections: "Mississippi's black codes, like those of other Southern states, reflected, chiefly, planters' attempts to resolve the problem of making the transition from mastery to management, a task for which they were fundamentally ill-prepared." See her "Freed People and Ex-Masters: Shaping a New Order in the Postbellum South, 1865–1868," ibid., 57.

4. McCain and Capers, *Memoirs of Ireys,* 31. Gavin Wright explores this change from labor lords to landlords in *Old South, New South: Revolutions in the Southern Economy since the Civil War* (New York, 1986).

5. C. Vann Woodward's essay "Equality: The Deferred Commitment" is still the best introduction to the challenges faced by emancipants, erstwhile liberators, and former owners. See his *The Burden of Southern History* (Baton Rouge, La., (1960; rev. ed., 1968), 69–88. For subsequent work on these issues, see Wright, *Old South, New South,* and Eric Foner, *Reconstruction: America's Unfinished Revolution, 1863–1877* (New York, 1988). For Mississippians' reluctant embrace of free labor, see Vernon L. Wharton, *The Negro in Mississippi, 1865–1890* (Chapel Hill, N.C., 1947); Michael Wayne, *The Reshaping of Plantation Society: The Natchez District, 1860–1880* (Baton Rouge, La., 1983); and Ronald L. F. Davis, *Good and Faithful Labor: From Slavery to Sharecropping in the Natchez District, 1860–1890* (Westport, Conn., 1982). A controversial work suggesting that slaves internalized the degradations of their bondage is Stanley M. Elkins, *Slavery: A Problem in American Institutional and Intellectual Life* (Chicago, 1959).

6. McCain and Capers, *Memoirs of Ireys,* 31; Wharton, *Negro in Mississippi,* 23–97.

7. Department of the Interior, Census Office, *Eighth Census of the United States,* "Agriculture" (Washington, D.C., 1864), 84; Department of the Interior, Census Office, *Tenth Census of the United States,* "Statistics of the Population" (Washington, D.C., 1883), 397–98; Willie D. Halsell, "Migration into, and Settlement of, Leflore County, 1833–1876," *Journal of Mississippi History* 9 (Oct. 1947): 221, 231.

8. Wirt A. Williams, ed., *History of Bolivar County, Mississippi* (Jackson, Miss., 1948), 2; *Greenville Times,* 8 Dec. 1883; Willie D. Halsell, "Migration into, and Settlement of, Leflore County, 1876–1920," *Journal of Mississippi History* 10 (Oct. 1948): 248; *Tenth Census,* "Agriculture," 3:66–67. Much of the Delta remained uncleared for decades, and some of its old forests persist in scattered remnants.

9. J. C. Burrus, "My Recollections of the Early Days of Bolivar County," in Williams, *Bolivar County,* 102–10; Robert W. Harrison, *Levee Districts and Levee Building in Mississippi: A Study of State and Local Efforts to Control Mississippi River Floods* (Stoneville, Miss., 1951); Illinois Central Railroad Company, *Prosperous Northern Settlements in Tennessee, Mississippi, and Louisiana on the Line of and Reached by the Illinois Central Railroad* (ca. 1888), 8–10, ICN. Antebellum settlers and those who arrived soon after the war burned off or deadened as much of the thick woods as possible. By the late 1870s, however, as railroads arrived to facilitate transportation and lumber companies began regarding the region as a profitable source of hardwood, many of the region's pioneers were harvesting and selling their land's timber.

10. Harrison, *Levee Districts and Levee Building in Mississippi;* Walter Sillers, "Levees of the Mississippi Levee District in Bolivar County," in Williams, *Bolivar County,* 84; *Greenville Times,* 14 Apr. 1877, 23 Mar. 1878.

11. Frederic Trautmann, ed. and trans., *Travels on the Lower Mississippi, 1879–1880: A Memoir by Ernst von Hesse-Wartegg* (Columbia, Mo., 1990), 54–63; Williams, *Bolivar County,* 134; *Greenville Times,* 26 July 1879, 1 Oct. 1887.

12. Deltans joined citizens from across the lower Mississippi in petitioning Congress for river and harbor improvements after 1865. Their first substantial victory was Congress's appropriation of funds to remove the hulks of ships sunk in the Yazoo River during the Civil War, and funds for snag removal and river dredging followed in later years. Brandfon, *Cotton Kingdom,* 67.

13. Gary B. Mills, "New Life for the River of Death: Development of the Yazoo River Basin, 1873–1977," *Journal of Mississippi History* 41 (Nov. 1979): 292; *Greenville Times,* 25 Aug. 1877, 11 Jan. 1879, 28 Nov. 1874, 18 Oct. 1884, 22 Feb. 1879. Transportation improvements could spring from unlikely sources, including vanity. One of the first gravel roads built in Bolivar County reveals the lengths to which a Delta husband might go to please his spouse. Mrs. J. C. Brooks, reared a belle in Natchez, expressed frequent regrets at having to live in a place where sticky mud roads necessitated that she be borne home from the nearby train station in a six-mule wagon. She convinced Dr. Brooks that it did not reflect well on her dignity to have so many beasts pull so mightily in her behalf alone. The county supervisors were amenable to his proposal for a gravel surface on the byway, but only if Dr. Brooks subsidized the thirty-two railcar loads of gravel needed for the job. He did so without regrets. Williams, *Bolivar County,* 64–65, 423.

14. Department of the Interior, Census Office, *Tenth Census of the United States,* "Report on Cotton Production in the United States, Also Embracing Agricultural and Physico-Geographical Descriptions" (Washington, D.C., 1884), 43; Washington Co. Land Tax Roll, 1870.

2. Reconstructing the Plantation District

1. William C. Harris, *The Day of the Carpetbagger: Republican Reconstruction in Mississippi* (Baton Rouge, La., 1979), 39; *Greenville Times,* 7 Apr. 1877; Wharton, *Negro in Mississippi,* 238; Edmund Richardson Papers, SHC, NcU.

2. For an example of Richardson's hard bargaining with a business partner, see his 1871 agreement with Fitz Lonsdale, Washington Co. Deed Records, X:404–7. White planters indebted to Richardson were required to purchase goods from him at credit prices, paying 2.5 percent above the usual charge. Ibid., 407–8. Richardson was a prominent Jackson merchant before investing in Delta plantations and became a major stockholder and president of Mississippi Mills, the state's preeminent textile manufacturing company. He doubled the factory's productive capacity between 1873 and 1876 and employed 500 operatives (paid from 30 to 75 cents per day) by the end of Reconstruction. Harris, *The Carpetbagger,* 571.

3. Greenville was not safe from competition with Richardson until the highly capitalized Southern Railway purchased the Greenville, Columbus and Birmingham Railroad and guaranteed the survival of the railroad and its riverside terminus. Editor J. S. McNeily of the *Greenville Times* expressed the community's relief and suggested that the threat of competition from Refuge accounted for Greenville's frenetic pursuit of interior rail connections in the 1870s. Richardson thereafter removed his cottonseed oil mill to Vicksburg and abandoned plans to extend his narrow-gauge railroad to Deer Creek. Although Richardson was thwarted in his expansion, he was not ruined. He still owned eleven plantations in Washington County and properties in several other Delta counties in 1884. Edmund Richardson's ambitions, methods, and success were well documented by McNeily's *Greenville Times.* For examples, see ibid., 7 Apr., 21 Apr. 1877, 27 Mar. 1880, 10 June, 19 Aug. 1882, 7 July 1883, and 18 Oct.–6 Dec. 1884.

4. Lillian A. Pereyra, *James Lusk Alcorn: Persistent Whig* (Baton Rouge, La., 1966); Halsell, "Leflore County, 1833–1876," 229.

5. See the diary of Henry W. Ball, Greenville newspaper editor and bon vivant, for a staggering recital of the little city's social attractions. SHC, NcU.

6. Ninth Census of the United States, Population and Agriculture MSS, Washington Co.; Tenth Census of the United States, Population and Agriculture MSS, Washington Co.; Twelfth Census of the United States, Population MSS, Washington Co.; McCain and Capers, *Memoirs of Ireys,* 36. Greenville's rapid urban development made the town an early center of absentee plantation owners, but other towns drew their own share of "urban planters" from the 1880s on. The relocation of planters to burgeoning towns was not unique to the Delta, for wealthy families across the South increasingly abandoned isolated plantations for the rush of town life. The tide was not reversed until paved roads made rapid and dependable transportation between town and country possible after 1920. Some of the social and political ramifications of planters' distance from their agricultural property and tenants are discussed in Raymond Arsenault's *The Wild Ass of the Ozarks: Jeff Davis and the Social Bases of Southern Politics* (Philadelphia, 1984).

7. Wharton, *Negro in Mississippi,* 238–40; J. H. Jones, "Penitentiary Reform in Mississippi," *Publications of the Mississippi Historical Society* 6 (1902): 128; Alex Lichtenstein, *Twice the Work of Free Labor: The Political Economy of Convict Labor in the New South* (London, 1996), 3.

8. Edward L. Ayers dissects the convict lease system in his *Vengeance and Justice: Crime and Punishment in the 19th-Century American South* (New York, 1984). He locates the convict lease within the continuum of southern experience on pp. 191–92. See also Paul M. Gaston, *The New South Creed: A Study in Southern Mythmaking* (New York, 1970); James Oakes's epilogue, "The Meaning of the Civil War," in *Slavery and Freedom: An Interpretation of the Old South* (New York, 1990); and Lichtenstein, *Twice the Work of Free Labor.* As Harold Woodman has reminded us, the "desire for a dependent, easily controlled, docile, and cheap labor force burns as fiercely in the heart of a bourgeois factory owner as it does in the heart of a plantation owner." "Sequel to Slavery: The New History Views the Postbellum South," *Journal of Southern History* 43 (1977): 550.

9. Harris, *The Carpetbagger,* 353; Wharton, *Negro in Mississippi,* 238; Pereyra, *Alcorn,* 116–17. The deal between Gillem and Richardson, though highly advantageous to the latter, was not the product of political affinity. Richardson was then and remained a staunch conservative. Harris, *The Carpetbagger,* 354.

10. Pereyra, *Alcorn,* 117; Harris, *Carpetbagger,* 353–54.

11. Pereyra, *Alcorn,* 117–18; Harris, *The Carpetbagger,* 353–56. Pereyra and Harris disagree over whether the bill was signed, with Pereyra arguing that Alcorn did approve the contract. But Harris's demonstration that the legislature had to revive the bill in its next session reveals the governor's maneuver. Ibid.

12. Harris, *The Carpetbagger,* 356–57.

13. Ibid., 359–61.

14. *Greenville Times,* 24 Apr. 1875, 3 July 1875.

15. Ibid., 14 Aug., 11 Sept. 1875, 15 Jan., 30 Sept., 7 Oct. 1876.

16. Jones, "Penitentiary Reform," 127–28. By contrast, only 1.76 percent of prisoners died among the combined penitentiary populations of New Hampshire, Iowa, Ohio, and Illinois in their deadliest year, 1885. That same year, Mississippi convicts experienced their second-healthiest year between 1881 and 1885: only 9.64 percent of the prisoners died. Ibid.

17. Wharton, *Negro in Mississippi,* 241–42; David M. Oshinsky, *"Worse than Slavery": Parchman Farm and the Ordeal of Jim Crow Justice* (New York, 1996). The leasing of county convicts was, if possible, even more invidious than the state levy. State law allowed the former employers of county prisoners the first option on leasing their labor. Planters must have been tempted to testify against laborers charged with offenses, for they could then lease them back from the county at a rate lower than local wages and treat them as they pleased. Wharton, *Negro in Mississippi,* 235–36.

18. Wharton, *Negro in Mississippi,* 84. Courts were allowed to apprentice minors whose parents were judged incapable of supporting them adequately. This amorphous provision was used to negate black parents' challenges to the forced apprenticeship of their children.

The law also provided strict penalties for anyone enticing an apprentice away from his master, a measure that might apply to parents or competing planters. Ibid. This clear attempt to resuscitate slavery contrasted sharply with the more equitable procedures used in traditional apprenticeship. See W. J. Rorabaugh's *The Craft Apprentice: From Franklin to the Machine Age in America* (New York, 1986).

19. Dorothy Vick Smith, "Black Reconstruction in Mississippi, 1862–1870" (Ph.D. diss., University of Kansas, 1985), 119–24; Laura Taylor, sworn and subscribed to Fred Moore, Sub-Assistant Commissioner, 31 July 1866, M-826, BRFAL.

20. Captain William L. Tidball (30 Sept. 1867) and Agent D. S. Harriman (1 Oct. 1867), Narrative Reports of Subordinate Officers, M-826, ibid.

21. J. M. Henderson to Alvan C. Gillem, 25 Jan. 1866, Letters Received, M-826, ibid.

22. Wharton, *Negro in Mississippi,* 92–93; Gillem's General Order Number 3 was printed in the *Jackson Clarion,* 23 Apr. 1867.

23. Smith, "Black Reconstruction," 127–28; Agent J. R. Webster (19 Nov. 1867) and Captain William L. Tidball (30 Sept. 1867), Narrative Reports, BRFAL.

24. Wharton, *Negro in Mississippi,* 97–98.

25. Ibid., 98–99.

26. On the basis of oral interviews with Delta Chinese in the 1960s, James Loewen has speculated that the first Chinese workers came to Mississippi after completing their work on the transcontinental railroad in 1869. Loewen found no evidence to support this claim, however, and the first Chinese in the region were sixteen workers imported from Hong Kong to Bolivar County's plantation district in 1870. The *Greenville Times* reported that these laborers had contracted to work for a Mr. Estill near Beulah for five years. James W. Loewen, *The Mississippi Chinese: Between Black and White* (Cambridge, Mass., 1971), 24–26, 187–91; *Greenville Times,* 25 June 1870. Frederick Metcalfe began employing Chinese laborers on his plantation in 1873. His plantation journals give an intriguing account of events on his Newstead and Brighton plantations after emancipation because, unlike many of his contemporaries, Metcalfe lived on his plantations and took an active hand in their daily management. He did not, however, specify how he obtained the services of the Chinese. Frederick A. Metcalfe Diary, Metcalfe Collection, Ms-Ar.

27. Metcalfe Diary, 17 Nov. 1873, 23 Jan., 18 Feb., 25 Dec. 1874. Theft of the Chinese workers' cigars—seven pounds of cigars, in fact—implies that they had more than a passing acquaintance with tobacco. Indeed, it suggests that Metcalfe obtained these workers through a labor agent dealing with Cuban planters. Many Chinese toiled in the sugar and tobacco fields of Cuba, and transportation from Cuba would have been significantly cheaper than bringing workers from China. Ibid., 18 Oct. 1874; Lucy M. Cohen, *Chinese in the Post-Civil War South: A People without a History* (Baton Rouge, La., 1984), 46–62, 109–10.

28. Metcalfe Diary, 17 Nov. 1873, 23 Jan., 27 Jan., 24 Feb., 25 May, 22 Aug., 26 Aug., 18 Oct., 25 Dec. 1874. Metcalfe did not mention the Chinese after the Christmas dinner of 1874. Those who had remained at Newstead to harvest the 1874 crops apparently sought work elsewhere for 1875.

29. Most of the fifty-one Chinese in the Delta in 1880 lived in Washington County. Loewen, *The Delta Chinese,* 25. There was a brief revival of interest in importing Chinese workers during the 1879 exodus of black farmers to Kansas. The *Greenville Times* and *Vicksburg Herald* advocated replacing the departed blacks with Chinese and English workers. Few Britons were interested in migrating to the Delta, however, and the recruitment of Chinese was abandoned after the Chinese consul in San Francisco informed planters that Asians in California received wages between two and four times what was offered in the Delta. By 1882 all but one member of Mississippi's congressional delegation voted to exclude Chinese from the United States. Wharton, *Negro in Mississippi,* 99; *Greenville Times,* 29 Mar. 1879.

30. Lieutenant D. M. White, 30 Sept. 1867, Narrative Reports, BRFAL.

31. A freedman's uninformed initiative, particularly where it involved cultivating someone else's land, could bring trouble. One ex-slave in Issaquena County went to work growing cotton on deserted fields in 1865. The property had been abandoned during the war, and it was his logical assumption that the owners had either died or forsaken the plantation. But after he had picked several hundred pounds of cotton, his activities were discovered, he was sent to jail, and his family was left without support. Lieutenant O. B. Foster, 12 Dec. 1865, ibid.

32. Captain W. F. Griffin, 21 Aug. 1865, ibid. We do not know the fate of Chasy or Atkins.

33. Lieutenant O. B. Foster (12 Dec. 1865) and agent Allen P. Huggins (31 Aug. 1867), ibid. The proportion of whites in Issaquena County's population rose from 8 to 12 percent between 1860 and 1870. *Tenth Census,* "Statistics of the Population," 397–98.

34. Lieutenant O. B. Foster (12 Dec. 1865) and Major George W. Corliss (31 Oct. 1867), Narrative Reports, BRFAL; Henry St. John Dixon Diary (10 Jan. 1866), SHC, NcU.

35. Sidney Nathans, "'Gotta Mind to Move, a Mind to Settle Down': Afro-Americans and the Plantation Frontier," in *A Master's Due: Essays in Honor of David Herbert Donald,* ed. William J. Cooper, Jr., Michael F. Holt, and John McCardell (Baton Rouge, La., 1985), 208; Dixon Diary, entries for Dec. 1865 and Jan. 1866, especially 10 Jan. 1866. The Dixons did not recover their worker and left the Delta for California in 1870. Henry St. John Dixon became a lawyer. Interview with Clinton Bagley, Aug. 1990.

36. Captain William L. Tidball, 30 Sept. 1867, Narrative Reports, BRFAL.

37. Agent J. D. Byers to Preston, 30 June 1866, Letters Received, reel 13, M-826, ibid.; Pereyra, *Alcorn,* 79.

38. The agents' Narrative Reports are filled with complaints against the local judiciary and estimates of the number of cases that were improperly decided or never admitted to the docket.

39. William S. McFeely, *Yankee Stepfather: General O. O. Howard and the Freedmen* (New Haven, 1968); Michael W. Fitzgerald, *The Union League Movement in the Deep South: Politics and Agricultural Change during Reconstruction* (Baton Rouge, La., 1989), 49–50; Ronald L. F. Davis, *Good and Faithful Labor,* 59; Dixon Diary, entries for Jan. 1866; Samuel G. French, *Two Wars: An Autobiography of Samuel G. French* (Nashville,

1901), 333–34. A partial list of scholars critical of the Bureau's agents would include Kenneth B. White, "Wager Swayne: Racist or Realist?" *Alabama Review* 33 (Apr. 1978): 92–109; James Oakes, "A Failure of Vision: The Collapse of the Freedmen's Bureau Courts," *Civil War History* 25 (Mar. 1979): 66–76; and Gaines M. Foster, "The Limitations of Federal Health Care for Freedmen, 1862–1868," *Journal of Southern History* 48 (Aug. 1982): 349–72.

40. Agents frequently failed to give the race of plaintiff or defendant, rendering many of their reports unsatisfactory for a race-focused inquiry. The above figures represent calculations based on thirty complaints lodged by black residents of Washington County in October 1867. Captain William L. Tidball, 31 Oct. 1867, Narrative Reports, BRFAL.

41. Captain William L. Tidball (30 Sept. 1867), Agent C. T. Lawson (31 Oct. 1867), Agent Allen P. Huggins (31 Aug. 1867), and Captain E. E. Platt (31 Aug. 1867), ibid.

42. Agent Allen P. Huggins (1 Sept. 1867), Agent Charles Walden (12 Oct. 1867), Captain E. E. Platt (31 Aug. 1867), and Lieutenant D. M. White (31 Oct. 1867), ibid.; Dixon Diary (10 Jan. 1866).

43. For a broader perspective on the regional process away from centralized labor control, see Ralph Shlomowitz, "The Squad System on Postbellum Cotton Plantations," in *Toward a New South: Studies in Post-Civil War Southern Communities,* ed. Orville Vernon Burton and Robert C. McMath, Jr. (Westport, Conn., 1982), 265–80.

44. Metcalfe apparently contracted with his squads for a monthly wage in the late 1860s and early 1870s. Metcalfe Diary. Some Delta planters did, however, compensate squads with a share of their crop. Shlomowitz, "Squad System," 269–70.

45. Metcalfe Diary. See 1874 and 1875 entries generally, and specific examples of Metcalfe's declining wealth on 3 Feb., 1 Mar., and 2 Mar. 1875.

46. Ibid., 2 Dec., 7 Dec. 1874, 3 Mar., 18 Mar., 29 Mar., 9 Apr. 1875. Although Metcalfe occasionally sold food and other basic items to his workers, he did not keep a plantation store. His squads were free to patronize area merchants and sometimes left work to spend the day shopping in Greenville. Like other cash-poor tenants and wage laborers, however, they needed credit for purchases. Merchants were eager for their trade but demanded they pay higher prices for goods bought on credit and sometimes charged interest on their debt balances. Ibid., 14 July 1877; Washington Co. Deed Records, X:396–99.

47. Metcalfe Diary, 13 Mar., 7 Apr. 1875, 31 Jan. 1876, 12 Dec. 1875.

48. Ibid., 26 Dec. 1876, 31 Jan., 21 Feb., 6 Apr. 1877. Metcalfe had difficulty supervising white workers, too. On Monday, 30 Oct. 1876, Metcalfe recorded that carpenter John Carlson "began to raise bridge, but got so drunk he could not work after breakfast. Wilson the plasterer [was] also drunk." The next day, "Wilson worked all day, but was drunk. Carlson worked on bridge." All Metcalfe recorded for Wednesday was "Wilson drunk in town." Ibid.

49. Nor was Metcalfe the only planter baffled by black initiative in labor negotiations. See Sidney Nathans's account of Tunica County planter George Collins and the enterprising freedmen who made him bargain for their services in "'Gotta Mind to Move,'" 208–12.

50. Washington Co. Deed Records, D2:307–8. This sharecropping contract for 1873 shows that the farmer in question concluded 1872 with no debt.

51. Wright, *Old South, New South*, 85; Harold Woodman, *New South—New Law: The Legal Foundations of Credit and Labor Relations in the Postbellum Agricultural South* (Baton Rouge, La., 1995), 45–48.

52. Agent Allen P. Huggins (1 Sept. 1867), Lieutenant D. M. White (31 Aug. 1867), Captain Ryan (1 Sept. 1867), Captain William L. Tidball (30 Sept. 1867), and Agent Charles Walden (12 Oct. 1867), Narrative Reports, BRFAL. Agent Walden opposed share-cropping because it left too "great a chance for the employer to defraud [tenants,] as in many instances the laborer is furnished provisions[&] etc.[,] and charged exorbitant prices." He favored paying wages to workers, despite white preferences (which he noted) and the region's shortage of cash and credit.

53. Joseph P. Reidy's examination of a more established agricultural area, by contrast, reveals that "in 1870 not more than 5 percent of black household heads in central Georgia possessed a mule, the *sine qua non* of rental tenancy." In 1880, however, 20 percent of black farmers in central Georgia owned mules. See his *From Slavery to Agrarian Capitalism in the Cotton Plantation South: Central Georgia, 1800–1880* (Chapel Hill, N.C., 1992), 235.

54. Captain Ryan (1 Sept. 1867) and Lieutenant D. M. White (31 Aug. 1867), Narrative Reports, BRFAL. The "bollworm" and "army worm" mysteriously infested much of the Delta after the Civil War. These insects were not, however, as debilitating as the boll weevil, which chewed its way through the Delta after 1908. See Frederick Metcalfe's sketches of the bollworm among his diary entries in the summer of 1875. Metcalfe Diary.

55. Alfred C. Downs's experience was related by his widow, Clara Muir Buckingham Downs Willson, in her unpublished memoir, "Autobiography of a Southern Lady," Downs Family Collection, Ms-Ar. Comparative figures are drawn from Ernest A. Boeger and Emanuel A. Goldenweiser, *A Study of the Tenant Systems of Farming in the Yazoo-Mississippi Delta*, U. S. Department of Agriculture Bulletin No. 337 (Washington, D.C., 1916), 2. Based on information from the 1913 crop year, Boeger and Goldenweiser found that landlords averaged a 13.6 percent return from sharecroppers, 11.8 percent from share renters, and 6.6 percent from cash renters. There are no studies comparing the returns of rented and sharecropped land in the Delta before the twentieth century.

56. Lieutenant D. M. White, 31 Aug. 1867, Narrative Reports, M-826, BRFAL.

57. Sidney Nathans examines the attractions of renting for both tenant and landlord in his "'Gotta Mind to Move,'" 208–18. Because many of the period's rental contracts are no longer extant, it is impossible to determine precisely an average rental fee per acre. For examples of the diverse prices and conditions imposed on rented land, see *Greenville Times*, 6 Mar. and 13 Nov. 1875; Washington Co. Deed Records, Z:254, 257, D2:341–42.

58. William Wiley's 1873 lease of thirty-five acres of Panola plantation was among the more restrictive; it included a lien on the crops, required Wiley to work "under the general supervision and directions" of his landlord's agent, called for fencing and ditching work, and prohibited the tenant from selling any of the property's timber. On the other

extreme in 1873, Lyman G. Aldrich's tenants could rent mules for the reasonable charge of only $2.50 per month at a time when mules were seldom purchased for less than $150. See Washington Co. Deed Records, E2:41–42, D2:341–42.

59. Agent John Hynes (15 July 1867), Captain E. E. Platt (31 Aug. 1867), and Lieutenant D. M. White (31 Aug. 1867), Narrative Reports, BRFAL.

60. Captain William L. Tidball (30 Sept. 1867) and Lieutenant D. M. White (31 Oct. 1867), ibid.

61. Whites' retention of riverside lands—and their loss of backcountry property—is treated at length in the next chapter.

62. The difficulties of one Delta planter, George Collins of Tunica County, are analyzed and writ large over the South in David H. Donald's "A Generation of Defeat," in *From the Old South to the New: Essays on the Transitional South,* ed. Walter J. Fraser, Jr., and Winfred B. Moore, Jr. (Westport, Conn., 1981), 3–20. Frederick Metcalfe's example suggests, however, that Collins's inability to manage newly freed laborers was not restricted to younger planters.

3. Away from the Riverside

1. Williams, *Bolivar County,* 84, 102–3.

2. Settlers found ways to avoid alligators, but there was no escape from the mosquitoes that swarmed out of the low-lying sloughs every summer. Ibid., 84, 102–4, 179; Linton Weeks, *Clarksdale and Coahoma County: A History* (Clarksdale, Miss., 1982), 4; Mary Hamilton, *Trials of the Earth: The Autobiography of Mary Hamilton* (Jackson, Miss., 1992).

3. Weeks, *Clarksdale and Coahoma County,* 6.

4. Williams, *Bolivar County,* 165–66.

5. Ibid., 407, 533.

6. *Greenville Times,* 29 May 1888. The road to Love's neighborhood was eventually built, but settlers complained that the surface was poorly maintained and frequently impassable. The editor of the *Greenville Times* grew so pestered by correspondence bemoaning the road's condition that he begged the town's merchants and wealthy citizens to bypass the Board of Supervisors, invest their own money, and "make the road a real highway." Ibid., 12 Mar. 1898.

7. John A. Hynes, 15 July 1867, Narrative Reports, M-826, BRFAL; Williams, *Bolivar County,* 329–30.

8. Although ridges seldom stood more than fifteen feet above the lowlands, that margin was often sufficient to separate crops that were merely dampened by floodwaters from those that were destroyed. *Tenth Census,* "Cotton Production," 39.

9. Ibid., 43–44; Halsell, "Leflore County, 1833–1876," 220, 227; McCain and Capers, *Memoirs of Ireys;* Williams, *Bolivar County,* 320–21.

10. Ibid.; Brandfon, *Cotton Kingdom,* 40. In Mississippi, as in much of nineteenth-century America, land speculation could prove enormously profitable. Antebellum land speculators in northern Mississippi sometimes reaped profits of over 500 percent. But the most substantial windfalls accrued to land companies, not individual speculators. Indeed,

many individuals would have been better served by investments in eastern commercial ventures than in frontier property. Still, wild rumors of fabulous profits—compounded by the rising international cotton market in the 1850s—underwrote a busy frontier land market in the last years before the Civil War. See James W. Silver, "Land Speculation Profits in the Chickasaw Cession," *Journal of Southern History* 10 (1944): 84–92.

11. Although the Delta's frontier state compounded local governments' responsibilities, many of the structural changes that brought about its new and increased tax levies were common throughout the South. The best study of Reconstruction-era taxation is J. Mills Thornton III's "Fiscal Policy and the Failure of Radical Reconstruction in the Lower South," in *Region, Race, and Reconstruction: Essays in Honor of C. Vann Woodward*, ed. J. Morgan Kousser and James M. McPherson (New York, 1982), 349–94.

12. *Greenville Times*, 2 Jan. 1875; Brandfon, *Cotton Kingdom*, 42–43; Washington Co. Deed Records.

13. *Greenville Times*, 7 Nov. 1874, etc. The tax burden issue was no mere illusory concern; Democrats slashed taxes and spending upon taking office. Between 1874 and 1879 the taxes imposed on Delta landowners fell precipitously. The combined state and local taxes on Washington County land, for example, fell from 37.5 mills in 1874 to only 18.5 mills in 1879. And the Democrats resisted subsequent increases—in 1884 the combined rate still stood at 18.5 mills. Ibid., 2 Jan. 1875, 20 Dec. 1879, 18 Oct.–6 Dec. 1884. J. Mills Thornton has demonstrated the importance of whites' increased tax burden (and their perceptions that freedmen were the primary beneficiaries of the new levies) in Deep South Democrats' redemption of state and local political offices from Republican control in the mid-1870s. See his "Fiscal Policy."

14. These calculations were derived from the assessed value of all land in Washington County in 1870. Washington Co. Land Tax Roll, 1870.

15. Halsell, "Leflore County, 1833–1876," 234; Washington Co. Land Tax Roll, 1870; Brandfon, *Cotton Kingdom*, 44.

16. See graph 4.

17. *Greenville Times*, Oct. 1874, 16 Jan., 27 Mar. 1875; Halsell, "Leflore County, 1833–1876," 234. Bolivar County's number of privately held acres fell 32 percent between 1870 and 1873, and Issaquena County lost 31 percent of its taxable land in the same period. Washington County's decline in privately owned land was mitigated by immigration into the area, but it too lost taxable acres as landowners defaulted on their tax bills: its number of taxable acres fell 24 percent from 1871 to 1873. *Greenville Times*, 2 Jan. 1875.

18. Brandfon details Mississippi's many efforts to return Delta lands to the tax rolls. See his *Cotton Kingdom*, 40–64. Many potential bidders may have abjured purchase in deference to their financially embarrassed neighbors. Moreover, the vociferous conservatism of the Taxpayers' League may have intimidated freedmen from buying the seized lands of prominent Democrats.

19. French, *Two Wars*, 341–42; McCain and Capers, *Memoirs of Ireys*, 31.

20. Lieutenant D. M. White, 31 Aug. 1867, Narrative Reports, M-826, BRFAL.

21. *Greenville Times*, 3 May 1879; Washington Co. Deed Records, M2:956–58. Washington County's "exodusters" quickly abandoned their departure plans when steamboats

refused to call at the bank. The 10 May 1879 *Greenville Times* reported that laborers had abandoned their plans to go to Kansas and returned to their former employers. The Agricultural and Immigration Company chartered by the state legislature in July 1881 never had much effect on immigration patterns. Many southern blacks continued to come to the Delta, but few whites could be convinced to immigrate. For more information on the short-lived popularity of Kansas with southern blacks, see Nell I. Painter's *Exodusters: Black Migration to Kansas after Reconstruction* (New York, 1977).

22. *Tenth Census,* "Cotton Production," 45; Richard A. O'Hea, civil engineer, *Map of Washington County, Mississippi; Compiled and Revised from Original Documents on Record* (New Orleans, 1871), RG 29, NA.

23. Robert Higgs has properly stressed the continuing diversity of southern agricultural contracts. In the Delta contractual diversity symbolized and fostered a dynamic and intricate economy. See Higgs's "Patterns of Farm Rental in the Georgia Cotton Belt, 1880–1900," *Journal of Economic History* 34 (June 1974): 468–82.

24. By contrast, the rest of Mississippi and the South were quickly falling into share-cropping. By 1880, 28 percent of farms in the cotton South were worked by sharecroppers, while only 17 percent supported renters. And the figures for the former states of the Confederacy show an even greater disparity: only 12 percent of farms in that area were rented, while 26 percent were sharecropped. See Joseph D. Reid, "Sharecropping as an Understandable Market Response: The Postbellum South," *Journal of Economic History* 33 (Mar. 1973): 111. As Harold Woodman has demonstrated, not all of the landless cultivators whose livelihood depended on a share of the cotton crop were properly termed *sharecroppers.* That designation correctly applies to laborers who were paid a share of their production, less deductions for any food and other supplies they were furnished. Share tenants, by contrast, paid the landlord a percentage of their crop. The former group enjoyed significantly less autonomy than did the latter. Woodman, *New South—New Law,* 67–94. However, few landlords were unambiguous in designating the terms on which their land would be worked, many leaving behind a variant of Frederick Metcalfe's notation: "Contracted with two freemen, named Williams, on the half share for 1876." Metcalfe Diary, 31 Jan. 1876.

25. Although sharecroppers should be classified as workers paid in kind rather than as tenants, this does not alter the fact that sharecroppers had more to lose (and gain) by their efforts than did wage laborers. Their assumption of risk placed them above laborers on the agricultural ladder, just as legal decisions placed them below renters by the third decade of the twentieth century. See Woodman's "Post-Civil War Southern Agriculture and the Law," *Agricultural History* 53 (Jan. 1979): 319–37; "Postbellum Social Change and Its Effects on Marketing the South's Cotton Crop," ibid., 56 (Jan. 1982): 215–30; and *New South—New Law.*

26. The disastrous effects of the short crop of 1867 for Delta agriculture are examined in the previous chapter.

27. In order to persuade Gordon Hicks and Martin Taylor to farm his property, absentee landowner Howard Falconer of Holly Springs agreed to a lease which favored the tenants and sold them two mules at a good price. Hicks and Taylor were, however, required

to haul their cotton to a specified gin for processing. Still, this small inconvenience was a minor detail when compared to the benefits of their lease. Hicks and Taylor were charged only 2,400 pounds of cotton as rent for the farm, although land in that area produced an average of 984 pounds of cotton per acre. See "Cotton Production," 39. A copy of the lease contract is found in the Washington Co. Deed Records, D2:387–88. For an anthropological perspective on the settlement efforts of African Americans in remote parts of South America, see Norman E. Whitten, Jr., *Black Frontiersmen: A South American Case* (Cambridge, Mass., 1974).

28. Samuel G. French's Matilda plantation leases are recorded in the Washington Co. Deed Records, D2:327–28, 369–70, E2:39–40, 75–76.

29. The gap between the rent charged for the small, cleared plot and the rates asked for the three larger tracts reminds us that the latter acreage would require more labor (to clear or plant around wooded areas) and still yield a smaller crop per acre. The experiences of these seven farmers would, therefore, be very different. One man could limit his activities to his cotton crop, but the other six struggled to wrest farmland from wilderness while raising sufficient cotton to cover their debts and obligations. Hence, calculation of the average plot per man creates a statistical aura of uniformity which did not conform to the divergent circumstances of these seven farmers. But those who take comfort in statistics should know that each of the seven men was responsible, on average, for 23.7 acres.

30. The problem of farm tenants' debts reached appalling levels during and after the agricultural depression of the 1890s. Many southern tenant farmers became trapped in "debt peonage," tied by debt to coercive landlords, restrained by law and the threat of violence from leaving lands that could never retire their obligations. See Pete Daniel, *The Shadow of Slavery: Peonage in the South, 1901–1969* (Urbana, Ill., 1972), and "The Metamorphosis of Slavery, 1865–1900," *Journal of American History* 66 (June 1979): 88–99. In the Delta peonage and coercion were largely confined to the plantation districts for most of the late nineteenth century. Labor shortages might tempt landlords to try trapping tenants on their land, but there was always a labor-hungry landowner on the frontier willing to offer poor farmers a better deal. Delta tenants became accustomed to moving about the region in search of a better lease, more fertile soil, and a less demanding landlord. Landlords realized by the 1870s that in this environment a bad reputation among potential tenants would only exacerbate their labor woes. Delta native David L. Cohn recorded the habitual relocation of the region's tenant farmers in his *Where I Was Born and Raised* (Boston, 1948).

31. The tenants' total cotton rent was multiplied by .12 (assuming their cotton would bring 12 cents per pound) to arrive at the figure of $9.64 per acre. The tenant on the 16-acre plot, Virgil McKee, paid $15.60 per acre to cultivate cleared land. French was less avaricious than most landlords; he did not charge interest on debts due or on money advanced to tenants.

32. Washington Co. Deed Records, C2:383. There is no way to ascertain whether Brown's work on the Sligo gin won better acreage for himself and his partners.

33. Ibid., F2:277. Henry T. Ireys was another landowner extending discounts to tenants paying their rent in cash. Ibid., U:208.

34. Ibid., A2:596. A large number of white women owned Delta plantations in the 1860s and 1870s. Some acquired the property through inheritance, and others, like Camille Bourges, held the land in their names to evade seizure should debt drive their husband into bankruptcy. Michael Wayne found a similar pattern in the Natchez District. See his *Reshaping of Plantation Society,* 93–94.

35. Washington Co. Deed Records, A2:467–68. Planter Frederick A. Metcalfe, by contrast, paid a carpenter $75 to build two tenant houses on his plantation. Metcalfe Diary, Sept. 1875.

36. Metcalfe Diary, 18 Aug., 19 Aug., 21 Aug., 25 Aug., 19 Dec. 1874, n.d. (1876 or 1877), 16 Apr. 1876, 16 June, 8 Sept. 1877, 7 Jan., 15 Jan., 22 Jan. 1880. Metcalfe paid less for fashioned materials in 1880 than he had in the mid-1870s, suggesting that more tenants were eager for cash labor in their spare time.

37. Interview with Wade S. Wineman, Sr., May 1990. A. G. Wineman & Company, founded by the father and uncle of Wade Wineman, was a major Greenville lumber company from the 1890s. Wade Wineman worked for decades as a timber agent and real estate appraiser in the Delta. For a representative lease contract allowing free use of cleared land in the 1870s, see Washington Co. Deed Records, A2:534–35.

38. John Hebron Moore, *Andrew Brown and Cypress Lumbering in the Old Southwest* (Baton Rouge, La., 1967); Halsell, "Leflore County, 1876–1920," 248; John R. Shipley, "The Story of the Chicago Mill and Lumber Company," *Washington County Historical Society Programs of 1980* (Greenville, Miss., 1980), 64–65; John P. Colletta, "Who Killed Joe Ring?" (work in progress), chap. 3; *Greenville Times,* 8 Mar. 1884.

39. Interview with Wade S. Wineman, Sr.; *Greenville Times,* 8 Aug. 1874; Charles Banks, *Negro Town and Colony, Mound Bayou, Bolivar County, Mississippi: Opportunities Open to Negro Farmers and Settlers* (Mound Bayou, Miss., n.d.), 5.

40. Halsell, "Leflore County, 1876–1920," 249; Banks, "Mound Bayou," 5; Metcalfe Diary, 21 May, 1 June, 1 July, 13 July 1875; *Greenville Times,* 24 Aug. 1878; interview with Wade S. Wineman, Sr. Coal was sold in the Delta during the 1870s, but large supplies of the ore were not available for several years. In 1875 fuel customers bought dry cordwood for only $3.50 per cord, while a bushel-sized box of coal cost 65 cents. Steam engines had no dependable supply of coal until Greenville merchant A. D. Pace began selling coal to steamboats in 1889. *Greenville Times,* 13 Nov. 1875, 2 Feb. 1889.

41. Halsell, "Leflore County, 1876–1920," 249, 250, 254; 1880 Census, population schedules, Greenville, Washington Co., Miss.; *Greenville Times,* 31 May 1884, 7 Feb. 1885; Williams, *Bolivar County,* 327–29. Halsell claims that between 5 and 6 million Delta acres were sold to lumber companies in this period. But only the timber rights, not full ownership, were conveyed in many cases. Still, it is not unreasonable to expect over 1 million acres sold for timber. Turn-of-the-century land tax records in several counties reveal lumber companies' ownership of tens of thousands of acres, much of it purchased over a decade earlier from the Louisville, New Orleans and Texas Railroad.

42. For William Faulkner's impression of these developments, see "The Bear" and "Delta Autumn" in his short story collection, *Go Down Moses* (New York, 1942).

43. Williams, *Bolivar County,* 327–28; Banks, *Mound Bayou,* 5; Hamilton, *Trials of the Earth,* 89; Twelfth Census, Population MSS, Washington Co.; *Greenville Times,* 17 Mar. 1883.

44. Brandfon discusses the provenance of lumber companies' land in *Cotton Kingdom,* 51–52.

4. The Rise of the Backcountry Farmer

1. A. J. Paxton, Sr., "Reminiscences," 35, 40, typed copy in the Carter Room, William Alexander Percy Memorial Library, Greenville, Miss.; Washington Co. Deed Records, D2:130.

2. Washington Co. Deed Records, Z:90.

3. Ibid., Z:90, D2:130, B2:202–3, E2:308–11, F2:287.

4. Ibid.

5. Washington Co. Probate Records, packet 423.

6. Ibid.; Washington Co. Deed Records, H2:393–95.

7. The deed of trust was not a mortgage. It did not automatically award property to the creditor upon the debtor's default but instead authorized a trustee to auction the property. The creditor was compensated from the proceeds of that sale. The deed of trust and other aspects of the frontier credit system are discussed in chap. 6.

8. Washington Co. Deed Records, Z:90, B2:202–3, E2:308–11, H2:393–95, I2:487–88.

9. *Greenville Times,* 21 Nov. 1874, 17 July 1875.

10. Ibid., 25 Sept.,, 30 Oct. 1875. Bohlen Lucas had announced as a Republican candidate for Washington County sheriff in 1871 but was not elected. Before his public alliance with the county's Redeemers, he referred to himself as a "liberal Republican" and admirer of Horace Greeley. Ibid., 15 July 1871, 25 Sept. 1875.

11. Ibid., 6 Nov., 13 Nov. 1875.

12. Washington Co. Deed Records, J2:328–29.

13. Wharton, *Negro in Mississippi,* 241–55; Neil R. McMillen, *Dark Journey: Black Mississippians in the Age of Jim Crow* (Urbana, Ill., 1989), 72–108. Chap. 6 examines white Democrats' use of literacy tests to disfranchise black Delta citizens.

14. By contrast, 85 percent of the region's white male farm owners were literate in 1880. These figures are drawn from the Federal Census MSS (Population and Agriculture) for Coahoma, Sunflower, and Washington Counties in 1870, 1880, and 1900. Information on all farm owners and a sample of farm tenants was evaluated to ascertain a variety of demographic attributes, including literacy, age, household size and composition, labor patterns, personal and real property, and farm production. This agglomeration of data, which includes information on approximately 25,000 of the region's white and black farm owners and laborers, is hereafter cited as Delta database.

15. Tenth Census, Agriculture and Population MSS, Washington Co.

16. Washington Co. Deed Records, D2:228, F2:573–74.

17. Delta database.

18. Washington Co. Deed Records, W2:120–21. Spearman's deed to the 119 acres was

not recorded in the county deed books, and its proximity to his original holdings cannot be determined, but his ownership of the property is verified by a subsequent deed of trust to the land. Ibid., J3:350–51.

19. Ninth Census, Population and Agriculture MSS, Washington Co.; Tenth Census, Population and Agriculture MSS, Washington Co..

20. Delta database.

21. Augmented households, containing the nuclear family, distant kin, boarders, and laborers, were not limited to the Delta frontier. Crandall A. Shifflett explores the emergence of similarly large households in the Virginia tobacco belt in his *Patronage and Poverty in the Tobacco South: Louisa County, Virginia, 1860–1900* (Knoxville, Tenn., 1982), 84–98.

22. The figures for black female farm owners are taken from 1900 because only three women held land in the source counties in 1880, an inadequate number for evaluation. Black farmers were not unique in their frequency of extranuclear households in this period: among white male farm-owning families in 1880, 24 percent housed relatives, 30 percent contained boarders, and 21 percent included servants or laborers. Delta database.

23. Tenth Census, Population and Agriculture MSS, Washington Co..

24. Washington Co. Deed Records, J3:350–51.

25. Ibid., Y2:766–70. Spearman's new creditors, Francis, Smith, Caldwell & Company, were less active in Washington County than in other sections of the Delta. See, for example, the deed record books of Coahoma and Sunflower Counties in this period. Their thin presence in Washington County is probably attributable to competition from Greenville's well-entrenched and prosperous banks, lending merchants, and cotton factorages.

26. Washington Co. Deed Records, C3:636–38.

27. Ibid., J3:350–51, 558–59, L3:245–47.

28. Lewis Spearman, Jr., was enumerated in the 1880, 1900, and 1910 census MSS of Washington County. He was identified as a farm renter in the latter two documents. There is no record of his father after 1895: Lewis Spearman, Sr., apparently died between losing his farm and the 1900 federal census.

29. Washington Co. Deed Records, J2:364–65. The deed to Toler's second 80-acre tract was not registered in the county deed books, but subsequent deeds of trust apply to the full 160 acres. See, for example, ibid., 136:637–39.

30. Ibid., L2:97–98, O2:710–11.

31. Ibid., A3:761–62. The increasingly acquisitive policies of the region's agricultural lenders during the late 1880s and 1890s are examined in chap. 6.

32. Ibid., D3:454–57, G3:93–94, I3:570–71, J3:371–72.

33. Ibid., J3:373.

34. Ibid., V3:258, 102:595–97.

35. Ibid., 114:298–99, 136:607–8, 637–39, 211:566–67; Ninth Census, Population MSS, Washington Co.; Tenth Census, Population MSS, Washington Co.; Twelfth Census, Population MSS, Washington Co. This ratio—with only one black farm owner in three holding his property until death— probably was representative of the Delta in its frontier period. William Toler died between March 1905 when he signed his last deed of trust

agreement and March 1908 when his heirs designated two of their number with power of attorney for the group. Toler's children continued in his tradition of innovative financing. They negotiated a $3,000 loan from a Mrs. Dora Ida Bullington of Memphis in 1912 and later obtained a $2,160 loan from an individual in Chicago who only asked 8 percent interest for the money. William Toler's children were still negotiating loans on his farm fifty years after he purchased the land.

36. Washington Co. Deed Records, K2:303, I2:696, L2:262–63, N2:126–27, E2:190, I2:180.

37. Donald L. Winters employs a similar hypothesis in evaluating the agricultural ladder in the Midwest. See his *Farmers without Farms: Agricultural Tenancy in Nineteenth-Century Iowa* (Westport, Conn., 1978).

38. Census enumerators were not instructed to distinguish between sharecropping farmers and other tenants, but several Washington and Coahoma County census takers did add this crucial fact in both 1880 and 1900. The figures for sharecroppers are drawn from those MS returns. Were all sharecroppers and renters delineated, age figures for the two groups would probably show greater differences.

39. Delta database.

40. Washington Co. Probate Records, packets 404 and 465; Washington Co. Will Book 2, 125; O'Hea, *Map of Washington County*. The Barefields intermarried regularly with the Ryals family, another backcountry clan of small landowners, lived together at or near the Colony, and lie in adjacent plots in the Hollandale cemetery. See Alice Wade and Katherine Branton, eds., *Early Mississippi Records: Washington County, 1860–1912* 4 (Leland, Miss., 1986), 130–31.

41. Ninth Census, Agriculture MSS, Washington Co.; Washington Co. Probate Records, packet 465; Washington Co. Will Book 2, 125; Washington Co. Deed Records; *Greenville Times*, 6 Nov. 1875. The Barefields were described as small farmers and lauded for their predictably Democratic phalanx during Redemption by the *Greenville Times*.

42. Washington Co. Probate Records, packet 465; Washington Co. Will Book 2, 125; Twelfth Census, Population MSS, Washington Co. The Barefields' frontier existence has several parallels to the backcountry republicanism outlined in Steven Hahn's study of upcountry Georgia in this period. I have not found any evidence, however, that members of the Colony opposed the stock and fence laws—a demarcating issue in the transition toward agricultural capitalism, according to Hahn—debated in Mississippi in the 1880s. See Hahn's *The Roots of Southern Populism: Yeoman Farmers and the Transformation of the Georgia Upcountry, 1850–1900* (New York, 1983).

43. Williams, *Bolivar County*, 293.

44. Ibid. Will A. Dockery recalled traveling to Cleveland in 1888; at that time, "there were no roads worth considering." Ibid., 170.

45. Ibid.

46. The Montgomery family is best described in Janet Sharp Hermann's *The Pursuit of a Dream* (New York, 1981). In 1890 Isaiah Montgomery recounted his story in the *New York World;* the text was reprinted in Williams, *Bolivar County*, 586–90. Joseph E. Davis was the older brother of Confederate president Jefferson Davis.

47. Hermann, *Pursuit of a Dream,* 219–22.

48. Ibid., 222. The LNO&T sold land to Mound Bayou colonists for only $7 per acre and allowed payments to be spread over five years. Ibid.

49. Ibid., 222–23.

50. Ibid., 222–24, 238–39.

51. Montgomery's participation in Mississippi's 1890 constitutional convention, where the founder of Mound Bayou (and only black representative to the convention) endorsed measures that he knew would be used to disfranchise many black voters, is examined in chap. 6.

52. Ibid., 225–45; Williams, *Bolivar County,* 586–90; *Memphis News-Scimitar,* 11 Feb. 1906; G. A. Lee, "Mound Bayou, the Negro City of Mississippi," *Voice of the Negro,* Jan. 1906, 36–41; Banks, "Negro Town and Colony."

53. Hermann and others blame the community's downfall in the early twentieth century on its financial overextension, especially the debt incurred to construct the cottonseed oil mill. See *Pursuit of a Dream,* 238–40. While the costly mill was the most vivid catalyst in Mound Bayou's decline, the colony was also a victim of the forces that narrowed all black Deltans' prospects in the two decades after 1900. These sequential disasters—blacks' loss of their political franchise at the turn of the century, the boll weevil's arrival after 1908, the floods of 1912 and 1913, the cotton crisis of 1914, and white planters' tightening grip on land throughout the region—are examined in detail in chaps. 6 and 7.

54. Ousley was named for his former master.

55. Hermann, *Pursuit of a Dream,* 229; Williams, *Bolivar County,* 35–37.

56. Nearby white planter Will A. Dockery, who knew both Ousleys well, is the source of this interpretation of Renova's failure. In comparing Joseph Ousley to the founders of Mound Bayou, Isaiah Montgomery and Ben Green, Dockery emphasized that Ousley "was not of the same type of man that those two were." Williams, *Bolivar County,* 173.

5. Joining Town and Country

1. William Alexander Percy, *Lanterns on the Levee: Recollections of a Planter's Son* (New York, 1941), 5–6.

2. *Greenville Times,* 17 July 1875, 5 Dec. 1874. Steamboats stopped at hundreds of landings on the Mississippi, Yazoo, and Sunflower Rivers at the beginning of the postbellum era. See Harry P. Owens, *Steamboats and the Cotton Economy: River Trade in the Yazoo-Mississippi Delta* (Jackson, Miss., 1990).

3. Harold D. Woodman, *King Cotton and His Retainers: Financing and Marketing the Cotton Crop of the South, 1800–1925* (Lexington, Ky., 1968); Lewis E. Atherton, *The Southern Country Store, 1800–1860* (Baton Rouge, La., 1949); Thomas D. Clark, *Pills, Petticoats, and Plows* (Indianapolis, 1944).

4. According to Atherton, "The factorage system undoubtedly retarded the development of interior towns and stores to a serious degree." See his *Southern Country Store,* 34, 38–62. In *Reshaping of Plantation Society,* 163–65, Michael Wayne concludes that the local merchants of the Natchez District were similarly restrained by the factor system. Woodman supports this interpretation in *King Cotton and His Retainers,* 154–64.

5. See Atherton, *Southern Country Store*. Frank L. Owsley discusses the antebellum yeoman farmers of Bolivar County in his *Plain Folk of the Old South* (Baton Rouge, La., 1949; rept., with an introduction by Grady McWhiney, 1985), 15–17. Even slaves "sold to Mississippi" found opportunities to earn cash. Planters like Frederick Metcalfe of Washington County paid slaves for extra work and found the practice improved morale and introduced incentive to bondsmen's efforts. Indeed, much of the work on Metcalfe's plantation during the last two weeks of each December was performed for small wages, and slaves and shopkeepers shared in this infusion of cash for Christmas gifts. Metcalfe Diary; John Hebron Moore, *The Emergence of the Cotton Kingdom in the Old Southwest: Mississippi, 1770–1860* (Baton Rouge, La., 1988), 105.

6. Harold Woodman demonstrates that many merchants compensated for the blockade by vigorously pursuing internal trade during the Civil War, and he shows how some continued to import goods and export cotton despite the exertions of the U.S. Navy. Still, the Civil War marked the beginning of the end for cotton factors. See *King Cotton and His Retainers*, 200–241. Michael Wayne surveys the deleterious effects of war and the collapse of factorage in *Reshaping of Plantation Society*, 160–63. The Confederates' voluntary cotton embargo is discussed in James McPherson, *Battle Cry of Freedom: The Civil War Era* (New York, 1988), 382–87.

7. Woodman, *King Cotton and His Retainers*, 244–314. Unlike most antebellum cotton traders, the ubiquitous Edmund Richardson contrived to resurrect his factorage after the war. His ownership of land (with 500 bales of cotton hidden away) and convict lease contracts from the Mississippi state government greatly aided his solvency. By the 1880s his company, Richardson & May, was reported to be the largest cotton factorage in the United States. Ibid., 259.

8. Ibid., 281–87; Ransom and Sutch, *One Kind of Freedom*, 117–25.

9. Although Ransom and Sutch regard the furnishing merchant (and crop liens) with unmitigated disdain, Woodman shows the initial advantages of merchant lending to both storekeeper and farmer. Ransom and Sutch, *One Kind of Freedom*, 117–70; Woodman, *King Cotton and His Retainers*, 296–98.

10. See William Faulkner's *The Hamlet* (New York, 1940), *The Town* (New York, 1957), or *The Mansion* (New York, 1959).

11. Colletta, *Who Killed Joe Ring?;* Dunbar Rowland, ed., *Mississippi . . .* 3 (Atlanta, 1907), 3:243–44, 259–60; Marie M. Hemphill, *Fevers, Floods, and Faith: A History of Sunflower County, Mississippi, 1844–1976* (privately printed, 1980), 115; Ninth Census, Population MSS, Sunflower Co.

12. A. E. Britt, "The Steamboat Era," MS in the collection of Sam J. Ely, Jr., Indianola, Miss.; Hemphill, *Fevers, Floods, and Faith*, 115–16; Rowland, *Mississippi* 3:259–60.

13. Hemphill, *Fevers, Floods, and Faith*, 116.

14. Ibid., 116; Rowland, *Mississippi* 3:243–44, 259–60; Sunflower Co. Deed Records. For example, see the deeds of trust issued by George W. Faison, Sr., James P. Faison, Edmund H. Faison, Walter B. Faison, William M. Faison, and George W. Faison, Jr., to the Scottish-American Mortgage Company, Ltd., an international concern represented in the United States by a Chicago agent. Sunflower Co. Deed Records, H2:368–84, R2:358–75,

441–50, 452–60. Despite the savings on interest charges, few Delta landowners of lesser wealth availed themselves of loans from beyond the region's boundaries. The Faisons paid 8 percent annual interest for these loans at a time when the local average was 10 percent per annum. The Delta's credit market is discussed in the next chapter.

15. Faison attempted to extend his commercial network to Greenville in the early 1880s but relinquished operations there after only two years, perhaps discouraged by the level of competition in the booming river town. At the turn of the century, Faison operated stores under the name of Faison & Son in Indianola, Shaw, and Faisonia. Rowland, *Mississippi* 3:243–44, 259–60.

16. Ninth Census, Population and Agriculture MSS, Washington Co.; Tenth Census, Population and Agriculture MSS, Washington Co..

17. The carpetbagger myth notwithstanding, foreign merchants—not northern new-comers—dominated Greenville shopkeeping in the postbellum era. Still, some northern-ers did migrate to the Delta in search of trading wealth after the Civil War. Honas B. Putman was one such newcomer. See his testimony to the Senate committee investigat-ing Mississippi's "redemption" from Republican control in *Mississippi in 1875,* Report No. 527, vol. 2, 44th Congress, 1st sess. (Washington, D.C., 1876), 1430–39.

18. Ninth Census, Population MSS, Washington Co.. Prior places of residence can be determined from the places of birth listed for the merchants' offspring. Foreign-born males accounted for twenty-one of Greenville's forty-two wholesale merchants, retail mer-chants, and grocers in 1870. Six of these were born in Prussia, three in Bavaria, one each in Baden and Hesse-Darmstadt, four in France, three in Italy, two in Ireland, and one in Poland. On average, these men were just under thirty-five years old, all but six were mar-ried, and they and their wives were literate. The average foreign-born merchant was al-most five years older than his spouse, compared to Faison's eleven years of seniority. Two-thirds of the American-born merchants hailed from the former slaveholding states. Just over half of these men were married as of 1870, but a similar age gap (four years) sep-arated them from their spouses. While one-third of the foreign-born merchants married American women, the native southerners all took American spouses. Ibid.

19. Of Greenville's fourteen southern-born merchants in 1870, three were black and eleven white. Ibid. Contrast Greenville's preponderance of nonnative merchants to Harold Woodman's claim that "most storekeepers were indigenous," and his assumption of "continuity in the history of the country store [because] . . . many of the postwar store-keepers were antebellum merchants who had survived the war." In his study of the Natchez District, however, Michael Wayne found that "the vast majority in the decade following the war were new to the district or the profession, in some cases both." Their common access to the Mississippi River suggests one explanation for the large number of nonsoutherners and foreign-born merchants in both the Delta and the Natchez District. Woodman's claim may hold for the more remote sections of the South. See Woodman, *King Cotton and His Retainers,* 303–4; Wayne, *Reshaping of Plantation Society,* 166.

20. Many of the foreign-born merchants listed in 1870 were still living and hawking their wares in Greenville in 1880. Their number and percentage of the town's commercial class would have been even larger had Greenville not suffered nearly 200 dead in the 1878

yellow fever epidemic. McCain and Capers, *Memoirs of Ireys;* Alice Wade and Katherine Branton, eds., *Early Mississippi Records: Issaquena County, Washington County* 2 (Leland, Miss., 1983), 121–24.

21. In 1880 twenty-seven of the forty-one listed as "dry goods merchant," "hardware dealer," "grocer," or "merchant" were born outside the United States. Of the fourteen American-born merchants, ten hailed from former slaveholding states. The number of black merchants recorded in Greenville fell from three in 1870 to none in 1880. Tenth Census, Population MSS, Washington Co..

22. In 1880 Greenville's foreign-born merchants hailed from Bavaria (5), Austria (5), Prussia (4), Baden (1), Posen (1), Hesse-Darmstadt (1), Alsace (1), France (3), China (3), Canada (1), Poland (1), and Russia (1). All three Chinese merchants were grocers, and most of the remaining storekeepers were described as "dry goods" merchants. Present-day Chinese-Americans in Greenville hypothesize that the Delta's first Chinese merchants arrived in the region as agricultural laborers, but I have found no way to verify that claim. Ibid.; interview with Raymond Wong, Sr., Aug. 1987.

23. Of Greenville's seventy-nine nonblack merchants, forty were born outside the United States. Almost half of these nonnatives (19) were Chinese, a dramatic increase since the three recorded in 1880. Fifty of Greenville's eighty-six merchants claimed at least one foreign-born parent. The town had seven black merchants, most grocers, in 1900. Twelfth Census, Population MSS, Washington Co..

24. Harold Woodman discounted the possibility of a large postbellum influx of Jewish merchants to the South and claimed that many Jewish storekeepers arrived in the region during the antebellum era. Unlike Woodman, Michael Wayne stressed the number and success of European Jews among the Natchez District's postbellum merchants. See Woodman, *King Cotton and His Retainers,* 304; Wayne, *Reshaping of Plantation Society,* 167–68.

25. Ninth Census, Population MSS, Washington Co.; Tenth Census, Population MSS, Washington Co.; *Greenville Times;* Louis Schmier, ed., *Reflections of Southern Jewry: The Letters of Charles Wessolowsky, 1878–1879* (Macon, Ga., 1982), 63–65; Harold W. Solomon, *The Early History of the Hebrew Union Congregation of Greenville, Mississippi* (Greenville, Miss., 1972). I am grateful to L. B. Stein for directing me to Solomon's history and for loaning me his copy of the work, among other kindnesses.

26. That support continued well into the twentieth century. Consider William Alexander Percy's description of the Delta Jewry. Jews arrived in the region "shortly after the Civil War with packs on their backs, peddlers from Russia, Poland, Germany, a few from Alsace. They sold trinkets to the Negroes and saved. Today they are plantation-owners, bankers, lawyers, doctors, merchants; their children attend the great universities, win prizes, become connoisseurs in the arts and radicals in politics. I was talking to one, an old-timer, not too successful, in front of his small store a short time ago. He suddenly asked in his thick Russian accent: 'Do you know Pushkin? Ah, beautiful, better than Shelley or Byron!' Why shouldn't such a people inherit the earth, not, surely, because of their meekness, but because of a steadier fire, a tension and tenacity that make all other whites seem stodgy and unintellectual." Percy, *Lanterns on the Levee,* 17.

27. Julius Lengsfield and Jacob Alexander were elected mayor, and Nathan Goldstein assumed the post after the 1878 yellow fever epidemic left him (a city councilman) the only surviving member of the city's government. *Greenville Times.*

28. Solomon, *Hebrew Union Congregation,* 38–39; Rabbi Leo E. Turitz and Evelyn Turitz, *Jews in Early Mississippi* (Jackson, Miss., 1983), 57–78; Bilbo's quote and the story behind the incident are in Hodding Carter's *Where Main Street Meets the River* (New York, 1953), 182–84. The large number of Delta Jews supported several temples in and near the region in this period. The Congregation B'nai Israel, formed in Greenville in 1869, was reorganized in 1879 as the Hebrew Union Congregation and still worships in an impressive pale brick and stone temple built in 1906. Vicksburg Jews dedicated their first temple in 1870, the first services in Clarksdale were begun in 1894 (with the B'nai B'rith Lodge organized in 1910 and Temple Beth Israel completed later), Lexington settlers formed Congregation Beth El in 1904, and the Cleveland Jewry completed construction of Temple Adath Israel (begun in 1921) in 1927. Turitz and Turitz, *Jews in Early Mississippi,* 44, 61, 66, 73, 76–77.

29. Compare the diverse pursuits of these white merchants, planters, and professionals to the comparable moonlighting of black farmers who cleared forests and sold the lumber to supplement their cotton earnings. See chaps. 3 and 4.

30. Percy, *Lanterns on the Levee,* 70–73; *Mississippi in 1875,* 1459–97; *Washington County Times,* 20 Mar. 1869.

31. Ninth Census, Population and Agriculture MSS, Washington Co.; Washington Co. Land Tax Roll, 1870; McCain and Capers, *Memoirs of Ireys;* Washington Co. Deed Records.

32. Contrast this to the self-consciously conflicting planters and merchants sketched by Jonathan M. Wiener in his *Social Origins of the New South: Alabama, 1860–1885* (Baton Rouge, La., 1978).

33. A. J. Paxton, Sr., "Reminiscences."

34. Most of the hyphenated commercialists had purchased land in the antebellum period or soon after the Civil War when property taxes were relatively low and cotton prices high. Washington Co. Deed Records.

35. Many acres, particularly in the backcountry, were lost for tax arrears in the 1870s. See chap. 3.

36. Quote from J. B. Killebrew, "The Relation of Railroads to Agriculture," *Southern Farm Magazine* 7:9 (Nov. 1899): 11–12. Leo Marx argues persuasively that many nineteenth-century Americans revered the steam locomotive as "the industrial revolution incarnate." See his *The Machine in the Garden: Technology and the Pastoral Ideal in America* (New York, 1964), 191. The political causes and effects of railroad mania are considered in Mark W. Summers, *Railroads, Reconstruction, and the Gospel of Prosperity: Aid under the Radical Republicans, 1865–1877* (Princeton, N.J., 1984).

37. *Greenville Times,* 7 Apr. 1883. Pollock's mention of Greenville's "debilitated social structure" probably referred to the town's loss of almost 200 residents in the yellow fever epidemic of 1878. Ironically, the disease "debilitated" Greenville just weeks after the local

railroad, the Greenville, Columbus and Birmingham Railroad, opened its first section of track to passengers and freight. Several early settlers discussed the mosquito-borne epidemic, which was initially blamed on contagions in the persons or belongings of railroad employees, in McCain and Capers, *Memoirs of Ireys.* For a list of Greenville's yellow fever victims, see Wade and Branton, *Early Mississippi Records* 2:121–24.

38. *Greenville Times,* 27 Jan. 1877, 23 Feb. 1878; McCain and Capers, *Memoirs of Ireys,* 46, 283; Williams, *Bolivar County.* Edmund Richardson's plans to extend his private railroad east from Refuge Landing to Deer Creek—and the likelihood that Greenville's role as regional entrepôt would thus be supplanted—gave immediacy to McNeily's suspicions of the town's commercial vulnerability. See chap. 2 for a discussion of Edmund Richardson and his efforts at Refuge.

39. Competition between railroads and steamboats sometimes went beyond efforts to win passengers or goods. In 1884 the *Jackson State-Ledger* revealed that the "steamer 'Deer Creek,' a few days since, cut the railroad bridge at Nittayuma on Deer Creek to enable her to get at some cotton. Returning, the 'Deer Creek' replaced the bridge, but was followed by the steamer 'Harry,' which also cut out a span. Maj. Edwards, superintendent, notified the attorneys of the road, Messrs. Percy, Yerger & Percy, instructing them to proceed against the boats. Mr. LeRoy Percy repaired to the scene of action and instituted prosecution against Capt. Sargeant of the steamer 'Harry,' who gave bond for his appearance before the Circuit Court. The bridge has been substantially repaired and cutting will be guarded against in the future. The steamer 'Ubet' is caught above the bridge, and will have an interesting voyage in getting out." *Greenville Times,* 12 Apr. 1884.

40. Boyer, "The Steamboat Era"; Hemphill, *Fevers, Floods, and Faith,* 110–11; Mrs. L. A. Little, "Sketch of Life in Bolivar County in 1872," and Evelyn Sillers Pearson, "Our Gracious Lady—Kate Adams," in Williams, *Bolivar County,* 168, 203–9; Dot Turk, "The History and Architecture of Leland," *Washington County Historical Society: Programs of 1981* (Greenville, Miss., 1981), 13. See Halsell, "Leflore County, 1876–1920," 241–42.

41. An absence of strong state support for postbellum railroad construction also hampered rail boosters' efforts. Even at the high tide of Mississippi's Reconstruction-era "railroad mania," the state refused to provide direct aid for railroad construction, either in land grants or monetary subsidies. Although the state offered cheap prices on land and tax relief to some railroads, funds for construction had to be drawn from private investors and local governments. See Brandfon, *Cotton Kingdom,* 96–98; Summers, *Railroads, Reconstruction, and the Gospel of Prosperity,* 48.

42. Alcorn owned approximately 20,000 acres around the hamlet of Jonestown in the mid-1870s, for which he paid a tax bill of $5,101 in 1876. Alcorn acquired much of the property, called Eagle's Nest, from a partner in a commercial venture. Alcorn, John Jones, and M. R. Mitchell opened a general store in the area in 1870, and when Jones found himself unable to pay Alcorn for legal services, he relinquished the plantation for his debt. Even after moving into their Victorian mansion at Eagle's Nest in 1879, Alcorn and his family continued to labor in the plantation store. Pereyra, *Alcorn,* 110, 183; Weeks, *Clarksdale and Coahoma County,* 77–78; James F. Brieger, *Hometown Mississippi* (Jackson, Miss., 1980), 108.

43. Notice the way riverine Deltans reshuffled the railroad's name to parallel the Mississippi's southward flow.

44. Williams, *Bolivar County,* 228.

45. Ninth Census, Population and Agriculture MSS, Coahoma Co.; Weeks, *Clarksdale and Coahoma County,* 32, 59–61.

46. Williams, *Bolivar County,* 228–30. Their plan to build a railroad from Memphis to the Gulf was not without merit. The vast region needed railroads to haul agricultural supplies and crops, to make large-scale lumber operations profitable in the thick hardwood forests, and to transport settlers into the alluvial basin. But Alcorn and his group were too far ahead of demand in 1870. As railroad magnates C. P. Huntington and Stuyvesant Fish later discovered, a main line passing from Memphis to Vicksburg could be very profitable. National railroad companies would later bring Alcorn's vision to earth, first as the Louisville, New Orleans and Texas Railroad in the 1880s and later under the ownership of the Illinois Central as the Yazoo and Mississippi Valley Railroad. On the profits of the LNO&T and the Y&MV, see Brandfon, *Cotton Kingdom,* 74–75, 80.

47. Weeks, *Clarksdale and Coahoma County,* 61; Louis R. Saillard, *Delta Route: A History of the Columbus and Greenville Railway* (Columbus, Miss., 1981), 10.

48. Weeks, *Clarksdale and Coahoma County,* 61.

49. Ibid. Clark, not incidentally, had married Alcorn's sister, Eliza Jane Alcorn, in 1854. The "future of Coahoma County was bridesmaid at the wedding," Linton Weeks believes, "for in that union of Clark and Alcorn lay alliances that foreshadowed the direction, the route, progress would take through the Mississippi Delta." Ibid., 28–29.

50. Ibid.

51. Henry T. Ireys, "County Seats and Early Railroads of Washington County," *Publications of the Mississippi Historical Society* 14 (1914): 269–81.

52. Bond trustee William E. Hunt's refusal to pay the full price of construction in 1874 may have been influenced by another national economic crisis, the panic of 1873.

53. Ireys, "County Seats and Early Railroads," 269–98; Saillard, *Delta Route;* McCain and Capers, *Memoirs of Ireys.*

54. *Washington County Times,* 2 Apr. 1870; Ireys, "County Seats and Early Railroads," 286–88; Corporation Charter and Minute Book of the Greenville, Deer Creek and Rolling Fork Railroad Company, Special Collections, ViBlbV; Act of Incorporation, Minute Book, and "An Act to Aid in the Construction of the Greenville, Columbus and Birmingham Railroad" of the Arkansas City and Grenada Railroad Company, ibid. Although the Greenville, Deer Creek and Rolling Fork Railroad maintained a separate corporate existence until 1880, the two companies were effectively joined when that railroad contributed the $20,000 it had raised for construction to the joint effort in 1873. Greenville, Deer Creek and Rolling Fork Minute Book.

55. Prominent Republicans among the Arkansas City and Grenada investors included the aforementioned Blanche K. Bruce, L. T. Webber (Bolivar County sheriff), and L. D. Vincent (Tallahatchie County's assistant tax assessor). The Greenville, Deer Creek and Rolling Fork was similarly dominated by well-known Democrats. Jacob Alexander and John H. Nelson were both Democratic mayors of Greenville in the 1870s, lawyer-planter

William A. Percy played a prominent role in Redemption, and anti-Republican election judge Samuel W. Ferguson were all early investors in the Greenville, Deer Creek and Rolling Fork. Ibid.; *Greenville Times,* 22 Aug., 10 Oct. 1874, 9 Jan., 8 May, 3 July, 10 July, 28 Aug., 25 Sept., 9 Oct., 6 Nov. 1875; Ninth Census, Population MSS, Bolivar, Coahoma, Hinds, Tallahatchie, and Washington Counties; Pereyra, *Alcorn,* 132, 160–61 n.46; Paxton, "Reminiscences," 35, 40; Senate Report, "Mississippi Elections of 1875," 1459–97.

56. Ninth Census, Population MSS, Coahoma, Hinds, and Washington Counties.

57. Despite investing in a railroad company partly owned by blacks and largely directed by Republicans, Nathan Bedford Forrest was hardly tamed. After retiring to his Coahoma County plantation in 1865, Forrest encountered trouble gaining and keeping black laborers. In 1866 his short temper snapped, and the ex-slave trader killed a black field hand during a "personal difficulty." Forrest was later tried and released from the homicide charge, but he sold his Green Grove plantation in 1867 and left the region. The purchaser of the estate, one Colonel Chambers, promptly resold the property to Edmund Richardson. Weeks, *Clarksdale and Coahoma County,* 43–45, 76; Brian Steel Wills, *A Battle from the Start: The Life of Nathan Bedford Forrest* (New York, 1992), 325–30.

58. LeRoy Valliant's investments in Delta land did not signify a lack of legal abilities; he was later selected to the Missouri Supreme Court. McCain and Capers, *Memoirs of Ireys;* Washington Co. Land Tax Roll, 1870; Ninth Census, Population MSS, Washington Co..

59. Samuel W. Ferguson, William A. Percy, Edward P. Byrnes, and William A. Haycraft were prominent examples. Ibid.; Ninth Census, Agriculture MSS, Washington Co.; Washington Co. Deed Records.

60. Greenville's first bond issue in support of the Greenville, Columbus and Birmingham Railroad provided $100,000 in 1874, with the railroad responsible for repaying the sum within twenty years at 8 percent interest. When the project was revived in 1877, the city again offered financial support. The second loan, for $50,000 payable plus 7 percent interest over twenty years, was approved by 311 of the town's 349 registered voters. Disagreements over which part of the county should first enjoy rail service prevented funding from Washington County. Ireys, "County Seats and Early Railroads," 287–90; Minute Book of the Greenville, Deer Creek and Rolling Fork Railroad; Minute Book of the Arkansas City and Grenada Railroad.

61. Richardson's operations and Greenville's collective anxiety at the prospect of his success are treated in chap. 2. Black farm owning and renting in the Deer Creek region are examined in chaps. 3 and 4.

62. *Greenville Times,* 13 Dec. 1879, 7 Apr. 1883; Saillard, *Delta Route,* 13–14; Minute Book of the Arkansas City and Grenada Railroad; Minute Book of the Richmond and Danville Extension Company, Special Collections, ViBlbV. Confidence born of their railroad success led Greenville merchants to underwrite a Mississippi River ferry to facilitate trade with Arkansas residents. *Greenville Times,* 3 Aug. 1878.

63. The railroad bond election that the intemperate planter spoke against was defeated, but for reasons that had little to do with railroads' lack of liquor "accommodations." Although growing rapidly, the Deer Creek region that would be served by the extension lacked sufficient voters to overcome the opposition of Mississippi River planters. The

riverside citizens refused to support railroads for the seminavigable lower Deer Creek because they feared aiding their competitors. Unless a railroad branch was run south from Greenville along the banks of the Mississippi, this large voting bloc would not approve county funds to aid settlers along Deer Creek's southern reaches. The lack of county funds did not delay construction, however, for planters eager for rail service underwrote extension by purchasing freight certificates redeemable once the Deer Creek branch was completed. *Greenville Times*, 26 Jan. 1878; Ireys, "County Seats and Early Railroads," 293, 298; Saillard, *Delta Route*, 13. Debate between Mississippi River planters and Deer Creek settlers erupted again in 1882 and 1883 as a trans-Delta railroad considered its route through Washington County. Then, as before, the banks along Deer Creek lured a railroad while the riverside planters grumbled enviously. The Louisville, New Orleans and Texas Railroad finally built a riverside branch in 1885. See the *Greenville Times*, 1882–83 (especially regarding the lopsided vote to underwrite a riverside branch, 14 Apr. 1883), 28 Feb., 7 Mar. 1885.

64. Ireys, "County Seats and Early Railroads," 297–98; *Greenville Times*, 16 June 1883, 31 May, 25 July, 21 Nov. 1885.

65. The GC&B's profits were healthy, in large part, because the stockholders continued to find public funds to underwrite the line's expansion. The road's extension east from Stoneville on Deer Creek to Johnsonville on the Sunflower River was subsidized by a $75,000 bond issue approved by Sunflower County. With construction supported by bonds from Greenville and Sunflower County, and freight certificates purchased to help construct the Deer Creek extension, the GC&B was able to build its thirty-seven-mile system with little initial capital investment. Saillard, *Delta Route*, 13–14.

66. Directors of the GC&B urged stockholders to approve the railroad's sale to the Georgia Pacific at an 11 Oct. 1881 meeting. The stockholders formally agreed to the transfer on 2 Nov. 1881. Editor J. S. McNeily approved of the decision, noting that the sale "marks an important era in the life of Greenville. Our railroad interests, and through their extension and direction the future growth and progress of the town . . . , are no longer in the hands of citizens of Greenville. They are now merged in a great trans-continental syndicate." *Greenville Times*, 15 Oct., 5 Nov. 1881.

67. Minute Book of the Arkansas City and Grenada Railroad; Minute Book of the Richmond and Danville Extension Company; Ireys, "County Seats and Early Railroads," 299–300; Saillard, *Delta Route*, 13–14, 26–30.

68. See Summers, *Railroads, Reconstruction, and the Gospel of Prosperity;* Robert W. Fogel, *Railroads and American Economic Growth* (Baltimore, 1964); George R. Taylor and Irene Neu, *The American Railroad Network, 1861–1890* (Cambridge, Mass., 1956); and Alfred D. Chandler, ed., *Railroads: The Nation's First Big Business* (New York, 1965).

69. Brandfon, *Cotton Kingdom*, 70–72. Collis Potter Huntington, the national railroad magnate, was not related to Charles Perrit Huntington, Washington County planter and onetime president of the Greenville, Columbus and Birmingham Railroad.

70. As this investment suggests, steam traffic on river and rail had reached a competitive understanding by the 1880s. Indeed, the Delta's thickening settlement (and concomitant rising cotton production) helped steamboats increase their freight traffic. In 1889

Greenwood—which was served by both the Georgia Pacific and the LNO&T railroads—shipped 35,000 bales of cotton to market on steamboats. Greenwood *Enterprise,* 30 Jan. 1890, in Halsell, "Leflore County, 1876–1929," 241.

71. Brandfon, *Cotton Kingdom,* 72–73, 78–80.

72. Williams, *Bolivar County,* 230; George F. Cram, *Cram's Standard American Railway System Atlas of the World* (New York, 1905), 299–308. By 1907 Washington County had the most railroad mileage—339—of any county in Mississippi. *The 39th Anniversary Edition of the Greenville Times* (Greenville, Miss., 1907), 2. The Pea Vine route was served by a train which left Cleveland at 4 A.M. on a two-mile run south to Boyle. Lacking a round-house, the Pea Vine was compelled to back its way from Boyle to Dockery's plantation depot. The train ran "head first" from Dockery's to Rosedale on the Mississippi and returned to Cleveland in the evening. Fans of Charley Patton's "Pea Vine Blues" will recognize the little doglegged railroad line's contributions to the region's culture. See Robert Palmer's *Deep Blues* (New York, 1981), 53.

73. Palmer, *Deep Blues,* 53; *Greenville Times,* 29 Nov. 1884, 25 May 1885. Railroad service, though appreciated, was soon subject to criticism. One Winterville resident who demanded dependably superior service wrote: "What is the matter with the mail agent on the LNO&T? Sometimes we get the mail from Memphis and Greenville in a few hours, and at other times our mail is four or five days old when we receive it." But at least he had an agent to complain about; three weeks earlier the station agent at Hampton in southwest Washington County abandoned his post and absconded with $800 of the railroad's funds. Ibid., 22 May, 1 May 1886.

74. Weeks, *Clarksdale and Coahoma County,* 79–80; Williams, *Bolivar County,* 282–83, 288.

75. Turk, "History and Architecture of Leland," 3–15; Twelfth Census, Population MSS, Washington Co..

76. Twelfth Census, Population MSS, Washington Co.; *Greenville Times,* 8 Apr. 1876, 13 Dec. 1879. After its initial north-south line was established through Leland, the LNO&T ran another line northwest to the Mississippi River in southern Bolivar County. This second line bisected Stoneville, but Leland was already entrenched as the primary railroad junction in Washington County. Two churches and seven or eight stores clustered at Stoneville at the turn of the century. Rowland, *Mississippi* 2:746.

77. Turk, "History and Architecture of Leland," 12; *75 Years in Leland* (Leland, Miss., 1974), n.p.

78. Weeks, *Clarksdale and Coahoma County,* 203. In both Clarksdale and Leland, the growth rate was spurred by more than just one passing rail line, for the two towns were junctions. Leland, of course, perched at the intersection of the Georgia Pacific and the Yazoo and Mississippi Valley railroads. Clarksdale became a junction in 1890, when a Y&MV line from Minter City joined the LNO&T within its town limits. Ibid., 99–100.

79. *Greenville Times,* 12 Mar. 1887, 7 Nov. 1895.

80. Although the Greenville paper printed the Arkansas City account of life at Huntington, it did so to ridicule its cross-river rival for envy at the Yazoo Delta's successful ex-

pansion. *Arkansas City Journal* in *Greenville Times,* 3 Oct. 1885; *Greenville Times,* 13 June 1885.

81. Williams, *Bolivar County,* 130, 135, 138; Halsell, "Leflore County, 1876–1920," 256. When the Y&MV bypassed Concordia, its inhabitants abandoned the site for the nearest railroad stop and established the town of Gunnison around A. N. Gunnison's plantation station.

82. Weeks, *Clarksdale and Coahoma County,* 61–66.

83. Ibid. Some present-day residents of sleepy Friars Point ("a collection of two gas stations, a small museum, and some antique stores in the shadow of the levee") confess to being surprised that their hamlet remains on maps. When a *New York Times* reporter researching tourist attractions in the Delta reached Friars Point, a surprised resident remarked, "If you're here, you must be lost." *New York Times,* 21 Apr. 1991.

84. Splitting the county government reduced some of Bolivar's political strain, but relations between the two sections remained tense. As Will Dockery recalled, "Politics were always one hundred and ten in the shade in Imperial Bolivar." Williams, *Bolivar County,* 52, 172, 451. By the time the Cleveland courthouse opened, the town had two newspapers, the *Progress* and the *Enterprise.* Ibid., 286.

85. Lawyers, often the most vocal advocates of county government "reform," cast their lots with Greenville. Members of influential planter-lawyer families, like the Percys and Yergers, resided in Greenville and either sold off or rented their Deer Creek property. The merchant community, another prominent coalition in the Coahoma and Bolivar divisions, often headquartered at Greenville and established branch stores in the interior. And despite its geographic centrality, Leland could never argue that it contained a majority of the county's population. Between 1900 and the following decennial, Greenville's population rose from 7,642 to 9,610. Leland, meanwhile, lagged with 762 and 1,547 in the same years. Department of the Interior, Census Office, *Twelfth Census of the United States,* "Population," pt. 1 (Washington, D.C., 1901), 230–35; Department of Commerce and Labor, Bureau of the Census, *Thirteenth Census of the United States,* "Population," 2 (Washington, D.C., 1913), 1028–36.

86. "The first shipment of freight to Greenville over the LNO&T railroad, without breaking bulk, was a car load of beer from the Christian Moerlien Brewing Company." *Greenville Times,* 18 Apr. 1885.

87. Privilege Tax Registers, State Auditor's Papers (RG 29), 290:69, Ms-Ar.

88. Ibid., 96. The town and county experienced a stagnant commercial economy in the early 1870s, as did much of the country after the panic of 1873. The 1878–79 figures were little changed from surveys of Greenville's business sector in the mid-1870s. See the *Greenville Times,* 6 Mar. 1875.

89. Railroads' role in Greenville's growth and Washington County's development were persistently proclaimed by members of the area's first historical society. See McCain and Capers, *Memoirs of Ireys.*

90. The brickmakers' trade was fueled by a Greenville ordinance banning wood construction in the town's business district, passed in the wake of two disastrous 1874 fires.

The city gained its first steam-powered brickworks in 1887; a steam-powered ice machine manufacturing five tons of ice per day (for sale at 1 cent per pound) was operating in 1881. Greenville was not alone in its surge in population and local manufacturing. The same was true in the interior counties of the Delta. Leflore County, for example, saw the number of manufacturing establishments within its borders grow from twelve to ninety-seven in only ten years. The average capitalization of these firms increased 292 percent in the same period, from $2,222 to $6,485. *Greenville Times,* 26 Dec. 1874, 1 Oct. 1887, 28 May 1881; Halsell, "Leflore County, 1876–1920," 254.

91. *Greenville Times,* 1 Oct. 1887. The quote is taken from Lamar Fontaine's *My Life and Lectures* (New York, 1908), 276. When Fontaine's home beside the Yazoo River burned in 1893, he moved his family to the Coahoma County railroad town of Lyon. Fontaine spent his retirement recounting real and imagined exploits to enthralled audiences. "And here, with my children and grandchildren around me, I sit in my great armchair, on the shaded gallery, with the balmy sea-born zephyrs, fresh from the Mexic Sea, fanning my brow; with the smoke curling up from my old meerschaum pipe, fragrant with the perfume of perique, I dream and retrospect." Weeks, *Clarksdale and Coahoma County,* 80–81.

92. *Greenville Times,* 29 May 1875, 6 Oct. 1877, 8 Apr. 1882, 29 Jan., 12 Feb., 16 Apr. 1887, May 1900, 6 May 1905; *Greenville Democrat,* 3 May 1894. The Greenville Electric Light and Power Company was organized to provide residential and commercial service in 1888. The town gained telegraph service in 1877, and twenty-five subscribers to the Bell telephone system's local office were talking by the end of 1881. Greenville's Hotel Cowan installed 100 telephones in guest rooms in 1904. *Greenville Times,* 3 Mar., 12 May, 19 May 1877, 3 Dec. 1881, 28 May 1904.

93. While Greenville's services were only slowly improved, those in other Delta towns lagged far behind. Greenville organized for electric lights in 1888; residents of Cleveland were without electricity until 1907. Greenville began constructing concrete sidewalks in 1905; Cleveland waited until 1910. The Washington County city's first graveled streets preceded Cleveland's by twenty-two years, and there is no evidence that Cleveland ever organized a streetcar system. Ibid.; Williams, *Bolivar County,* 288–89.

94. The electric streetcar system may have caused anxiety in some quarters: a "veterinary sanitorium" capable of holding 150 horses was constructed in Greenville in 1904. Rowland, *Mississippi* 3:47–48.

95. *Greenville Times,* 11 Sept. 1886.

96. Ibid.

97. Ibid.

6. Closing the New South Frontier

1. See the *Greenville Times,* 25 Sept. 1875, for description of an early bipartisan, biracial nominating committee.

2. According to Vernon Wharton, "The fusion system did work to the general satisfaction of a majority of both races." Stephen Cresswell's more recent work takes a dimmer

view of the practice. Wharton, *Negro in Mississippi,* 203; Stephen Cresswell, *Multiparty Politics in Mississippi, 1877–1902* (Jackson, Miss., 1995).

3. *Greenville Times,* 21 Nov. 1874, 25 Sept. 1875. Lucas's path to financial and political prominence in Washington County is detailed in chap. 4.

4. Ibid., 3 July, 10 July, 6 Nov. 1875.

5. Ibid., 11 Sept. 1875.

6. Ibid., 23 Sept. 1876.

7. *Greenville Times,* 30 Sept., 14 Oct. 1876. Lynch was defeated in his 1876 bid for Congress by James R. Chalmers, the ex-Confederate general who led the white troops from Memphis against Austin's black rioters in 1874. The Austin disturbances are examined later in this chapter.

8. Of 18,652 Bolivar County inhabitants in 1880, 15,958 were black and 2,694 were white. In 1890 the county had grown to 29,980, with 26,737 black and 3,222 white residents. *Tenth Census,* "Population," 67–68, 233–37, 397–98; Department of the Interior, Census Office, *Eleventh Census of the United States,* "Report on Population," pt. 1 (Washington, D.C., 1895), 27, 206–11, 417–18.

9. Williams, *Bolivar County,* 33–37.

10. Ibid., 162–63.

11. Ibid.

12. Ibid.

13. Ibid., 33–37, 162–63. Black magistrates were numerous throughout the Delta during Reconstruction and continued to dominate judicial proceedings in the backcountry until the 1890s. Samuel G. French describes two of Greenville's black Reconstruction-era justices of the peace in his *Two Wars,* 333–37. Bolivar County's black judges and constables are mentioned in Williams, *Bolivar County,* 337, 594, and in Banks, "Mound Bayou," 8.

14. C. Vann Woodward, *Origins of the New South, 1877–1913* (Baton Rouge, La., 1951), 185. For compelling examinations of the southern cotton economy in the 1860s and early 1870s, see Willie Lee Rose, *Rehearsal for Reconstruction: The Port Royal Experiment* (New York, 1964); Lawrence Powell, *New Masters.*

15. The figures for the average Delta farmer are taken from a Department of Agriculture examination of the region's 1896 crop. Because the study did not consider the farmer's need for credit to operate in the months between planting and marketing his cotton, these figures probably understate the costs of Delta farming in this period. See John Hyde and James L. Watkins, *The Cost of Cotton Production,* Department of Agriculture, Division of Statistics, Miscellaneous Bulletin no. 16 (Washington, D.C., 1899), 78. Average cotton prices (both real and adjusted figures) are available in Bureau of the Census, *Historical Statistics of the United States,* pt. 1 (Washington, D.C., 1975), 200–201, 517–18.

16. U.S. Senate, Committee on Agriculture and Forestry, *Condition of Cotton Growers in the United States, the Present Prices of Cotton, and the Remedy . . . ,* 53d Congress, 3d sess. (Washington, D.C., 1895), 344–47.

17. Ibid.

18. Ibid.

19. This description of Delta agricultural credit in the 1870s and early 1880s is drawn from my examination of the deed records, liens, and auction records of Coahoma, Sunflower, and Washington Counties. The most common credit instrument was the deed of trust, where the borrower conveyed his property to a third party (the trustee) in the event he failed to retire his loan. The trustee then held the land, goods, and crops "in trust" and supervised the auction. The deed of trust guaranteed the trustee either a specified fee or a percentage of the auction price in payment for his services. Trustees who were not called on to dispose of property for arrears did no work and hence were not compensated.

20. Ibid.

21. For examples, see Washington Co. Deed Records, X:403–4, 407–8, E2:125–26. Liens were also employed to safeguard a variety of nonagricultural credit transactions in the Delta. When V. F. P. Alexander sold his wharf boat to N. J. Nelson in 1869, he demanded a lien on the boat and its landing rights at the Greenville dock to ensure full payment of pending installments. Ibid., X:58–59.

22. Deed records, Coahoma, Sunflower, and Washington Counties.

23. Delta database.

24. Percy, "Negro Education," 730–32. Note how Percy's memorial to honesty is largely predicated on his calculation of whites' interest in fair dealing.

25. Whites' use of "the pencil" to enhance their profits at blacks' expense continued in the Delta. Works Progress Administration interviewers in the 1930s heard stories like this one, recorded and transcribed in the dialect, in Tunica County. Two men, one white and the other black, came upon two boxes at a crossroads. The black, "he spied it first," and "he run erhead and grab de *bigger* box and he speck he hab sumpin. Well, he opin hit and fine picks en shubbles en hoes and de res ob hit, and den he turn erowun to see wot de Wite man got. Well de Wite man he got de little box and when he open hit dar war pens and pencils and paper an er big count book wat he keeps wat de niggars owes em in. And dats de way hits been eber since. De Niggar just caint outfigger de Wite man for he sure ter cut yer down." Sydney Nathans also uses this tale to demonstrate the mendacity of white merchants, but he does not consider how patterns of fraud, like other aspects of life, might have been as affected by chronology and context as by race. Nathans, "Gotta Mind to Move," 215 n.18.

26. See the lien history of black farmer Benjamin Williams for a concrete example of the increasing specificity demanded by lenders in preparing deeds of trust. These instruments span the period from Williams's purchase of thirty-seven acres (in 1880) through his last deed of trust (in 1899). Washington Co. Deed Records, L2:855, R2:11–12, V2:119–21, X2:673–74, A3:449–51, D3:238–41, G3:71–74, H3:142–45, K3:38–42, L3:66–69, M3:666–69, R3:56–60, T3:317–21, V3:718–20. Williams, having survived the 1890s agricultural depression with holdings intact, finally sold his property in 1919. Ibid., 172:7–8, 477–78.

27. Bliss was an exceptional debtor in other ways, too, for in purchasing his land from a local planter in 1878, he negotiated to pay only 6 percent interest on his principal installments. And during the agricultural depression Bliss was faring better than many of his

neighbors. The year after he negotiated the English loan, the black farmer convinced a local planter to sell him an additional fifty-seven acres over an extended period with no down payment. Sunflower Co. Deed Records, D:390, Q:126–31, 470–71.

28. Washington Co. Deed Records, L3:617–20.

29. Ibid., O3:258–61, Q3:86–89.

30. Ibid., T3:404–5. The cotton market did eventually improve. The staple's price jumped upward in 1898 and merchant Wong quickly unloaded the property. He sold the forty acres to local land speculator L. F. Roach for $350 cash on 14 Jan. 1899, probably emerging with at least a small profit on the five-year series of transactions. Ibid., V3:42. The land market's quickening in the wake of rising cotton prices is examined in the next chapter.

31. Ninth Census, Population MSS, Washington Co.; Tenth Census, Population MSS, Washington Co.; Solomon, *The Hebrew Union Congregation.*

32. Washington Co. Deed Records, V2:160–62, L2:882–83, N2:608–9, P2:347–48, S2:782–86; Washington County Circuit Court Records, suit 6400, Washington County Courthouse, Greenville, Miss.

33. Washington Co. Deed Records, F3:617–18.

34. Other Wilczinski properties were also loaded with multiple liens in this period. Ibid., F3:613–14.

35. Because Mississippi did not require registration of land deeds (and still does not), other farmers may have purchased property in this period but left no official record. Despite this element of imprecision, the dramatic decline in registered purchases indicates the dire consequences of economic downturn and mercantile mendacity for black Delta farmers in the 1890s.

36. In Washington County, the Delta's largest jurisdiction, black farmers registered no land purchases in 1891, 1892, or 1894. Washington Co. Deed Records.

37. A number of writers have attempted to understand the foundations, character, and implications of the Populist movement. C. Vann Woodward's *Origins of the New South* and *Tom Watson: Agrarian Rebel* (New York, 1938) remain crucial for understanding political and economic aspects of the agrarian revolt. Lawrence L. Goodwyn's ambitious *Democratic Promise: The Populist Movement in America* (New York, 1976) examines (and may overstate) the movement's unique culture. More specialized studies include Robert C. McMath, *American Populism: A Social History, 1877–1898* (New York, 1993); Albert D. Kirwan, *Revolt of the Rednecks: Mississippi Politics, 1876–1925* (Lexington, Ky., 1951); and James Sharbrough Ferguson, "Agrarianism in Mississippi, 1871–1900: A Study in Nonconformity" (Ph.D. diss., University of North Carolina, 1952).

38. I have found no records of loans from the Tchula Cooperative Store to landless farmers in the deed records of Sunflower, Coahoma, and Washington Counties. Although the store may have extended credit to tenants without requiring them to sign binding contracts for repayment, the specificity of its relations with landowners casts doubt on the possibility of easier terms for tenants.

39. Sunflower Co. Deed Records, L:163–64.

40. Ibid., Q:289–91.

41. Ibid., U:356–58, V:522–24, X:261–64.

42. I reached this conclusion after an examination of the deed records of Sunflower County, which reveal several other farmers with credit experiences similar to those of the Cross family. None of the borrowers from the Tchula Cooperative Store lost their land or other property to default auctions between 1890 and 1897. Ibid., L:161–63, Q:235–37, 561–63, U:472–75, V:232–35, J2:431–33, 437–38, U2:551–52.

43. The Sunflower County Deed Records contain no deeds of trust or other borrowing instruments naming W. P. or R. G. Cross between the 1897 Tchula negotiation and a 1902 deed of trust to the Union Central Life Insurance Company of Ohio. In 1902 the Crosses borrowed $400 from the Union Central on extended terms, promising to repay the full amount with 10 percent interest by 1912. W. P. Cross sold the farm a few months before the debt came due, receiving $574.45 cash and assumption of the Union Central loan in compensation for his eighty acres. Although Cross only received about $17 per acre for the land (including the loan principal and interest), this was a good sum in 1912, for the boll weevil had just reached the area, and many small farm owners were unable to hold their property in the face of the insect's voracious appetite. Ibid., J2:434–36, X3:630–31. The effects of the boll weevil's arrival are examined in the next chapter.

44. The Leflore incidents are most thoroughly explored in Clark L. Miller, "'Let Us Die to Make Men Free': Political Terrorism in Post-Reconstruction Mississippi, 1877–1896" (Ph.D. diss., University of Minnesota, 1983), and William F. Holmes, "The Leflore County Massacre and the Demise of the Colored Farmers' Alliance," *Phylon* 4 (1973): 267–74.

45. Holmes, "Leflore County," 270.

46. Ibid.; Miller, "'Let Us Die,'" 530.

47. Holmes, "Leflore County," 271.

48. Ibid.

49. Ibid.; Miller, "'Let Us Die,'" 530–31.

50. Ibid. Shell Mound was located on the site of a battle between the Chakchiuma tribe and the allied forces of the Choctaw and Chickasaw nations. The fierce fighting left so many dead that their bodies choked the nearby river. The watercourse was subsequently renamed "Yazoo," meaning river of death. Brieger, *Hometown Mississippi,* 303.

51. In Leflore County the 2,597 whites were outnumbered by 14,276 blacks. Holmes, "Leflore County," 270; *Eleventh Census,* "Population," pt. 1, 27, 206–11, 417–18; Miller, "'Let Us Die,'" 530. Eugene D. Genovese describes whites' antebellum terror of slave uprisings in his *Roll, Jordan, Roll: The World the Slaves Made* (New York, 1974).

52. *Greenville Times,* 15 Aug. 1874.

53. Ibid., 15 Aug., 12 Sept. 1874. Chalmers, who served under Nathan Bedford Forrest during the Civil War, represented the Delta in Congress from 1877 to 1883.

54. Although evidence about the affray remains obscure, it seems that Leflore County witnessed its own version of the Austin debacle during Reconstruction. White resident Benjamin G. Humphreys later recounted a pitched battle between ex-Confederate sol-

diers and "three or four hundred organized, armed negroes" which left some freedmen dead on the field and an untold number of wounded. Humphreys did not explain the cause of the conflict. See Percy L. Rainwater, ed., "The Autobiography of Benjamin G. Humphreys," *Mississippi Valley Historical Review* 21 (Sept. 1934): 252–54.

55. Holmes, "Leflore County," 271.

56. Ibid.

57. *Greenville Times,* 14 Sept. 1889.

58. Ibid.; Holmes, "Leflore County," 271.

59. Ibid.; Miller, "'Let Us Die,'" 532–34.

60. Miller, "'Let Us Die,'" 538. Wharton postulates a pattern in which racial tension, armed confrontation with few casualties, and the execution of leading blacks emerged from numerous such confrontations in post–Civil War Mississippi. See his *Negro in Mississippi,* 222–23.

61. Miller, "'Let Us Die,'" 535–38.

62. Holmes, "Leflore County," 272.

63. Ibid., 273; NAACP, *Thirty Years of Lynching in the United States, 1889–1918* (New York, 1919), 75; Miller, "'Let Us Die,'" 537. Curiously, Holmes states that "what happened to Allen is unknown," despite the NAACP's published documentation of his 1889 lynching. Holmes, "Leflore County," 272–73.

64. The Tchula Cooperative Store, mentioned earlier in this chapter, is the only such emporium I have been able to locate in the Delta after 1889. Fear of retaliation from local white merchants may have inspired the Tchula store to charge credit prices for its goods and limit loans to landowners, lest it succeed too well in gathering the business of area black farmers.

65. Miller, "'Let Us Die,'" 538.

66. Miller, who has most thoroughly examined the Leflore County bloodshed, demonstrates the importance of Delta votes in approving the 1890 state constitutional convention and the region's power in blocking calls for a gathering two years before. "'Let Us Die,'" 579–81.

67. In Wharton, *Negro in Mississippi,* 207.

68. See ibid., Miller's "'Let Us Die,'" and Ferguson's "Agrarianism" for the best analyses of the factors leading to and governing the 1890 constitutional convention.

69. Quoted in McMillen, *Dark Journey,* 53.

70. As in 1861, white Mississippians in 1889 overreacted to the prospect of federal intervention in local race relations: the Lodge bill bogged down in the Senate after passing the House. Wharton, *Negro in Mississippi,* 208; Kirwan, *Revolt of the Rednecks,* 59.

71. Hermann, *Pursuit of a Dream,* 229.

72. Wharton, *Negro in Mississippi,* 211.

73. Ibid.

74. The *New York World* reprinted Montgomery's speech on 28 Sept. 1890.

75. Quoted in Wharton, *Negro in Mississippi,* 210.

76. *Clarion-Ledger* quote in McMillen, *Dark Journey,* 53; *Greenville Times* quote from

William F. Holmes, *The White Chief: James Kimble Vardaman* (Baton Rouge, La., 1970), 39; Hermann, *Pursuit of a Dream,* 229–32. Vardaman and his Greenville colleague may have been motivated by less exalted motives, however, for both Leflore and Washington Counties were strenuously eliminating blacks from their voting rolls. Their support for Montgomery's Bolivar County school plan did not lead them to champion improved black education in their home counties, and their approbation for Mound Bayou's founder may have been grounded in a cynical attempt to distract attention from the disfranchising efforts of local Democrats.

77. Hermann, *Pursuit of a Dream,* 229–32.

78. These estimates of the number of literate white and black males age twenty-one and older were derived from figures in the published census. Because the census figures lumped native-born male and female literates together by race, the number of males able to read and write were estimated: the proportion of males among Mississippi's literate black population over age twenty was determined to be 56.24457 percent. That figure was then applied to the aggregate numbers of black literates for the nine counties fully within the Delta in 1900. Of the 23,922 native-born blacks over age twenty who were able to read and write in 1900, 13,455 were thus estimated to be males. A similar process was followed to arrive at the estimate of 3,474 native-born white males over age twenty. These combined for a total of 16,929 native-born males over age twenty from whom voters might have been selected if the literacy strictures were interpreted without prejudice: this would have resulted in an regional electorate 20.5 percent white and 79.5 percent black. *Twelfth Census,* "Population," pt. 1, 190–91, 986–87; Department of the Interior, Census Office, *Twelfth Census of the United States,* "Population," pt. 2 (Washington, D.C., 1901), 436–37, 56–57.

79. Kirwan, *Revolt of the Rednecks,* 74.

80. Sallis, "Color Line," 327; Kirwan, *Revolt of the Rednecks,* 74; Wharton, *Negro in Mississippi,* 213. In the 1875 elections that overturned Reconstruction, many blacks were prevented from voting, and others had their ballots discarded in a dispute over precinct boundaries. *Mississippi in 1875,* 1461–62. In fact, county boundary lines were so uncertain in the densely forested region that many land purchasers in the 1870s and 1880s registered their deeds in adjacent counties.

81. Freedmen's Bureau agents described widely divergent interpretations of the sanctity of marriage in the late 1860s. Major George W. Corliss reported from Lake Station in Coahoma County that "marital relations among some of the freed people are not so sacredly observed as would be in keeping with their advancement in other respects." Other agents were, predictably, more negative in their appraisals. Captain Tidball claimed that among his Washington County charges "cohabitation without marriage is quite common" and related that "in two cases the men contended that they had a right to have as many women as they could support." Lieutenant D. M. White was, however, among the most critical of ex-slaves' relationships. He insisted that the freed people of Yazoo County "have no regard for any moral obligations, and in my opinion, nothing but stringent laws will remedy the evil." If the appointed advocates of the freedmen judged black behavior this

harshly, one can imagine the reactions of local whites. Major Corliss, 31 Oct. 1867, Captain Tidball, 30 Sept. 1867, Lieutenant White, 31 Oct. 1867, Narrative Reports, BRFAL.

82. Quotes from Judge R. H. Thompson and James K. Vardaman in McMillen, *Dark Journey,* 43.

83. The number of black and white voters registered in each of the nine counties fully within the Delta is taken from James H. Stone's "A Note on Voter Registration under the Mississippi Understanding Clause, 1892," *Journal of Southern History* 38 (1972): 293–96. My estimates of literate blacks and whites over age twenty are explained in note 78 above.

84. Stone, "A Note on Voter Registration," 293–96; Wharton, *Negro in Mississippi,* 215. Some of the counties that most ruthlessly disfranchised black voters before the 1892 election actually increased the number of blacks eligible to cast ballots in the 1896 contest. Thus, Washington County augmented its black electorate by 200 registrants and Tunica added 64. These additions did not, however, endanger white control of local politics. McMillen, *Dark Journey,* 47.

85. Wharton, *Negro in Mississippi,* 215.

7. The Plantation Empire

1. The role of honor in southern life and thought has been the subject of extended examination in recent years. See Ayers, *Vengeance and Justice;* Bertram Wyatt-Brown, *Southern Honor: Ethics and Behavior in the Old South* (New York, 1982); John C. Willis, "From the Dictates of Pride to the Paths of Righteousness: Slave Honor and Christianity in Antebellum Virginia," in *The Edge of the South: Life in Nineteenth-Century Virginia,* ed. Edward L. Ayers and John C. Willis (Charlottesville, Va., 1991), 37–55; Kenneth S. Greenberg, *Honor and Slavery: Lies, Duels, Noses, Masks, Dressing as a Woman, Gifts, Strangers, Humanitarianism, Death, Slave Rebellions, the Proslavery Argument, Baseball, Hunting, and Gambling in the Old South* (Princeton, N.J., 1996).

2. Local historian Eunice J. Stockwell wrote that "those best informed never voiced their opinion as to who shot the soldier and Holt went to his grave without telling his secret." *Greenville Times,* 31 Dec. 1943. Stockwell refers to the murdered man as a "soldier," but research by Katharine Branton indicates that the victim was Captain Stanley King, white commander of a detachment of black Union troops stationed in Washington County in 1866. Interview with Katharine Branton, June 1991.

3. Collier, who had become one of the region's most renowned hunting guides, was engaged to lead a bear-hunting party after the turn of the century. The group included President Theodore Roosevelt, and his local hosts were determined that the celebrated slayer of beasts not leave the Delta without at least one bear kill to his credit. Although Collier tied a black bear to a tree near their path so Roosevelt could take home a trophy from the day, the squint-eyed Progressive exercised uncharacteristic restraint (for he was accustomed to shooting first and asking questions later). He refused to kill the bound animal. The tale of "Teddy's bear" was widely reported, an entrepreneur seized upon the story to promote the sale of stuffed bear dolls, and a marketing legend was born. The captive bear was dispatched after the president's departure, however, for no one in the hunting party

dared unleash the enraged and ungrateful carnivore. The story of Holt Collier and Theodore Roosevelt is periodically revived, as in Paul Schullery's "The Great Bear Men, Part IV: Holt Collier," *Outdoor Life,* Sept. 1988, 94–95, 106, 108, 110, 112, 114.

4. Friends or relatives of the stabbed Bradshaw must have demanded official action, for although Gordon was not apprehended, his three supporters were incarcerated as accomplices in his escape. *Greenville Times,* 12 Sept. 1874. Samuel G. French described a similar bloody confrontation in his *Two Wars,* 326–27.

5. *Greenville Times,* 9 Jan. 1875.

6. Ibid., 16 Oct. 1875.

7. Ibid., 14 Nov. 1874.

8. Ibid., 12 Sept. 1874, 9 Jan. 1875, 14 Nov. 1874.

9. See Ayers's *Vengeance and Justice,* especially pp. 266–76, for an examination of the subsidence of honorific violence among southern whites.

10. This account is based on reports in the *Greenville Times,* 26 June 1897.

11. In most Delta marriages at this time, the husband was several years his wife's senior. White male farm owners, for example, averaged more than seven and one-half years older than their spouse. Similarly, the average black male farm owner was just over six and one-third years his wife's elder. Delta database.

12. *Greenville Times,* 14 Aug., 6 Nov. 1875; Ayers, *Vengeance and Justice,* 234.

13. These motivations and misdeeds were doubtless replicated among the Delta's white population. Extant copies of the region's planter-dominated newspapers bequeath a one-sided view of these transgressions. Whites were, it seems, eager to highlight the domestic disturbances of freed people as evidence of black inferiority.

14. *Greenville Times,* 10 July 1875. The same newspaper reported a shocking child abuse later that month. "One of the most inhuman acts we have ever been called upon to record, was committed here during this week," the *Times* declared. "A negro named John Sweeney, with his paramour, beat a child of some seven or eight years, (the daughter of the woman) in so inhuman a manner that it died from the beating. Those who saw the child say that it was literally covered with the marks of the lash from head to foot. The little thing lingered in agony a few days before death came to its relief. The inhuman fiends were arrested and are now in jail, but the severest penalty of the law will be too mild a punishment for such barbarous wretches." Ibid., 31 July 1875.

15. Ayers, *Vengeance and Justice,* 231.

16. Wills, *A Battle from the Start,* 325–30; Weeks, *Clarksdale and Coahoma County,* 44–45. Wills, Forrest's most objective biographer, points out that the jury's carefully worded decision did not exactly exonerate the ex-general. Rather than find him innocent, the jurors held that Forrest was "not guilty in the manner and form as charged in the Indictment." Wills, *A Battle from the Start,* 330. Wills also presents a perceptive analysis of Forrest's Klan activities. Ibid., 331–39.

17. Two Washington County freedmen were arrested after a failed attempt to kill their employer, a levee contractor named Winter. Other laborers in Winter's employ testified to the plotters' guilt. *Greenville Times,* 18 Sept. 1875.

18. Ibid., 16 Jan., 23 Jan. 1875.

19. Ibid., 24 July 1875. Although Myers was arrested, I can find no record of a trial or lynching.

20. Ibid., 19 Jan. 1878.

21. Ibid., 10 July 1875; Colletta, *Who Killed Joe Ring?* chap. 3. Lowenstein's murderers, Rolla Bell and Alfred Brannon, were captured, convicted, and hanged in 1875.

22. *Greenville Times,* 2 Jan. 1875. The uninsured store and stock of a Sharkey County merchant, one Mr. Ostroffsky, were burned in December 1876. Several other planters and merchants, most of them similarly uninsured (thus lacking financial incentive to commit arson against their own property), also reported devastating fires in this period. For examples, see ibid., 16 Dec. 1876, 13 Feb. 1875, and 9 Dec. 1876. Significantly, most of these fires occurred in the months when merchants and planters settled the year's accounts with tenants and in the period when contracts for the coming crop were negotiated. The Delta receives frequent, heavy rains from November through April, and it is very unlikely that all of these fires resulted from spontaneous combustion.

23. Bohlen Lucas's experiences are recounted in detail in chap. 4.

24. *Greenville Times,* 16 Sept. 1876.

25. Ibid., 29 Aug. 1874. This rare negative critique was probably motivated by the specter of race war in the riverside town of Austin. That incident is examined in chap. 6.

26. The victims were William M. Morgan and W. Luther Ervin. The accused, Thomas Wallace, was represented before Justice of the Peace J. L. Griffin by J. W. Shields and J. D. Werles. Percy joined District Attorney Clarke in the prosecution. This account is drawn from the *Greenville Times,* 9 Oct. 1875.

27. The editor of the *Times* stressed that the "forbearance" of the would-be lynchers merited "the highest encomiums, for the Sheriff and his officers were powerless to stop them."

28. Ibid., 24 Mar. 1877.

29. Between 1889 and 1901, the earliest years for which dependable figures on lynching are available, there were forty-two lynchings in the Delta. Of the victims, thirty-five were black and seven were white. These numbers were drawn from the NAACP study, *Thirty Years of Lynching in the United States, 1889–1918,* 15, 22, 74–80. In arriving at these figures, I did not include lynchings that occurred outside the geographic boundaries of the alluvial Delta. The population statistics are drawn from the 1900 census because that was the decennial nearest the majority of white lynchings. In 1900 there were 171,209 blacks and 23,970 whites living in the counties fully within the Delta. *Twelfth Census,* "Population," pt. 1, 26–27, 545.

30. Stewart E. Tolnay and E. M. Beck, *A Festival of Violence: An Analysis of Southern Lynchings, 1882–1930* (Urbana, Ill., 1995), ix.

31. As in the Delta, the largest number of blacks lynched in other parts of the South were also accused of crimes against persons. Almost 40 percent of the South's black lynching victims were accused of murder (compared to 58 percent blamed for murder or attempted murder in the Delta), and approximately one-third of the black lynchings in the

larger region followed accusations of rape (compared with 15 percent in the Delta). Thus, the general patterns in the South were also present in the Delta, although the mobs lynching blacks in the subregion seem to have been more often punishing murderous activity than sexual assault. The patterns for white lynching victims in region and subregion were more distinct. White lynching victims in the Delta were only half as likely to have been accused of murder as in the remainder of the South, where almost 60 percent of white victims were blamed for that crime. *Thirty Years of Lynching*, 74–80; Tolnay and Beck, *Violence*, 48, 94.

32. This is another point on which Delta experience diverged from patterns in the larger South. Indeed, the periods of greatest lynching in the Delta (from September through March) were times of comparatively little lynching in the rest of the South. Data collected by sociologists Tolnay and Beck show that the larger region suffered the worst periods of lynching from May through September. The sociologists conclude that the intense labor needs of cotton-culture landlords contributed to summertime dangers in the remainder of the South. Tolnay and Beck, *Violence*, 142–49.

33. Interview with Wade Wineman, Sr.

34. *Thirty Years of Lynching*, 74–80. Transients and the unknown comprised a large number of the lynching victims in the larger South, as well. Edward L. Ayers, *The Promise of the New South: Life after Reconstruction* (New York, 1992), 157–58.

35. Few scholars now argue that any single factor motivated or justified lynchings in the postbellum South. Although monocausal explanations once dominated the literature, most recent studies emphasize multiple influences, including the inequities of the agricultural economy, the South's honor culture, isolated settlers' vigilantism, transiency, cotton price fluctuations and economic instability, and the growing bitterness of whites' racism in the late nineteenth century. See Ayers, *Promise;* Ayers, *Vengeance and Justice;* Tolnay and Beck, *Violence;* and W. Fitzhugh Brundage, *Lynching in the New South: Georgia and Virginia, 1880–1930* (Urbana, Ill., 1993). Brundage's survey of earlier writings about lynching is particularly helpful. See his Introduction, ibid., 1–16.

36. In the remainder of the South, by contrast, the tide of lynchings crested in the late 1880s and early 1890s. Ayers, *Vengeance and Justice,* 238–55; Ayers, *Promise,* 156; Tolnay and Beck, *Violence,* 29–32.

37. From 1901 through 1908 an average of 5.44 blacks were lynched each year in the Delta. *Thirty Years of Lynching,* 74–80.

38. Ibid.

39. J. William Harris explores the volatile combination of white supremacy and the demands of wartime patriotism in his article on Vicksburg violence during World War I, "Etiquette, Lynching, and Racial Boundaries: A Mississippi Example," *American Historical Review* 100:2 (Apr. 1995): 387–410.

40. *Statistical History of the United States,* 301; Alfred Holt Stone, "A Plantation Experiment," *Quarterly Journal of Economics* 19 (Feb. 1905): 287; Brandfon, *Cotton Kingdom,* 107–8; Williams, *Bolivar County,* 170; *Thirteenth Census,* "Agriculture," 870–71. Although cotton prices did not increase every year after 1900, the value of the fiber did not fall

below seven cents per pound until 1931. The average land price for 1900 reflects sales in Washington County.

41. Counties containing large sections of land for sale by the Yazoo and Mississippi Valley Railroad, black speculators with farm acreage for sale, or overworked soil (preventing rapid price escalation) saw significant increases in their black farm-owning populations. Between 1900 and 1910 these factors applied to Coahoma, Bolivar, and Issaquena Counties, respectively. But this was an ephemeral prosperity, for between 1910 and 1920 these same counties saw the region's largest declines in the number of black landowners. In Bolivar County the number of landowning blacks declined sharply after 1910, and by 1920 the area was home to 14 percent fewer black farm owners than in 1900. The number of black landholders in Coahoma County fell almost 20 percent in the same period. *Twelfth Census,* "Agriculture," vol. 5, pt. 1, 96–97; *Thirteenth Census,* "Agriculture," 6:872–79; *Fourteenth Census,* "Agriculture," vol. 6, pt. 2, 522–29. See Clifton L. Taulbert's *Once upon a Time When We Were Colored* (Tulsa, Okla., 1989) for the memoir of an African American whose family bought Washington County land from the Yazoo and Mississippi Valley Railroad in this period.

42. Sunflower Co. Deed Records, H2:368–84, R2:358–75, 441–50, 452–60; Rowland, *Mississippi,* 243–44, 259–60. Northern life insurance companies also began making loans to Delta farmers in this period. Bruce S. Cheeseman argues that these entities preferred to deal with wealthy, white borrowers. See his "New England Capital in Southern Agriculture: Connecticut General Life Insurance Company's Farm Loans in Texas, Alabama, and Mississippi, 1900–1940," paper presented at the 54th annual meeting of the Southern Historical Association, Nov. 1988.

43. The Illinois Central Railroad, which owned the Yazoo and Mississippi Valley Railroad and its dowry of cleared and uncleared Delta acreage, was especially eager to sell. To lure buyers, the railroad company placed advertisements in both local and national publications. For example, the railroad routinely ran a three-quarter-page advertisement on page 4 of the *Southern Farm Magazine.* "The Yazoo Valley in Mississippi," the ad exclaimed, "Beats the World for Farming Lands!" White farmer W. E. Litton of Centerville, Tenn., on the other hand, learned of the railroad's land department through an ad their agent placed in the *Hickman County News.* Litton took the bait, journeyed to the Delta to examine the property, and bought a quarter section at $7 per acre. *Southern Farm Magazine* 7:1–12 (Mar. 1899–Feb. 1900); Williams, *Bolivar County,* 324.

44. Black farmers' incentives for working partially wooded acreage are examined in chaps. 3 and 4, above.

45. Washington Co. Deed Records; Washington Co. Land Tax Roll, 1892; George T. Houston & Company Map (ca. 1904), MSS, Ms-Ar. Despite numerous sales to white planters, the Houston Company was still the largest single landowner in the backcountry in 1904, when it paid taxes on 35,000 Washington County acres. Washington Co. Land Tax Roll, 1904.

46. Alfred Holt Stone, *The Negro in the Yazoo-Mississippi Delta,* Publications of the American Economic Association 3 (1902).

47. Stone, "A Plantation Experiment," 271–72.

48. Ibid., 272, 274, 287.

49. Ibid., 276. Successful tenants in this era of rapidly escalating land prices may have spent much of their disposable income for personal property because they doubted their ability to ever purchase real estate.

50. Ibid., 275, 278–80, 287. Sharecropping did not stop the problem of "removals," as Stone termed tenants' departure from his plantation, but he was satisfied that fewer would leave with money and valuable goods. In the first two years, with renters, Stone's plantation lost 44.8 and 22 percent of its tenant families, respectively. With sharecroppers, the operation lost 26.2 percent of its workers after the third year, 24.6 percent after the fourth year, and 41.3 percent following the final experimental crop. Ibid., 287.

51. Pete Daniel, *The Shadow of Slavery: Peonage in the South, 1901–1969* (Urbana, Ill., 1972); William Cohen, *At Freedom's Edge: Black Mobility and the Southern White Quest for Racial Control, 1861–1915* (Baton Rouge, La., 1991). Cohen describes the Tunica case on pp. 284–85. The Tunica conviction is well established, but Bertram Wyatt-Brown and Randolph Boehm must be credited for bringing the Sunnyside, Ark., operations of O. B. Crittenden, LeRoy Percy, and Morris Rosenstock to light. See their contributions in Jeannie M. Whayne, ed., *Shadows over Sunnyside: An Arkansas Plantation in Transition, 1830–1945* (Fayetteville, Ark., 1993).

52. Agricultural agent Alexander E. Cance, who studied the region in 1911, observed Delta planters' practice of "buying labor" from weevil-infested areas and commented that the effort had become common in the preceding three years. Alexander E. Cance, "Report on Sub-District I: The Yazoo-Mississippi Delta," dated 3 Sept. 1911, 6, 8, typescript, Alexander E. Cance Papers, box 5, folder 41, University of Massachusetts at Amherst. I am grateful to William H. Harbaugh for drawing my attention to this valuable source.

53. Cance, "Report," 4–5.

54. Ibid., 13; *Greenville Times,* 24 July 1909. That same day, the *Times* reported a rumor that some of the wholesale merchants of the region would equip traveling salesmen with cars in order to speed and extend their business.

55. Brandfon, *Cotton Kingdom,* 121–24; Cance, "Report."

56. J. B. Wilson, "Farming in the Yazoo: Characteristics of Different Soils in the Delta," *Southern Farm Magazine* 7:3 (May 1899): 18. See also Robert Higgs, "The Boll Weevil, the Cotton Economy, and Black Migration, 1910–1930," *Agricultural History* 50:2 (1976): 335–50.

57. Coahoma, Sunflower, and Washington Co. Deed Records. Cance found planters openly preferring sharecroppers and wage laborers in his 1911 inspection. Cance, "Report," 17. Harold Woodman's latest work demonstrates how planters were able to accumulate ever more power in their relationships with sharecroppers, especially after the legislature and state courts of Mississippi came to regard the landlord's crop lien as primary to a tenant's other obligations in the 1880s. Woodman specifically considers William Alexander Percy's self-serving (or shockingly uninformed) statements on sharecropping in the same volume. See his *New South—New Law,* 67–70.

58. *Twelfth Census,* "Agriculture," vol. 5, pt. 1, 96–97; *Thirteenth Census,* "Agriculture," 6:872–79; *Fourteenth Census,* "Agriculture," vol. 6, pt. 2, 522–29.

59. Cance, "Report," 16–17.

60. Ibid., 19.

61. Wineman interview; Ayers, *Promise,* 123–31.

62. Boeger and Goldenweiser, "Tenant Systems of Farming in the Yazoo-Mississippi Delta," 2.

63. Stone's philosophy of race relations and agriculture is expressed in his *Studies in the American Race Problem* (New York, 1908). The quotes in this paragraph are drawn from pp. 115–16. Although published in book form in 1908, Stone's essay on the Delta was written in 1901. See ibid., 118n.

64. For planters like Stone, who urged a modicum of agricultural diversification, the problem with allowing tenants to determine their crop mixes was the resulting emphasis on cotton: the black renter, he stressed, wanted "to put practically all his land in cotton because it is a cash crop." Ibid., 116.

65. This extreme sentiment was not limited to Stone and his day; subsequent generations of Delta whites have blamed the automobile for tempting blacks away from their work. I have heard present-day whites of the region conclude that "getting cars was the worst thing that ever happened to the blacks."

66. Stone, *American Race Problem,* 116.

67. Cance, "Report," 19.

68. The region's roads did not yet admit motorized transport during muddy weather and would not until after World War I.

69. Cance reported that Delta planters in this era were convinced that several holdings of 800 to 1,200 acres each were more profitable than a unified plantation. The region's haphazard development, moreover, made it unlikely that any individual would then own an undivided tract of 3,000 or 4,000 cleared acres. Cance, "Report," 13–15.

70. Ibid., 15–16.

71. Ibid., 16–17.

72. Agent Cance reported that "not 5 percent seem to be acquiring either cows or mules—except where they are urged to do so by the planter." Ibid., 11.

73. Ibid., 9–12.

74. Ibid., 10–11. See Ayers, *Promise,* 13–17, 55–59, for consideration of the importance of plantation stores, general stores, and the rural market towns of the postbellum South.

75. Cance, "Report," 6–7; M. A. Crosby, "Report on Delta Farms Company," 4, U.S. Department of Agriculture, Bureau of Agricultural Economics, Office of Farm Management, MSS, ser. 133, Record Group 83, NA.

76. Cance, "Report," 6–7.

77. Despite the boll weevil's Delta depredations between 1908 and 1915, the pest did not reach much of the South's cotton until after World War I. Robert Higgs stresses examining local conditions in specific years when evaluating the boll weevil problem in his "The Boll Weevil, The Cotton Economy, and Black Migration, 1910–1930." Although

Higgs is correct in his claim that boll weevil infestation was a greater problem for the entire South in the 1920s than in the 1910s, the reverse was true in the Delta. As agricultural
agent Alexander E. Cance reported in 1911, the boll weevil was "responsible for the movement to closer control" of plantation operations, which led to the abandonment of renting in the region. Cance, "Report," 20.

78. Johnson owed over $5,000 in principal and interest to one creditor. Washington
Co. Deed Records, V2:141–43, 629–31, A3:197, K3:665–71, L3:425–27, P3:258–61,
Z2:664–66, G3:370–72, R3:769–74, S3:58–59, T3:23–26, 234–37, V3:674–75, Z3:209–14,
83:208–13, 89:58–60, 92:548–51, 93:117–18, 95:487–92, 99:487–89, 102:34, 104:1–3,
107:403–6, 112:63–65, 113:395–96, 422–24, 117:65–68, 118:148–51, 124:398–401, 135:274–75.

79. H. A. Turner, "An Account of Dunleith Plantation, Washington County, Mississippi, 1916," U.S. Department of Agriculture, Bureau of Agricultural Economics, Office
of Farm Management, MSS, ser. 133, RG 83, NA. Some of the region's promoters, including Stone, insisted that the Delta suffered less from the weevil's attention than did other
areas due to its favorable dew moisture, unique vegetation, and soil conditions. The report was published before the pest struck Dunleith, and we do not know if Stone later reconsidered his claim of Delta immunity. See Alfred H. Stone and Julian Fort, *The Truth
about the Boll Weevil* (Greenville, Miss., 1911).

80. Robert W. Harrison, *Levee Districts and Levee Building in Mississippi: A Study of
State and Local Efforts to Control Mississippi River Floods* (Stoneville, Miss., 1951), 212, 215.
Between boll weevils and floodwaters, Stone's Dunleith plantation had its smallest crop
on record in 1912. In that year tenants gathered an average of only 171 pounds of lint per
acre. This represented a 45 percent reduction from the plantation's (below average) crop
two years before. Turner, "Dunleith," 6.

81. Manning Marable, "The Politics of Black Land Tenure, 1877–1915," *Agricultural
History* 53:1 (1979): 148–49; Department of Commerce, Bureau of the Census, *Cotton Pro-
duction and Distribution, Season of 1915–16,* Bulletin no. 134 (Washington, D.C., 1916), 23;
Department of Commerce, Bureau of the Census, *Cotton Production and Distribution,
Season of 1920–21,* Bulletin no. 147 (Washington, D.C., 1921), 31.

82. Washington Co. Deed Records, M2:842, 126:586, 127:434, 139:89, 152:475–77,
153:481.

83. *Cotton Production, 1915–16,* 23; *Cotton Production, 1920–21,* 31; *Thirteenth Census,*
"Agriculture," 6:872–79; *Fourteenth Census,* "Agriculture," vol. 6, pt. 2, 522–29. The number of black farm owners in the region fell from 2,524 in 1910 to 2,462 in 1920. The largest
declines were seen in Coahoma and Bolivar Counties.

84. Luandrew, a Delta bluesman also known as "Sunnyland Slim," recalled the scene
for Robert Palmer. See the latter's *Deep Blues,* 148. Although Luandrew gave no date for
this incident, internal evidence suggests it happened in the latter half of the 1910s.

85. Quote in James R. Grossman, *Land of Hope: Chicago, Black Southerners, and the
Great Migration* (Chicago, 1989), 3.

86. Charles S. Johnson, "How Much Is the Migration a Flight from Persecution?" *Opportunity: A Journal of Negro Life* 1:9 (Sept. 1923): 272–74; Grossman, *Land of Hope,* 1–97.

87. The exact number contributed by the Delta to the Great Migration cannot be determined. The closest student of the movement, James Grossman, does not attempt an estimate of state totals in his *Land of Hope.*

88. Grossman, *Land of Hope,* 98–160.

89. Ibid., 51, 107–8.

90. D. A. McCandliss, "Movement of Farm Labor, 20 April 1923," Department of Agriculture, Bureau of Crop Estimates, MSS, ser. 133, RG 83, NA.

Conclusion

1. The *Greenville Times* was notably reticent on the identity of Lucas's attackers and failed to make an issue of the crime in subsequent editions. Some doubtless assumed that Lucas was a victim of the sort of black lawlessness that the Republicans were accused of tolerating; others may have wondered if the attack was whites' way of reminding Lucas not to confuse his newly won office with true power in the Redeemer government. Bohlen Lucas left no record of his views on the incident. The careers of Bohlen Lucas, Lewis Spearman, and William Toler are treated at length in chap. 4.

2. Toler's son, Dr. Q. Leon Toler, was a relentless thorn in the side of the patrician Percy family. In 1906 LeRoy Percy instructed his foreman, "I don't mind your being rough with [Leon] Toler if you find him on the place" in response to the doctor's agitation for sharecroppers' rights. See John M. Barry, *Rising Tide: The Great Mississippi Flood of 1927 and How It Changed America* (New York, 1997), 326.

3. Clive Metcalfe Diary, microfilm copy, SHC, NcU. Edward L. Ayers quotes two 1890 revelations in the younger Metcalfe's diary that might have been written by a harsh antebellum master: "Caught a negro girl stealing clothes from one of my darkeys, and I gave her a good whipping"; and after returning from a failed hunt, "Did not see a coon. Came home and whipped Harrison for feeding the dogs on the gallery." See *Promise,* 135.

4. C. Vann Woodward, *American Counterpoint: Slavery and Racism in the North/South Dialogue* (Boston, 1971), 40; Woodman, "The Reconstruction of the Cotton Plantation in the New South," 100–101; Barbara Jeanne Fields, "The Advent of Capitalist Agriculture: The New South in a Bourgeois World," in Glymph and Kushma, *Essays on the Postbellum Southern Economy,* 74.

5. Hahn, "Class and State in Postemancipation Societies," 84–85.

6. Altina L. Waller's *Feud: Hatfields, McCoys, and Social Change in Appalachia, 1860–1900* (Chapel Hill, N.C., 1982) captures the swirl of life in the southern mountains; Neil Foley's *The White Scourge: Mexicans, Blacks, and Poor Whites in Texas Cotton Culture* (Berkeley, Calif., 1997) depicts the tumultuous Southwest in stark terms.

7. Ayers, *Promise,* 196–97. Of course, there were some exceptions. In 1870 blacks constituted only 2 percent of the landowners in tobacco-growing Louisa County, Va.; by 1900, African Americans owned 39 percent of the county's farms. This meant that an astounding 88 percent of Louisa County's black heads of households owned land at the turn of the century. See Crandall A. Shifflett, *Patronage and Poverty in the Tobacco South: Louisa County, Virginia, 1860–1900* (Knoxville, Tenn., 1982), 52–53.

8. Steven Hahn's work on the politics of migration promises to add another dimension to the meaning of postbellum relocation. See his "Politics by Other Means: Grassroots Emigrationism in the Post-Reconstruction South," paper presented at the annual meeting of the Southern Historical Association, 7 Nov. 1997.

9. Some blacks still own land in the region, parcels carefully handed down from generation to generation. Yet these tracts are often too small to justify independent cultivation with the chemicals and machines presently in vogue throughout the region, and black farmers are seldom successful in negotiating favorable credit terms from local agricultural lenders. Many black landowners thus rent their land to wealthier farmers and nearby cotton-growing corporations. Despite the efforts of Mike Espy, the first black representative elected from the Delta since Reconstruction and later secretary of agriculture in the Clinton administration, nonwhite farmers remain at a disadvantage in their search for agricultural credit. Mike Espy interview, 25 July 1990.

10. Mississippi Authority for Educational Television, "Good Morning Blues," Walt Lowe, director, and B. B. King, narrator (Alexandria, Va.: PBS Video, 1978). For the Delta's role as birthplace of the blues, see Palmer, *Deep Blues,* and William Ferris, *Blues from the Delta* (Garden City, N.Y., 1978).

Index

Able, Will, 147–48

African Americans: and apprentice law, 20–23, 192–93; commercial activity by, 72–73; as convict laborers, 15–20; in cooperative settlements, 70–77, 205; disarmed, 26; economic mobility of, 16, 68–69, 75, 119, 127–28, 158, 160–61, 173, 174–81, 204; education of, 63–64, 77, 140, 175–76; in elective offices, 61–62, 73, 117, 119, 175, 217; farm owners profiled, 63, 64, 68, 123, 178–79, 188, 219, 224, 227, 232; as farm tenants, 36–38, 50–53, 160–61, 163–68, 175; and Freedmen's Bureau, 20–23, 25–31, 36; and household economy, 63–64, 175–76, 203; as landlords, 59–62, 150, 175; literacy among, 62, 68, 123, 177, 178; losing land, 60–62, 66, 68, 129, 168–69, 170, 175, 176, 178–79, 203, 230; in regional perspective, 188, 231; as sharecroppers, 33–36, 39, 49–50, 121–22, 161, 164–65, 179–80, 188, 199; as squatters, 194; voting rights of, 137–42, 178, 180, 181; and wage labor, 16, 196

Alcorn, Eliza Jane, 211

Alcorn, James L., 14, 15, 17, 92–95, 96, 97, 98, 99, 100, 101, 109, 210, 211

Aldrich, Lyman G., 197

Alexander, Jacob, 211

Alexander, Leopold, 10

Alexander, V. F. P., 218

Allen, George, 135

Apprentice law, 20–23; black parents' opposition to, 20–22, 192–93; provisions of, 20;

Arkansas City and Grenada Railroad, 97–98, 99–00

Atkins, C. P., 25–26

Austin riot (1874), 132–33

Ayers, Edward L.: on postbellum honor, 148; on subregions and opportunity, 183–84

Backcountry, 8–9, 41–57, 58–75; agricultural opportunity, 41; arson in, 151; black farm owners in, 58–69, 70–75, 101, 150; cooperative settlements in, 69–75; dangers, 8–9, 41–42; free use for clearing, 201; improved land, 56, 158–59; land prices, 157–58; land rental, 47–48, 49–50, 50–53, 201; land sales, 47, 49; land speculation, 44, 89–90, 99, 158–59, 197–98; land taxes' impact, 47, 180–81; plantations expand into, 158–59, 162–63, 166–67, 171, 173, 178, 190; politics in, 117, 217; railroad construction and, 109–10; ridges, 44; settlers' isolation, 42–43; soil fertility, 42, 43–44; tenants' extra duties, 52; tenants' incentives, 53; tenants' restrictions, 52–53; timber extraction, 9, 53–55, 56, 63, 72, 190; wilderness, 9, 41–42, 190

Ball, Henry W., 191

Banks, Charles, 73

Barefield, Jesse H., 69–70

Index

Barefield, John, 69–70

Barefield, Samuel, 70

Barefield, Steven T., 70

Barefield Colony, Miss., 69–70, 204

Baskett, L. T., 134–35

Bell, Rolla, 225

Beller, W. H., 147

Bilbo, Theodore, 87

Blanton, Dr., 27–28

Bliss, Nelson, 124, 218–19

Blues, 3–4

Bolton, William H., 27–28

Bourges, Camille, 52, 53, 201

Boyle, L. V., and Company, 105

Bradshaw, E. T., 146, 224

Brannon, Alfred, 225

Brooks, Mrs. J. C., 190

Brown, Bazil, 170

Brown, George H., 52, 68–69

Brown, T. L., 146, 147

Bruce, Blanche K., 98, 119, 211

Buford, J. H., 119

Bureau of Refugees, Freedmen, and Abandoned Lands ("Freedmen's Bureau"): agents' class prejudices, 31; agents' opposition to apprentice law, 21–23; agents' racial prejudices, 28–29, 39; arbitration efforts, 36; and court system, 194; fraud reported, 29–30; limitations of, 28–29; misconduct reported to, 29–30, 36, 195; negotiating labor contracts, 26–27; planters' view of, 27–30, 31

Burton, John, 63

Byrnes, Edward P., 89, 212

Campbell, William, 52, 69

Cance, Alexander E., 163, 164–65, 166–68, 228, 229, 230

Careers: multiple ("hyphenated commercialists"), 87–90, 99, 209

Cargil, Bill, 148

Chalmers, James R., 133, 217, 220

Chicago Defender, 171–72

Chinese immigrants, 124–26, 180, 193; conflict with freedpeople, 24; in 1880 census, 24; at Newstead plantation, 23–24, 193; recruited as farm laborers, 23

Chism Brothers' Store, 78

Chung, Wong, 124–26, 127

Clark, John, 95, 107, 109, 211

Cole, Aaron, 69

Collier, Holt, 145, 146, 223–24

Collier, James, 58, 59, 60, 107

Collins, George, 197

Colored Farmers' Alliance, 128, 130–31, 136

Constitutional convention (1890), 137–39, 140, 141, 142, 221; impact of, 142–44, 223

Convict labor, 180; applications, 17; escaped prisoners, 18–19; investigations of conditions, 17–18; legislation regarding, 17–20, 192; lessees of, 17, 18; opposition to, 18–19; prisoners' profile, 15–16; treatment of, 16, 18, 19–20, 192

Corliss, George W., 27, 222

Corn: production, 120–21

Cotton: army worm, 196; boll weevil, 162, 163–64, 168, 169, 170, 196, 229–30; bollworm, 36, 38, 196; business plantations, 181–82, 184–85; 1867 crop year, 36–38, 39; overproduction of, 119–20; price decline, 65–66, 119–21, 176; price increases, 157, 170, 219, 226–27; production costs, 120, 217; yields, 3; and World War I, 169–72

Credit: debtors' auctions, 60–61, 66, 67, 122, 125–26, 169, 170, 176, 178–79, 218; debtors' flight, 124; debt peonage, 121, 162, 200; deed of trust, 60, 65, 66, 67, 87, 121–22, 125, 128–29, 170, 202, 218; fraud, 123, 127, 218; interest rates, 122; and insurance, 124; international sources, 124, 158, 206–7, 218; liens, 37, 121–22, 128, 219; merchants' losses, 125–26, 127; merchants' sources of, 83, 85; negotiations, 66–68, 123–24, 176–78; practices (1870s–1880s), 121–22, 218; practices (late 1880s–early 1900s), 122–24, 218; purchase prices, 122, 191, 195

Cress, D. N., 147

Index

The American South Series

Anne Goodwyn Jones and Susan V. Donaldson, editors
  Haunted Bodies: Gender and Southern Texts

M. M. Manring
  Slave in a Box: The Strange Career of Aunt Jemima

Stephen Cushman
  Bloody Promenade: Reflections on a Civil War Battle

John C. Willis
  Forgotten Time: The Yazoo-Mississippi Delta after the Civil War